Feathers for Arrows

Feathers for Arrows

Illustrations for Preachers and Teachers

Charles H. Spurgeon

Reformation Heritage Books
Grand Rapids, Michigan

Reformation Heritage Books
2965 Leonard St. NE
Grand Rapids, MI 49525
616-977-0889 / Fax 616-285-3246
orders@heritagebooks.org
www.heritagebooks.org

Printed in the United States of America
16 17 18 19 20 21/10 9 8 7 6 5 4 3 2 1

ISBN 978-1-60178-504-6

*For additional Reformed literature, request a free book list
from Reformation Heritage Books at the above regular or
e-mail address.*

PREFACE.

(T)HERE is no necessity in these times to advocate the free use of similitudes in public teaching. Far more needful is it to assist our brethren to find a supply of these indispensable aids to understanding. To some it is difficult to create a comparison, although they know how to use it with effect when it is once suggested to them ; and the most fertile minds are frequently stimulated to further production by reading the thoughts of others. It is not, therefore, I hope, an impertinence on my part to present to the Christian public a bundle of illustrations original and collected. My aim has not been to amuse the reader, but to furnish FEATHERS FOR ARROWS for the servants of Christ Jesus.

Whenever I have been permitted sufficient respite from my ministerial duties to enjoy a lengthened tour, or even a short excursion, I have been in the habit of carrying with me a small *Note Book*, in which I have jotted down any illustrations which have occurred to me by the way. My recreations have been all the more pleasant because I have made them subservient to my life-work. The *Note Book* has been useful in my travels as a mental purse. If not fixed upon paper, ideas are apt to vanish with the occasion which suggested them. A word or two will suffice to bring an incident or train of thought to remembrance ; and therefore, it would be inexcusable in a minister, who needs so much, not to preserve all that comes in his way.

From the pencil-marks of the pocket-book my notes have
been enlarged into more permanent manuscript, and have been
of great service to me. Out of hundreds of metaphors and
anecdotes thus collected, I have used the main body in my
constant sermonisings ; but as enough remained unused to
make me feel competently rich in illustrations, I determined
to offer a portion of my hoard to my fellow workers, feeling
the less difficulty in so doing because the ingatherings of
continual observation more than replace the material expended
in this distribution. Moreover, indebted as every preacher
must be to the illustrations of others, it is but just, that, if he
be able, he should make some return : in that spirit my
contribution is hereby offered.

To the nucleus formed by cullings from my *Note Book*, my
readings, in an attempt to expound the Psalms,* have enabled
me to add many quaint comparisons and ancient stories,
which from their very age are probably newer than the latest
novelties to modern readers. A few clippings from favourite
writers, such as James Hamilton and William Arnot have
been thrown in almost of necessity, for one feels a sort of
obligation, by the exhibition of golden nuggets, to give note
to others of the mines where treasure lies piled up in
glittering heaps. To make the gathering still more varied,
scraps from newspapers and magazines are interspersed,
—fragments preserved in such odd times and circumstances, that out of what basket they first fell I cannot say,
whether they are new or old I know not; I can only say that
they were new to me. The whole collection is now presented
to teachers and preachers as a sincere offering of hearty
"brother-help." If there be here a single illustration which
shall assist one of my Master's servants in his efforts to
impart truth, I shall be greatly gratified. Desiring to do this
and every other word and deed, "in the name of the Lord

* "The Treasury of David." By C. H. SPURGEON. Vol. 1. Psalm I. to XXVI.
London : Passmore and Alabaster, 18, Paternoster Row. Price 8s.

Jesus, giving thanks unto God and the Father by him,"
I prepared these figures and metaphors, that they may serve
as *feathers for arrows*—arrows of gospel truth which I pray
may be made sharp in the hearts of the King's enemies.

According to D'Israeli's canon, "a preface being the
entrance to a book, should invite by its beauty," but he might
have equally well remarked that a preface being merely a
porch, no one ought to be long detained in it.   Believing in
this last rule, and begging the reader's lenient criticism, I
invite him to such entertainment as this little volume may
afford : being myself,

His willing servant,

CLAPHAM,
February, 1870.

MY NOTE BOOK.

ABASEMENT—To be rejoiced in.

WHEN Latimer resigned his bishopric, Foxe tells us that as he put off his rochet from his shoulders he gave a skip on the floor for joy, "feeling his shoulders so light at being discharged of such a burden." To be relieved of our wealth or high position is to be unloaded of weighty responsibilities, and should not cause us to fret, but rather to rejoice as those who are lightened of a great load. If we cease from office in the church, or from public honours, or from power of any sort, we may be consoled by the thought that there is just so much the less for us to answer for at the great audit, when we must give an account of our stewardship.

ABSENCE FROM WEEK-NIGHT SERVICES.

"PRAYER-MEETING and lecture as usual on Wednesday evening, in the lecture-room. Dear brethren, I urge you all to attend the weekly meetings. 'Forsake not the assembling of yourselves together.'" Some of the "dear brethren" deported themselves in this way : Brother A. *thought it looked like rain,* and concluded that his family, including himself of course, had better remain at home. On Thursday evening it was raining very hard, and the same brother hired a carriage,

1

and took his whole family to the Academy of Music, to hear
M. Agassiz lecture on the "Intelligence of the Lobster."
Brother B. *thought he was too tired to go,* so he stayed at
home and *worked* at the sledge he had promised to make for
Billy.   Sister C. *thought the pavements were too slippery.*   It
would be very dangerous for her to venture out.   I saw her
next morning, going down street to get her old bonnet
"done up."   She had an old pair of stockings drawn over
her shoes.   Three-fourths of the members stayed at home.
God was at the prayer-meeting.   The pastor was there, and
God blessed them.   The persons who stayed at home were
each represented by a vacant seat.   God don't bless empty
seats.—*United Presbyterian.*

ACCESS.

THERE are many locks in my house and all with different
keys, but I have one master-key which opens all.   So the
Lord has many treasuries and secrets all shut up from carnal
minds with locks which they cannot open; but he who walks
in fellowship with Jesus possesses the master-key which will
admit him to all the blessings of the covenant; yea, to the very
heart of God.   Through the Wellbeloved we have access to
God, to heaven, to every secret of the Lord.

ACTIVITY—a Help to Courage.

COURAGE maintains itself by its ardent action, as some
birds rest on the wing.   There is an energy about agility that
will often give a man a fortitude which otherwise he might
not have possessed.   We can picture the gallant regiment at
Balaclava riding into the valley of death at a dashing gallop,
but we could scarcely imagine their marching slowly up to the
guns, coolly calculating all the deadly odds of the adventure.
There is much in our obeying as our Lord did, "straightway."
When the Lord gives his servants grace to follow out their convictions as soon as they feel them, then they act courageously.

First thoughts are best in the service of God, they are like Gideon's men that lapped. Second thoughts come up timorously and limpingly, and incite us to make provision for the flesh, they are like those men whom Gideon discarded because they went down on their knees to drink, they took things too leisurely to be fit for the Lord's battles.

ADVENT—Looking for the.

I WAS told of a poor peasant on the Welsh mountains who, month after month, year after year, through a long period of declining life, was used every morning, as soon as he awoke, to open his casement window, towards the east, and look out to see if Jesus Christ was coming. He was no calculator, or he need not have looked so long ; he was no student of prophecy, or he need not have looked at all ; he was ready, or he would not have been in so much haste ; he was willing, or he would rather have looked another way ; he loved, or it would not have been the first thought of the morning. His Master did not come, but a messenger did, to fetch the ready one home. The same preparation sufficed for both, the longing soul was satisfied with either. Often when, in the morning, the child of God awakes, weary and encumbered with the flesh, perhaps from troubled dreams, perhaps with troubled thoughts, his Father's secret comes presently across him, he looks up, if not out, to feel, if not to see, the glories of that last morning when the trumpet shall sound, and the dead shall arise indestructible ; no weary limbs to bear the spirit down ; no feverish dreams to haunt the vision ; no dark forecasting of the day's events, or returning memory of the griefs of yesterday.—*Fry.*

AFFLICTION—Attendant upon Honour.

IN the ancient times, a box on the ear given by a master to a slave meant liberty, little would the freedman care how hard was the blow. By a stroke from the sword the warrior was

knighted by his monarch, small matter was it to the new-made
knight if the royal hand was heavy.   When the Lord intends
to lift his servants into a higher stage of spiritual life, he
frequently sends them a severe trial ; he makes his Jacobs to
be prevailing princes, but he confers the honour after a night
of wrestling, and accompanies it with a shrunken sinew.   Be
it so, who among us would wish to be deprived of the trials
if they are the necessary attendants of spiritual advancement?

AFFLICTION—Awakening Gratitude.

AFFLICTIONS when sanctified make us grateful for mercies
which aforetime we treated with indifference.   We sat for
half-an-hour in a calf's shed the other day, quite grateful
for the shelter from the driving rain, yet at no other time
would we have entered such a hovel.   Discontented persons
need a course of the bread of adversity and the water of
affliction, to cure them of the wretched habit of murmuring.
Even things which we loathed before, we shall learn to prize
when in troublous circumstances.   We are no lovers of
lizards, and yet at Pont St. Martin, in the Val D'Aosta, where
the mosquitoes, flies, and insects of all sorts drove us nearly
to distraction, we prized the little green fellows, and felt quite
an attachment to them as they darted out their tongues and
devoured our worrying enemies.   Sweet are the uses of
adversity, and this among them—that it brings into proper
estimation mercies aforetime lightly esteemed.

AFFLICTION—Endears the Promises.

WE never prize the precious words of promise till we are
placed in conditions in which their suitability and sweetness
are manifested.   We all of us value those golden words, " *When
thou walkest through the fire thou shalt not be burned, neither
shall the flame kindle upon thee,*" but few if any of us have
read them with the delight of the martyr Bilney, to whom this
passage was a stay, while he was in prison awaiting his

execution at the stake. His Bible, still preserved in the library of Corpus Christi College, Cambridge, has the passage marked with a pen in the margin. Perhaps, if all were known, every promise in the Bible has borne a special message to some one saint, and so the whole volume might be scored in the margin with mementoes of Christian experience, every one appropriate to the very letter.

AFFLICTION—Effects of, in different People.

" How different are summer storms from winter ones ! In winter they rush over the earth with their violence; and if any poor remnants of foliage or flowers have lingered behind, these are swept along at one gust. Nothing is left but desolation; and long after the rain has ceased, pools of water and mud bear tokens of what has been. But when the clouds have poured out their torrents in summer, when the winds have spent their fury, and the sun breaks forth again in glory, all things seem to rise with renewed loveliness from their refreshing bath. The flowers, glistening with rainbows, smell sweeter than before; the grass seems to have gained another brighter shade of green ; and the young plants which had hardly come into sight, have taken their place among their fellows in the borders, so quickly have they sprung among the showers. The air, too, which may previously have been oppressive, is become clear, and soft, and fresh. Such, too, is the difference when the storms of affliction fall on hearts unrenewed by Christian faith, and on those who abide in Christ. In the former they bring out the dreariness and desolation which may before have been unapparent. The gloom is not relieved by the prospect of any cheering ray to follow it; of any flowers or fruits to show its beneficence. But in the true Christian soul, 'though weeping may endure for a night, joy cometh in the morning.' A sweet smile of hope and love follows every tear; and tribulation itself is turned into the chief of blessings."

AFFLICTION—an Incentive to Zeal.

THERE is an old story in the Greek annals of a soldier under Antigonus who had a disease about him, an extremely painful one, likely to bring him soon to the grave. Always first in the charge was this soldier, rushing into the hottest part of the fray, as the bravest of the brave. His pain prompted him to fight, that he might forget it ; and he feared not death, because he knew that in any case he had not long to live. Antigonus, who greatly admired the valour of his soldier, discovering his malady, had him cured by one of the most eminent physicians of the day ; but, alas ! from that moment the warrior was absent from the front of the battle. He now sought his ease ; for, as he remarked to his companions, he had something worth living for—health, home, family, and other comforts, and he would not risk his life now as aforetime. So, when our troubles are many we are often by grace made courageous in serving our God ; we feel that we have nothing to live for in this world, and we are driven, by hope of the world to come, to exhibit zeal, self-denial, and industry. But how often is it otherwise in better times ! for then the joys and pleasures of this world make it hard for us to remember the world to come, and we sink into inglorious ease.

AFFLICTION—Increased with our Strength.

" I HAD," said Latimer, describing the way in which his father trained him as a yeoman's son, " my bows bought me according to my age and strength; as I increased in them so my bows were made bigger and bigger." Thus boys grew into cross-bowmen, and by a similar increase in the force of their trials, Christians become veterans in the Lord's host. The affliction which is suitable for a babe in grace would little serve the young man, and even the well-developed man needs severer trials as his strength increases. God, like a wise father, trains us wisely, and as we are able to bear it he makes our service and our suffering more arduous. As boys rejoice to be treated like men, so will we rejoice in our greater tribulations, for here is man's work for us, and by God's help we will not flinch from doing it.

AFFLICTION—Making us long for Heaven.

WE had traversed the Great Aletsch Glacier, and were very hungry when we reached the mountain tarn half-way between the Bel Alp and the hotel at the foot of the Æggischorn; there a peasant undertook to descend the mountain, and bring us bread and milk. It was a very Marah to us when he brought us back milk too sour for us to drink, and bread black as a coal, too hard to bite, and sour as the curds. What then? Why, we longed the more eagerly to reach the hotel towards which we were travelling. We mounted our horses, and made no more halts till we reached the hospitable table where our hunger was abundantly satisfied. Thus our disappointments on the road to heaven whet our appetites for the better country, and quicken the pace of our pilgrimage to the celestial city.

AFFLICTION—Noble Piety nourished amid.

" THE pine, placed nearly always among scenes disordered and desolate, brings into them all possible elements of order and precision. Lowland trees may lean to this side and that, though it is but a meadow breeze that bends them, or a bank of cowslips from which their trunks lean aslope. But let storm and avalanche do their worst, and let the pine find only a ledge of vertical precipice to cling to, it will nevertheless grow straight. Thrust a rod from its last shoot down the stem, it shall point to the centre of the earth as long as the tree lives." Amid the sternest trials the most upright Christians are usually reared. The divine life within them so triumphs over every difficulty as to render the men, above all others, true and exact. What a noble spectacle is a man whom nothing can warp, a firm, decided servant of God, defying hurricanes of temptation!

AFFLICTION—Overruled to promote Joy.

OUR afflictions are like weights, and have a tendency to bow us to the dust, but there is a way of arranging weights by means of wheels and pulleys, so that they will even lift us up.   Grace, by its matchless art, has often turned the heaviest of our trials into occasions for heavenly joy.   " We glory in tribulations also."   We gather honey out of the rock, and oil out of the flinty rock.

AFFLICTION—Revealing Christians.

WHEN the green leaves bedeck the trees and all is fair, one cannot readily find the birds' nests, but when the winter lays bare the trees, anyone, with half-an-eye, may see them. Thus amid the press of business and prosperity the Christian may scarcely be discerned, his hidden life is concealed amid the thick and throng of the things of earth ; but let affliction come, a general sickness, or severe losses in the family, and you shall see the Christian man plainly enough in the gracious patience by which he rises superior to trial.   The sick bed reveals the man ; the burning house, the sinking ship, the panic on the exchange, all these make manifest the hidden ones.   In many a true believer, true piety is like a drum which nobody hears of unless it be beaten.

AFFLICTION—Right View of.

OUR crosses are not made of iron, though painted sometimes with iron colours ; they are formed of nothing heavier than wood.   Yet they are not made of pasteboard, and will never be light in themselves, though our Lord can lighten them by his presence.   The Papists foolishly worship pieces of wood supposed to be parts of the true cross ; but he who has borne the really true cross, and known its sanctifying power, will value every sliver of it, counting his trials to be his treasures, his afflictions argosies of wealth, and his losses his best gains.

AFFLICTIONS—Tokens of Divine Regard.

LAWNS which we would keep in the best condition are very frequently mown; the grass has scarcely any respite from the scythe. Out in the meadows there is no such repeated cutting, they are mown but once or twice in the year. Even thus the nearer we are to God, and the more regard he has for us, the more frequent will be our adversities. To be very dear to God, involves no small degree of chastisement.

AFFLICTIONS—Winning the Heart for God.

PAYSON thus beautifully writes :—" I have been all my life like a child whose father wishes to fix his undivided attention. At first the child runs about the room, but his father ties up his feet; he then plays with his hands until they likewise are tied. Thus he continues to do, till he is completely tied up. Then, when he can do nothing else, he will attend to his father. Just so has God been dealing with me, to induce me to place my happiness in him alone. But I blindly continued to look for it here, and God has kept cutting off one source of enjoyment after another, till I find that I can do without them all, and yet enjoy more happiness than ever in my life before."

AGE—No Cure for Sin.

ACCORDING to Æsop, an old woman found an empty jar which had lately been full of prime old wine, and which still retained the fragrant smell of its former contents. She greedily placed it several times to her nose, and drawing it backwards and forwards said, " Oh, most delicious! How nice must the wine itself have been, when it leaves behind in the very vessel which contained it so sweet a perfume !"

Men often hug their vices when their power to enjoy them is gone. The memories of revelling and wantonness appear to be sweet to the ungodly in their old age. They sniff the empty bottles of their follies, and only wish they could again be drunken with them. Age cures not the evil heart, but exhibits in a ridiculous but deeply painful light the indelible perversity of human nature.

AMBITION.

AMBITION is like the sea which swallows all the rivers and is none the fuller ; or like the grave whose insatiable maw for ever craves for the bodies of men. It is not like an amphora, which being full receives no more, but its fulness swells it till a still-greater vacuum is formed. In all probability, Napoleon never longed for a sceptre till he had gained the bâton, nor dreamed of being emperor of Europe till he had gained the crown of France. Caligula, with the world at his feet, was mad with a longing for the moon, and could he have gained it the imperial lunatic would have coveted the sun. It is in vain to feed a fire which grows the more voracious the more it is supplied with fuel ; he who lives to satisfy his ambition has before him the labour of Sisyphus, who rolled up hill an ever-rebounding stone, and the task of the daughters of Danaus, who are condemned for ever to attempt to fill a bottomless vessel with buckets full of holes. Could we know the secret heart-breaks and wearinesses of ambitious men, we should need no Wolsey's voice crying, " I charge thee, fling away ambition," but we should flee from it as from the most accursed blood-sucking vampire which ever uprose from the caverns of hell.

APOSTATES.

IN the long line of portraits of the Doges, in the palace at Venice, one space is empty, and the semblance of a black curtain remains as a melancholy record of glory forfeited. Found guilty of treason against the state, Marino Falieri was beheaded, and his image as far as possible blotted from remembrance. As we regarded the singular memorial we thought of Judas and Demas, and then, as we heard in spirit the Master's warning word, " One of you shall betray me," we asked within our soul the solemn question, "Lord, is it I?" Every one's eye rests longer upon the one dark vacancy than upon any one of the many fine portraits of the merchant monarchs ; and so the apostates of the church are far more frequently the theme of the world's talk than the thousands of good men and true who adorn the doctrine of God our Saviour in all things. Hence the more need of care on the part of those of us whose portraits are publicly exhibited as saints, lest we should one day be painted out of the church's gallery, and our persons only remembered as having been detestable hypocrites.

APPEARANCE—We must Not Judge by.

WHATEVER truth there may be in phrenology, or in Lavater's kindred science of physiognomy, we shall do well scrupulously to avoid forming an opinion against a man from his personal appearance. If we so judge we shall often commit the greatest injustice, which may, if we should ever live to be disfigured by sickness or marred by age, be returned into our own bosom to our bitter sorrow. Plato compared Socrates to the gallipots of the Athenian apothecaries, on the outside of which were painted grotesque figures of apes and owls, but they contained within precious balsams. All the beauty of a Cleopatra cannot save her name from being infamous ; personal attractions have adorned some of the grossest monsters that ever cursed humanity. Judge then no man or woman after their outward fashion, but with purified eye behold the hidden beauty of the heart and life.

ASSURANCE—Excellence of.

BELIEVE me, the life of grace is no dead level, it is not a fen country, a vast flat. There are mountains, and there are valleys. There are tribes of Christians who live in the lowlands, like the poor Swiss of the Valais, who live between the lofty ranges of mountains in the midst of the miasma, where the air is stagnant and fever has its lair, and the human frame grows languid and enfeebled. Such dwellers in the lowlands of unbelief are for ever doubting, fearing, troubled about their interest in Christ, and tossed to and fro ; but there are other believers, who, by God's grace, have climbed the mountain of full assurance and near communion, their place is with the eagle in his eyrie, high aloft ; they are like the strong mountaineer, who has trodden the virgin snow, who has breathed the fresh, free air of the Alpine regions, and therefore his sinews are braced, and his limbs are vigorous ; these are they who do great exploits, being mighty men, men of renown.

ATTENDANCE AT PUBLIC WORSHIP—Invitations to.

IN Edinburgh a Sabbath-school teacher was once visiting in a close, and in one of the top flats of a stair, found a poor family living in a small but clean room. From conversation with the father and mother, she soon discovered that it was one of those cases where, from the long illness of the father, the family had fallen from comparative comfort to poverty. He was now, however, better, and had been able for some time to work a little, so as to keep his family from destitution, but by no means to enable them to live in comfort. Having learned so much of their worldly concerns, their visitor next began to speak of their souls' interests. She asked them if they went to any church. "No," said the father, "We used to go long ago, before I took ill ; but we went no more after that." "But," said she, "you have been better for a good while." "Oh," said the father, "nobody ever asked us to come !" "Well," said the visitor, "I'll ask you now," and she directed him to a church where he would hear the glad tidings from a faithful minister. Next Sabbath several of the children were at her Sabbath-school, and told her that that day their family had been at church. Since that day they have been hearers of the Word. How many souls are perishing in Edinburgh and other towns, "because, though all things are now ready, NOBODY EVER ASKED THEM TO COME!" Will not the blood of their souls be required at the hand of those who profess to have tasted a Saviour's love, and yet make not one effort to pluck brands out of the fire?—*Scottish Sunday School Teacher's Magazine.*

ATTENDANCE AT PUBLIC WORSHIP—Young should be Trained.

THE question is often asked how shall we get our working-classes to attend public worship. The answer may be supplied by an incident of my boyhood. On the mantel-shelf of my grandmother's best parlour, among other marvels was an apple in a phial. It quite filled up the body of the bottle, and my wondering enquiry was, "How could it have been got into its place?" By stealth I climbed a chair to see if the bottom would unscrew, or if there had been a join in the glass throughout the length of the phial. I was satisfied by careful observation that neither of these theories could be supported, and the apple remained to me an enigma and a mystery. But as it was said of that other wonder, the source of the Nile—

"Nature well known no mystery remains,"—

so was it here. Walking in the garden I saw a phial placed on a tree bearing within it a tiny apple, which was growing within the crystal; now I saw it all; the apple was put into the bottle while it was little, and it grew there. Just so must we catch the little men and women who swarm our streets— we call them boys and girls—and introduce them within the influence of the church, for alas! it is hard indeed to reach them when they have ripened in carelessness and sin.

ATTENTION—Difficulty of Winning.

BÜCHSELL, in his "Ministerial Experiences," says, "I was surprised to observe that for some Sundays a rustic, whom I had never seen there before, now regularly made his appearance in church, but in the most open way in the world settled himself to sleep as soon as he was seated, and snored so loud that one heard him even during the singing.   A boy, to whom I had often spoken, and who had an open, merry expression of face, was in the habit of placing himself not far from the snorer, and I now requested him to sit more immediately behind him, and to touch him from time to time in order to keep him awake.   At first the lad refused to do this, but the promise of a *groschen* led him to comply.   During the whole service, I could see the contest carried on between the little fellow and his somnolent neighbour, and by a glance of my eye I sought to encourage the former to keep up the rousing process.   On the following Sunday the rustic came again, and so did the boy, whom I begged to continue his good offices as before, but he declined ; and when I held out the bribe of the *groschen*, he told me that the peasant had already given him two, on condition that he should not be disturbed."

Let us do what we will to enlist the attention of our hearers, we shall not find it an easy task.   With our illustrations and anecdotes we may as it were be giving ONE *groschen* to secure the ear, but the world, the flesh, and the devil, with their cares, pleasures, and distractions, will always be offering TWO *groschen* to our one.   Yet by God's grace we shall win the day, and conquer not alone the ear but the heart.

BIBLE.

THE *historical* matters of Scripture, both narrative and prophecy, constitute as it were the *bones* of its system ; whereas the *spiritual* matters are as its muscles, blood-vessels and nerves.   As the *bones* are necessary to the human system, so Scripture *must* have its *historical* matters.   The expositor who nullifies the *historical* ground-work of Scripture for the sake of finding only spiritual truths everywhere, brings death on all correct interpretation.—*J. A. Bengel.*

BIBLE—Cause of Interest in it.

THE lifeboat may have a tasteful bend and beautiful decoration, but these are not the qualities for which I prize it; it was my salvation from the howling sea! So the interest which a regenerate soul takes in the Bible, is founded on a personal application to the heart of the saving truth which it contains. If there is no taste for this truth, there can be no relish for the Scriptures.—*J. W. Alexander, D.D.*

BIBLE—How to Deal with its Difficulties.

AN old man once said, "For a long period I puzzled myself about the difficulties of Scripture, until at last I came to the resolution that reading the Bible was like eating fish. When I find a difficulty I lay it aside, and call it a bone. Why should I choke on the bone when there is so much nutritious meat for me? Some day, perhaps, I may find that even the bone may afford me nourishment."

BIBLE—How to Read.

TO some the Bible is uninteresting and unprofitable, because they read too fast. Amongst the insects which subsist on the sweet sap of flowers, there are two very different classes. One is remarkable for its imposing plumage, which shows in the sunbeams like the dust of gems; and as you watch its jaunty gyrations over the fields, and its minuet dance from flower to flower, you cannot help admiring its graceful activity, for it is plainly getting over a great deal of ground. But, in the same field there is another worker, whose brown vest and business-like straight-forward flight may not have arrested your eye. His fluttering neighbour darts down here and there, and sips elegantly wherever he can find a drop of ready nectar; but this dingy plodder makes a point of alighting everywhere, and wherever he alights he either finds honey or makes it. If the flower-cup be deep, he goes down to the bottom; if its dragon-mouth be shut, he

thrusts its lips asunder; and if the nectar be peculiar or re-
condite, he explores all about till he discovers it, and then
having ascertained the knack of it, joyful as one who has
found great spoil, he sings his way down into its luscious
recesses. His rival, of the painted velvet wing, has no
patience for such dull and long-winded details. But what is
the end? Why, the one died last October along with the
flowers; the other is warm in his hive to-night, amidst the
fragrant stores which he gathered beneath the bright beams
of summer.

Reader, to which do you belong?—the butterflies or bees?
Do you search the Scriptures, or do you only skim them?
Do you dwell on a passage till you bring out some meaning,
or till you can carry away some memorable truth or immediate
lesson? or do you flit along on heedless wing, only on the
look-out for novelty, and too frivolous to explore or ponder
the Scriptures? Does the Word of God dwell in you so
richly, that in the vigils of a restless night, or in the bookless
solitude of a sick room, or in the winter of old age or exclusion
from ordinances, its treasured truths would perpetuate
summer round you, and give you meat to eat which the world
knows not of?—*James Hamilton, D.D.*

BIBLE—Judged by its Fruits.

A ROMAN Catholic priest in Belgium rebuked a young
woman and her brother for reading that "*bad book*,"
pointing to the Bible. "Mr. Priest," she replied, "a little
while ago my brother was an idler, a gambler, a drunkard,
and made such a noise in the house that no one could stay
in it. Since he began to read the Bible, he works with
industry, goes no longer to the tavern, no longer touches
cards, brings home money to his poor old mother, and our
life at home is quiet and delightful. How comes it, Mr. Priest,
that a bad book produces such good fruits?"

BIBLE—Power of its Authority.

THE mother of a family was married to an infidel who made jest of religion in the presence of his own children ; yet she succeeded in bringing them all up in the fear of the Lord. I asked her one day how she preserved them from the influence of a father whose sentiments were so opposed to her own. This was her answer : " Because to the authority of a *father* I do not oppose the authority of a *mother*, but that of God. From their earliest years my children have always seen the Bible upon my table. This holy book has constituted the whole of their religious instruction. I was silent that I might allow it to speak. Did they propose a question, did they commit a fault, did they perform a good action, I opened the Bible, and the Bible answered, reproved, or encouraged them. The constant reading of the Scriptures has wrought the prodigy which surprises you.—*Adolphe Monod.*

BIBLE—To be Read with Delight.

WHEN Mr. Hone, who wrote the " Every-day Book," and was of sceptical views, was travelling through Wales, he stopped at a cottage to ask for a drink of water, and a little girl answered him, " Oh, yes ! sir, I have no doubt mother will give you some milk. Come in." He went in and sat down. The little girl was reading her Bible. Mr. Hone said, " Well, my little girl, you are getting your task?" " No, sir, I am not," she replied, " I am reading the Bible." " Yes," said he, " you are getting your task out of the Bible?" " Oh, no," she replied, " it is no task to read the Bible ; I love the Bible." " And why do you love the Bible?" said he. Her simple, child-like answer was, " I thought everybody loved the Bible." Her own love to the precious volume had made her innocently believe that everybody else was equally delighted to read God's Word. Mr. Hone was so touched with the sincerity of that expression, that he read the Bible himself,

2

and instead of being an opponent to the things of God, came to be a friend of divine truth.

BIBLE—The Spirit more than the Letter.

IT is easy enough to be learned in the letter of the Word, and yet to miss the spirit. If no other instance were before us, the Jewish people would furnish us with a most convincing one, for they have wholly missed the meaning of the Scriptures, and yet, Lightfoot tells us, " They have summed up all the letters in the Bible to show that one hair of that sacred head is not perished. Eight hundred and forty-eight marginal notes are observed and preserved, for the more facility of the text: the middle verse of every book noted; the number of the verses in every book reckoned: and not a vowel that misseth ordinary grammer which is not marked."

BIBLE—Why Priests Withhold it.

THE true reason why the Papists forbid the Scriptures to be read is not to keep men from errors and heresies, but to keep them from discovering those which they themselves impose upon them. Such trash as they trade in would never go off their hands if they did not keep their shops thus dark ; which made one of their shavelings so bitterly complain of Luther for spoiling their market, saying that but for him they might have persuaded the people of Germany to eat hay. Anything, indeed, will go down a blind man's throat.— *Gurnal.*

BIGOTRY.

SOME men magnify the importance of their own little clique of believers by denying the godliness of all who differ from them. They remind one of Bishop Hacket's story. " At Wimbledon," says he, " not far from me, a warrener promised Thomas, Earl of Exeter, that he should have a burrow of rabbits, all of them of what colour he pleased. ' Let them be all white,' said that good Earl. Whereupon the warrener *killed up all the rest* but the white rabbits, and sold them away, and left not enough to serve the earl's table."

A sorry few would be left to serve the Lord, and preserve the name of Christ upon earth, if some men's judgments could be final. Blessed be God, the Judge of saints is not the rabbi of any of the rival synagogues.

BODY AND SOUL

"Two things a master commits to his servants' care," saith one, "the child and the child's clothes." It will be a poor excuse for the servant to say, at his master's return, "Sir, here are all the child's clothes, neat and clean, but the child is lost!" Much so with the account that many will give to God of their souls and bodies at the great day. "Lord, here is my body; I was very grateful for it; I neglected nothing that belonged to its content and welfare; but as for my soul, that is lost and cast away for ever. I took little care and thought about it!"—*Flavel.*

BOOKS—How to make them Intelligible.

JOHN KEBLE, the author of "The Christian Year," in a letter to Mr. (afterwards Sir) J. T. Coleridge, thus writes:— "Have you read a little publication of Miller's, which I sent to James Coleridge, and if you have, how do you like it? Lest you should think his style in this new book too obscure for the 'Plain People,' I must tell you that he made Molière's experiment, for he gave the sermons to his servant, quite a rustic lad, to read before he printed them, and the man said he understood them all except the fifth, which accordingly M. made plainer, till the youth professed himself satisfied with it. And his father, the clerk of the parish, had given the greatest proof of his understanding even of this the obscurest part, for he said to Miller, 'Oh, yes! sir, I see what you mean, you mean such-and-such people (naming them) by the one of your two classes, and such-and-such by the other.' I call this a very satisfactory experiment, quite as much so as most of Sir Humphrey Davy's." In a letter to another friend on the same subject, Keble further adds :—" I wonder whether people that write tracts for the poor, generally take this method ; it seems mere common sense for them to do so, and yet one can hardly think they do."

BOOKS—Tried by Time and Posterity.

CALL it by what name you please—dream, vision, or revery—we found ourselves in a large room, the walls of which were concealed by well-packed shelves of books, from the ponderous folio to the minute thirty-two-mo, and in all the variety of dress which a skilful handicraft could devise. While cursorily gazing on these intellectual stores, our attention was arrested by the entrance of two personages of mild· and venerable aspect, who very courteously introduced themselves, and stated the object of their visit. They bore the significant names of TIME and POSTERITY, and intimated that they had come to pay their semi-centennial visit, to weigh the merits of authors, and determine their destiny. The task seemed to us an herculean one, where the volumes were numbered by thousands ; and we were curious to know by what process they were to ascertain the character of so many candidates for fame. We might, however, have spared our surprise, had we reflected that TIME was a gentlemen who had seen much of the world, and professed great experience, and POSTERITY was no less distinguished for the solidity of his judgment. They were well prepared for an expeditious performance of their work, and, in truth, we felt no small degree of horror in witnessing the results of their *essay*. By the way, we should have mentioned that they were provided with a capacious crucible, under which was burning a large and steady flame. Into it volume after volume was thrown, and the ordeal through which they had to pass was one of fire. "Goodly volumes, these," said TIME, taking up a brace of octavos on metaphysics, "let us test their quality." Placed in the crucible, they were instantly converted into cinders. "Dust and ashes," said POSTERITY. This was the doom of many an ostentatious volume, whose promising title availed as little as its interior embellishments. TIME rather soliloquised than addressed POSTERITY, while subjecting volume after volume. He would remark,-"Deadborn this; its claims for perpetuity died amidst the types." "An old heresy under the slight disguise of a new dress." "Nonsense, fustian, bombast." A whole row of poets succeeded each other in their descent into the heated crucible, with no more sympathy on the part of the executioner than a contemptuous exclamation. What is called *light literature* could scarcely be kept in the crucible long enough to be converted into thin smoke. Whole tons of periodicals and reviews shared the same fate. Occasionally we observed an unscorched leaf or two remained in the crucible, which POSTERITY carefully gathered and deposited in his *portefeuille*. At intervals, a whole volume would escape—this, however, was very rare; for in the instances in which they preserved their original shape, large portions of these fortunate volumes were burned out. For the most part, the large books fared worse than the smaller ones, from which we were led to infer, that facility in writing was quite a different thing from ability, and that a lumbering ship may be dashed on the rocks, over which a small boat may safely ride. Whole piles of periodicals (our own did not entirely escape) were soon converted into ashes. "Fabrications," said TIME, as he hurled volume after volume of history into the crucible. Some leaves, however, of most of them escaped, out of which POSTERITY remarked, he would make up a small volume of true history worthy of preservation. Many books of religious controversy, and many more of worldly controversies on all subjects went in with the ominously expressed doom, "Dust and ashes," and so they came out. We perceived a most offensive effluvium arise, as certain "Philosophical Disquisitions," and "Light of Reason" were submitted to the fiery test. Thus went forward the process, the further details of which might be tedious to enumerate, and in a very brief time the great library had so far disappeared that POSTERITY carried off what was left in a small but beautiful cabinet, made of enduring materials. We were left to wonder how human brains and iron presses worked to so little effect in this world of ours.—*Presbyterian.*

BOLDNESS (holy)—Congruous with the Gospel.

HOLY boldness honours the gospel. In the olden times, when Oriental despots had things pretty much their own way, they expected all ambassadors from the West to lay their mouths in the dust if permitted to appear before his Celestial Brightness, the Brother of the Sun and the Cousin of the Moon. Certain money-loving traders agreed to all this, and ate dust as readily as reptiles ; but, when England sent her ambassadors abroad, the daring islanders stood bolt-upright. They were told that they could not be indulged with a vision of the Brother of the Sun and Cousin of the Moon, without going down on their hands and knees. "Very well," said the Englishmen, "we will dispense with the luxury ; but tell his Celestial Splendour, that it is very likely that his Serenity will hear our cannon at his palace gates before long, and that their booming is not quite so harmless as the cooing of his Sublimity's doves." When it was seen that ambassadors of the British Crown were no cringing petitioners, our empire rose in the respect of Oriental nations. It must be just so with the cross of Christ. Our cowardice has subjected the gospel to contempt. Jesus was humble, and his servants must not be proud; but Jesus was never mean or cowardly, nor must his servants be. There was no braver man than Christ upon earth. He could stoop to save a soul, but he would stoop to nothing by which his character might be compromised, or truth and righteousness insulted. To preach the gospel boldly is to deliver it as such a message ought to be delivered. Blush to preach of a dying Saviour? Apologise for talking of the Son of God condescending to be made man, that he might redeem us from all iniquity? *Never!* Oh! by the grace of God let us purpose, with Paul, "to be yet more bold," that the gospel may be yet more fully preached throughout all ranks of mankind.

"I'll preach thy Word though kings should hear,
Nor yield to sinful shame."

BREVITY.

DR. COTTON MATHER wrote over his study-door in large letters, BE SHORT. Callers upon ministers will please make a note of this; as also brethren who are lengthy at the prayer-meeting; Sunday-school teachers, in all their devotional exercises and addresses; speakers at public meetings, who have nothing to say; and ministers who are given to prosiness.

CARNAL SECURITY.

A NUMBER of men are upstairs in a house, amusing themselves with a game of cards. What is that? The window is red! What is that cry in the streets? " *The house is on fire!*" says one. "Oh," answers another, "shuffle the cards again, let us finish the game; we have plenty of time." " *Fire! Fire! Fire!*" The cry rises more sharply from the streets, but the gamblers continue their game. One of them swaggeringly boasts, "It's all right, my brave boys, yon door leads to the roof, and we can get out at the last minute. I know the way over the leads—it's all right, go ahead with the game." Presently one of them nervously enquires, "Are you sure that we can get through that door?" and he goes to try, but finds it locked. "Never mind," is the answer,

"I have the key." "But are you sure you have the key?" "Oh, yes! I am sure I have, here it is ; try it for yourself, and do not be such a coward, man ; try it." The man tries the key. "It will not turn," says he. "Let me try," says his friend. He puts it in the lock, but lo, it will not turn! "*O God!*" he shrieks, "*it's the wrong key!*" Now, sirs, will ye go back to your game again? No, now they will strain every nerve, and labour with might and main to open the door, only to find that it is all too late for them to escape.

So many of our hearers are saying, "Oh, yes! what the preacher says is well enough, but you know we can repent whenever we like ; we have power to obtain the grace of God whenever we please ; we know the way ; have we not been told over and over again simply to trust Christ?— and we can do that whenever we please—we are safe enough." *Ah, but suppose you cannot believe whenever you please?* Suppose the day shall come when you shall call upon the Lord, and he will not answer ; when you shall stretch out your hand, but no man shall regard! Suppose you should one day cry, "Lord, Lord, open to us," and the answer should be, "I never knew you, depart, ye cursed!" O procrastinator, if you think that you can repent now, *why do you not repent now?* You believe that you have full power to do so! Oh, do it, do it, and do not trifle with that power, lest when the power is gone, you find, too late, that in one sense you never possessed it!

CENSORIOUSNESS—Who most Guilty of.

PEDLEY, who was a well-known natural simpleton, was wont to say, "God help the fool." None are more ready to pity the folly of others than those who have a small share of wit themselves. "There is no love among Christians," cries the man who is destitute of true charity. "Zeal has vanished," exclaims the idle talker. "O for more consistency," groans out the hypocrite. "We want more vital godliness," protests the false pretender. As in the old legend, the wolf preached against sheep-stealing, so very many hunt down those sins in others which they gladly shelter in themselves.

CHANGE—Love of.

IT will be found that they are the weakest-minded and the hardest-hearted men that most love variety and change; for the weakest-minded are those who both wonder most at things new, and digest worst things old; in so far that everything they have lies rusty, and loses lustre from want of use. Neither do they make any stir among their possessions, nor look over them to see what may be made of them, nor keep any great store, nor are householders with storehouses of things new and old; but they catch at the new-fashioned garments, and let the moth and thief look after the rest; and the hardest-hearted men are those that least feel the endearing and binding power of custom, and hold on by no cords of affection to any shore, but drive with the waves that cast up mire and dirt.— *John Ruskin.*

CHARITY—Spies out the Good Points in all.

MR. Jameson says, " The following beautiful epilogue had a powerful effect on my mind :"—" Jesus," says the story, " arrived one evening at the gates of a certain city, and he sent his disciples forward to prepare supper while he himself, intent on doing good, walked through the streets into the market-place. And he saw, at the corner of the market, some people gathered together looking at some object on the ground; and he drew near to see what it might be. It was a dead dog with a halter round his neck, by which he appeared to have been dragged through the dirt; and a viler, a more abject, a more unclean thing never met the eyes of man. And those who stood by looked on with abhorrence. 'Faugh !' said one, stopping his nose, 'it pollutes the air !' 'How long,' said another, 'shall this foul beast offend our sight?' 'Look at his torn hide,' said a third, 'one could not even cut a shoe out of it.' 'And his ears,' said a fourth, 'all draggled and bleeding.' 'No doubt,' said a fifth, 'he has been hanged for thieving.' And Jesus heard them, and looking down compassionately on the dead creature, he said, 'Pearls are not equal to the whiteness of his teeth.' Then the people turned to him with amazement, and said among themselves, 'Who is this? This must be Jesus of Nazareth, for only he could find something to pity and approve even in a dead dog.' And, being ashamed, they bowed their heads before him, and went each on his way."

"I can recall at this hour the vivid, yet softening and pathetic, impression left on my fancy by this old Eastern story. It gave me pain in my conscience, for it seemed thenceforward so easy and so vulgar to say satirical things, and so much nobler to be benign and merciful ; and I took the lesson so home that I was in great danger of falling into the opposite extreme—of seeking the beautiful even in the midst of the corrupt and the repulsive."

CHILDREN—Perseverance Needed in Teaching.

In dibbling beans the old practice was to put three in each hole: one for the worm, one for the crow, and one to live and produce the crop. In teaching children, we must give line upon line, and precept upon precept, repeating the truth which we would inculcate, till it becomes impossible for the child to forget it. We may well give the lesson once expecting the child's frail memory to lose it ; twice, reckoning that the devil, like an ill bird, will steal it ; thrice, hoping that it will take root downward, and bring forth fruit upward to the glory of God.

CHILDREN—their Future.

In the early French revolution, the schoolboys of Bourges, from twelve to seventeen years of age, formed themselves into a Band of Hope. They wore a uniform, and were taught drill. On their holidays, their flag was unfurled, displaying in shining letters the sentence—" TREMBLEZ, TYRANS, NOUS GRAND-IRONS !" (*Tremble, Tyrants, we shall grow up!*). Without any charge of spurious enthusiasm, we may, in imagination, hear the shouts of confidence and courage, uttered by the young Christians of the future, as they say, "Tremble, O enemy, *we* are growing up for God !"—*Mr. S. R. Pattison's Address at the Meeting of the Baptist Union*, 1869.

CHRIST—his Eye our Stimulus.

THERE is a touching fact related in a history of a Highland chief, of the noble house of M'Gregor, who fell wounded by two balls, at the battle of Prestonpans. Seeing their chief fall, the clan wavered, and gave the enemy an advantage. The old chieftain, beholding the effect of his disaster, raised himself up on his elbow, while the blood gushed in streams from his wounds, and cried aloud, "I am not dead, my children ; I am looking at you to see you do your duty." These words revived the sinking courage of his brave High-landers. There was a charm in the fact that they still fought under the eye of their chief. It roused them to put forth their mightiest energies, and they did all that human strength could do to turn and stem the dreadful tide of battle.

And is there not a charm to thee, O believer, in the fact that you contend in the battle-field of life under the eye of your Saviour ? Wherever you are, however you are oppressed by foes, however exhausted by the stern strife with evil, the eye of Christ is fixed most lovingly upon thee. Nor is Jesus the only observer of your conduct. You are also "a spectacle unto angels." You are "compassed about by a cloud of wit-nesses." Human and angelic minds, animated, the good by love, and the evil by hate, are the spectators of your deeds. Thus is the theatre of your life made sublime ; and you con-tend for salvation under circumstances sufficiently grand, and with results before you sufficiently awful, to arouse your most latent powers, and to stimulate you to strive bravely, vigorously, and perseveringly even unto victory.—*D. Wise.*

CHRIST—To be Followed above all.

IN a letter of Abelard to Eloisa, the following paragraph occurs :—" I will be no philosopher, if so be I must needs fight against St. Paul ; I will be no Aristotle, if so be I be separated from Christ." If all students were thus resolved to hold with the great Teacher at all hazards, we should not see such frequent victims of "philosophy, falsely so called." Unlettered ignorance is a great evil, but learned ignorance is worse, and such is all learning which decoys the heart from Jesus.

CHRIST—Love of, Proved.

IN the French revolution, a young man was condemned to the guillotine, and shut up in one of the prisons. He was greatly loved by many, but there was one who loved him more than all put together. How know we this ? It was his own father, and the love he bore his son was proved in this way : when the lists were called, the father, whose name was exactly the same as the son's, answered to the name, and the father rode in the gloomy tumbril out to the place of execution, and his head rolled beneath the axe instead of his son's, a victim to mighty love. See here an image of the love of Christ to sinners ; for thus Jesus died for the ungodly.

CHRIST—the Soul's only Defence.

THERE is an ancient parable which says that the dove once made a piteous complaint to her fellow birds, that the hawk was a most cruel tyrant, and was thirsting for her blood. One counselled her to keep below—but the hawk can stoop for its prey ; another advised her to soar aloft—

but the hawk can mount as high as she. A third bade her hide herself in the woods, but alas ! these are the hawk's own estates, where he holds his court. A fourth recommended her to keep in the town, but there man hunted her, and she feared that her eyes would be put out by the cruel falconer to make sport for the hawk. At last one told her to rest herself in the clefts of the rock, there she would be safe, violence itself could not surprise her there.

The meaning is easy ; reader, do not fail to catch it, and to act upon it. The dove is thy poor defenceless soul. Satan is · thy cruel foe ; wouldst thou not escape from him? Thy poverty cannot protect thee, for sin can stoop to the poor man's level and devour him in the cottage, and drag him to hell from a hovel. Thy riches are no security, for Satan can make these a snare to thee, and if thou shouldst mount ever so high, the bird of prey can follow thee and rend thee in pieces ! The busy world with all its cares cannot shelter thee, for here it is that the great enemy is most at home ; he is the prince of this world, and seizes men who find their joys therein as easily as a kite lays hold upon a sparrow. Nor can retirement secure you, for there are sins peculiar to quietude, and hell's dread vulture soars over lonely solitudes to find defenceless souls, and rend them in pieces. There is but one defence. O may you and I fly to it at once ! Jesus was wounded for sin ; faith in him saves at once and for ever.

CHRIST JESUS—the Marrow of Theology.

THE late venerable and godly Dr. Archibald Alexander, of Princeton, United States, had been a preacher of Christ for sixty years, and a professor of divinity for forty. He died on the 22nd October, 1851. On his death-bed, he was heard to say to a friend, "All my theology is reduced to this narrow compass—*Jesus Christ came into the world to save sinners.*"

CHRIST—our only Hope.

ON a huge cross by the side of an Italian highway hung a
hideous caricature of the Beloved of our souls, who poured
out his life for our redemption. Out of reverence to the
living Christ we turned aside, disgusted from the revolting
image, but not until we had espied the words SPES UNICA,
in capitals over its head. Here was truth emblazoned on an
idol. Yes, indeed, Jesus, our now exalted, but once crucified
Lord is the sole and *only hope* of man. Assuredly, O Lord
Jesus, thou art *spes unica* to our soul.

> " Other refuge have we none,
>   Hangs our helpless soul on thee."

We found this diamond in the mire of superstition : does it
sparkle any the less ?

CHRIST—our only Rest.

MY heart can have no rest, unless it leans on Jesus Christ
wholly, and then it feels his peace. But I am apt to leave
my resting-place, and when I ramble from it, my heart will
quickly brew up mischief. Some evil temper now begins to
boil, or some care would fain perplex me, or some idol wants
to please me, or some deadness or some lightness creeps upon
my spirit, and communion with my Saviour is withdrawn.
When these thorns stick in my flesh, I do not try, as hereto-
fore, to pick them out with my own needle, but carry all
complaints to Jesus, casting every care upon him. His office
is to save, and mine to look for help.—*John Berridge.*

CHRIST—Riches of his Grace.

SIR Richard Whittington entertained King Henry V. at
the Guildhall with unparalleled magnificence. The braziers
in the hall were supplied with logs of rare, sweet-scented
wood for fuel ; but they burned with a far more delicious
fragrance when the noble citizen bringing forth the king's

bonds for the repayment of the large sum of £60,000 (equal to £900,000 now), thrust them into the blazing fire, saying, that he was too happy thus to discharge the king's obligations. When the handwriting which was against us is put away, we receive a choice mercy indeed. That blessed fire of Christ's most fragrant sufferings hath consumed all his people's sins ; this is royal bounty with an emphasis.

CHRIST—Sympathy with his People.

" IF," says Augustine, " a man should come up to embrace thee, to kiss and honour thee upward, and beneath with a pair of shoes beaten full of nails, tread upon thy bare foot ; the head shall despise the honour done unto it, and for the foot that smarteth, say, Why treadest thou upon me ? So when feigned gospellers honour Christ our Head, sitting in heaven, and oppress his members on earth, the Head shall speak for the feet that smart, and say, Why treadest thou on me ?" Paul had a zeal toward God, but he did tread upon Christ's feet on earth, for whom the Head crieth forth of heaven, " Saul, Saul, why persecutest thou me ?" Although Christ sitteth on the right hand of his Father, yet lieth he on earth ; he suffereth all calamities here on earth, he is many times evil entreated here on earth.—*Bernard Gilpin.*

CHRIST—the Preacher's Theme.

THE pulpit is intended to be a pedestal for the cross, though, alas ! even the cross itself, it is to be feared, is sometimes used as a mere pedestal for the preacher's fame. We may roll the thunders of eloquence, we may dart the coruscations of genius, we may scatter the flowers of poetry, we may diffuse the light of science, we may enforce the precepts of morality, from the pulpit ; but if we do not make Christ the great subject of our preaching, we have forgotten our errand, and shall do no good. Satan trembles at nothing but the cross : at this he does tremble ; and if we would destroy his power, and extend that holy and benevolent kingdom, which is righteousness, peace, and joy in the Holy Ghost, it must be by means of the CROSS.—*J. A. James.*

CHRIST—the Preacher's great Theme.

THE best sermon is that which is fullest of Christ. A Welsh minister, when preaching at the chapel of my dear brother Jonathan George, was saying that Christ was the sum and substance of the gospel, and he broke out into the following story :—A young man had been preaching in the presence of a venerable divine, and after he had done, he foolishly went to the old minister and enquired, "What do you think of my sermon, sir?" "A very poor sermon indeed," said he. "A poor sermon!" said the young man, "it took me a long time to study it." "Ay, no doubt of it." "Why, then, do you say it was poor ; did you not think my explanation of the text to be accurate?" "Oh, yes," said the old preacher, "very correct indeed." "Well, then, why do you say it is a poor sermon? Didn't you think the metaphors were appropriate, and the arguments conclusive?" "Yes, they were very good, as far as that goes, but still it was a very poor sermon." "Will you tell me why you think it a poor sermon?" "Because," said he, "there was no Christ in it." "Well," said the young man, "Christ was not in the text ; we are not to be preaching Christ always, we must preach what is in the text." So the old man said, "Don't you know, young man, that from every town, and every village, and every little hamlet in England, wherever it may be, there is a road to London?" "Yes," said the young man. "Ah!" said the old divine, "and so from every text in Scripture there is a road to the metropolis of the Scriptures, that is Christ. And, my dear brother, your business is, when you get to a text, to say, 'Now, what is the road to Christ?' and then preach a sermon, running along the road towards the great metropolis—Christ. And," said he, "I have never yet found a text that had not a plain and direct road to Christ in it; and if ever I should find one that has no such road, I will make a road, I would go over hedge and ditch but I would get at my Master, for a sermon is neither fit for the land nor yet for the dunghill, unless there is a savour of Christ in it."

CHRIST—Trophies of his Power.

BEFORE many a Popish shrine on the Continent one sees exhibited a great variety of crutches, together with wax models of arms, legs, and other limbs. These are supposed to represent the cures wrought by devotion at that altar ; the memorials of the healing power of the saint. Poor miserable superstition all of it, and yet what a reminder to the believer in Jesus as to his duty and his privilege ! Having pleaded at the feet of Jesus, we have found salvation; have we remembered to record this wonder of his hand ? If we hung up memorials of all his matchless grace, what crutches, and bandages, and trophies of every sort should we pile together ! Temper subdued, pride humbled, unbelief slain, sin cast down, sloth ashamed, carelessness rebuked. The cross has healed all manner of diseases, and its honours should be proclaimed with every rising and setting sun.

CHRIST—Welcoming Sinners.

WE are told that in stormy weather it is not unusual for small birds to be blown out of sight of land on to the sea. They are often seen by voyagers out of their reckoning and far from the coast, hovering over the masts on weary wings as if they wanted to alight and rest themselves, but fearing to do so. A traveller tells us that on one occasion, a little lark, which followed the ship for a considerable distance, was at last compelled through sheer weariness to alight. He was so worn out as to be easily caught. The warmth of the hand was so agreeable to him that he sat down on it, burying his little cold feet in his feathers, and looking about with his

3

bright eye not in the least afraid, and as if feeling assured that he had been cast amongst good kind people whom he had no occasion to be so backward in trusting. A touching picture of the soul who is aroused by the Spirit of God and blown out of its own reckoning by the winds of conviction; and the warm reception which the weary little bird received at the hands of the passengers conveys but a faint idea of that welcome which will greet the worn-out, sin-sick souls who will commit themselves into the hands of the only Saviour.

CHRIST—With us in Trial.

ONE thing which contributed to make Cæsar's soldiers invincible was their seeing him always take his share in danger, and never desire any exemption from labour and fatigue. We have a far higher incentive in the war for truth and goodness when we consider him who endured such contradiction of sinners against himself.

CHRISTIAN—Manifest by his Life.

LONGFELLOW in his Hiawatha sings of—

" The pleasant watercourses,
　You could trace them through the valley,
　By the rushing in the Spring-time,
　By the alders in the Summer,
　By the white fog in the Autumn,
　By the black line in the Winter."

So traceable are the lives of really gracious men and women. They are not solicitous to be observed, but the gracious "signs following" are sure to reveal them. Like their Master they cannot be hid.

CHRISTIAN—Professor cannot be Neutral.

IT appears that Themistocles, when a boy, was full of spirit and fire, quick of apprehension, naturally inclined to bold attempts, and likely to make a great statesman. His hours of leisure and vacation he spent not, like other boys, in idleness and play, but he was always inventing and composing declamations, the subjects of which were either impeachments or defences of some of his schoolfellows ; so that his master would often say, " Boy, you will be nothing common or indifferent, you will either be a blessing or a curse to the community." So remember, you who profess to be followers of the Lord Jesus, that to you indifference is impossible ; you *must* bless the church and the world by your holiness, or you will curse them both by your hypocrisy and inconsistency. In the visible church it is most true that "no man liveth unto himself, and no man dieth unto himself."

CHRISTIAN—a Royal Personage.

A POOR but pious woman called upon two elegant young ladies, who, regardless of her poverty, invited her to sit down with them in the drawing-room, and entered into conversation with her upon religious subjects. While thus employed, their brother, a dashing youth, by chance entered, and appeared astonished to see his sisters thus engaged. One of them instantly exclaimed, " Brother, don't be surprised ; this is a king's daughter, though she has not yet put on her fine clothes."—*Pioneer.*

CHRISTIAN—What he should be.

A CHILD of God should be a *visible Beatitude*, for joy and happiness, and a *living Doxology*, for gratitude and adoration.

CHRISTIAN'S LIFE—The Power of.

THERE is a spot on the Lago Lugano, where the song of the nightingale swells sweetly from the thickets on the shore in matchless rush of music, so that the oar lies motionless and the listener is hushed into silent entrancement ; yet we did not see a single bird, the orchestra was as hidden as the notes

were clear. Such is a virtuous life, and such the influence of
modest holiness ; the voice of excellence is heard when the
excellent themselves are not seen.

CHURCH—her Glory in Tribulation.

LOOKING from the little wooden bridge which passes over
the brow of the beautiful waterfall of Handeck, on the Grimsel,
one will at a certain hour of a bright day be surprised to see
a rainbow making an entire circle, surrounding the fall like a
coronet of gems, or a ring set with all the brilliants of the
jeweller.   Every hue is there

> "In fair proportion, running from the red
> To where the violet fades into the sky."

We saw two such bows, one within the other, and we fancied
that we discovered traces of a third. We had looked upon such
a sight but once before, and were greatly delighted with "that
arch of light, born of the spray, and coloured by the sun."   It
was a fair vision to gaze upon, and reminded us of the mystic
rainbow, which the seer of Patmos beheld, which was round
about the throne, for it strikes us that it was seen by John as
a complete circle, of which we see but the half on earth ; the
upper arch of manifest glory we rejoice to gaze upon, but the
lower and foundation arch of the eternal purpose, upon which
the visible display of grace is founded, is reserved for our
contemplation in another world. When we read in the first
verse of the tenth chapter of Revelation, "I saw another
mighty angel come down from heaven, clothed with a cloud :
and a rainbow was upon his head," it greatly assists the imagination to conceive of a many-coloured circlet, rather than
a semicircle.

We lingered long watching the flashing crystal, dashed
and broken upon a hundred craggy rocks, and tossed into
the air in sheets of foam, to fall in wreaths of spray ; we

should not have tired for hours if we could have tarried to admire the harmonious hues of that wheel within a wheel,

> " Of colours changing from the splendid rose,
>   To the pale violet's dejected hue ;"

but we were on a journey, and were summoned to advance. As we mounted our mule and rode silently down the pass, amid the pine forests and the over-hanging mountains, we compared the little stream to the church of God, which in peaceful times flows on like a village brook, quiet and obscure, blessed and blessing others, but yet little known or considered by the sons of men. Abana and Pharpar, rivers of Damascus, are greater than all the waters of Israel, and the proud ones of the earth despise that brook which flows "hard by the oracle of God," because her waters go softly and in solitary places ; but when the church advances over the steeps of opposition, and is dashed adown the crags of persecution, then, in her hour of sorrow, her glory is revealed. Then she lifts up her voice, like the sea, and roars as a boiling torrent, quickening her pace till that mighty river, the river Kishon, sweeps not with such vehemence of power. Her sons and daughters are led to the slaughter, and her blood is cast abroad, like the foam of the waters, but onward she dashes with irresistible energy, fearing no leap of peril ; and then it is that the eternal God glorifies her with the rainbow of his everlasting grace, makes the beauty of her holiness to shine forth, and, in the patience of the saints, reveals a heavenly radiance, which all men behold with astonishment. The golden age of true religion is the martyr period ; war breeds heroes, and suffering unto blood in striving against sin draws forth men of whom the world is not worthy. So far from enduring loss by opposition, it is then that the cause of God receives its coronation. The rainbow of the divine presence in the fulness of majesty encircles the chosen people when tribulation, affliction, and distress break them, as the stream

is broken by the precipitous rocks adown which it boldly
casts itself, that its current may advance in its predestined
channel.   When, at any time, our forebodings foretell the
coming of evil times for the church, let us remember that before the Spirit revealed to the beloved disciple the terrible
beasts, the thundering trumpets, the falling stars, and the
dreadful vials, he bade him mark with attention that the
covenant rainbow was round about the throne. All is well, for
God is true.

CHURCH—To be Purged.

WHEN Oliver Cromwell was about to turn the Members of
Parliament out of their chamber, he pointed to the mace, and
cried, "Take away that bauble!"   When HE shall come, who
will effectually purge the church, he will say much the same
of many ecclesiastical ornaments, now held in high repute.
Gowns, and altars, and banners, and painted windows, will
all go at one sweep with "take away those baubles."   Nor
will the rhetorical embellishments and philosophies of modern
pulpits be any more tenderly dealt with.   "Take away this
bauble" will be the signal for turning many a treasured folly
into perpetual contempt.

CIRCUMSTANCES.

HORACE SMITH truly and wittily remarks, " If a letter were
to be addressed to that most influential word, *circumstances,*
concluding thus—'I am, sir, your very obedient humble
servant,' the greater part of the world might subscribe it
without deviating from the strictest veracity."

COMING TO CHRIST—as a Sinner.

A GREAT monarch was accustomed on certain set occasions
to entertain all the beggars of the city. Around him were placed
his courtiers, all clothed in rich apparel ; the beggars sat at
the same table in their rags of poverty. Now it came to pass,
that on a certain day, one of the courtiers had spoiled his

silken apparel, so that he dared not put it on, and he felt, " I cannot go to the king's feast to-day, for my robe is foul." He sat weeping till the thought struck him, " To-morrow when the king holds his feast, some will come as courtiers happily decked in their beautiful array, but others will come and be made quite as welcome who will be dressed in rags. Well, well," said he, "so long as I may see the king's face, and sit at the royal table, I will enter among the beggars." So without mourning because he had lost his silken habit, he put on the rags of a beggar, and he saw the king's face as well as if he had worn his scarlet and fine linen. My soul has done this full many a time, when her evidences of salvation have been dim; and I bid you do the same when you are in like case : if you cannot come to Jesus as a saint, come as a sinner ; only do come with simple faith to him, and you shall receive joy and peace.

COMING TO CHRIST—as a Sinner.

IN one of the coal-pits of the north, while a considerable number of the miners were down below, the top of the pit fell in, and the shaft was completely blocked up. Those who were in the mine, gathered to a spot where the last remains of air could be breathed. There they sat and sang and prayed after the lights had gone out because the air was unable to support the flame. They were in total darkness, but a gleam of hope cheered them when one of them said he had heard that there was a connection between that pit and an old pit which had been worked years ago. He said it was a long passage through which a man might get by crawling all the way, lying flat upon the ground ; he would go and see if it were passable. The passage was very long, but they crept through it, and at last they came out to light at the bottom of the other shaft, and their lives were saved.

If my present way of access to Christ as a saint is blocked

up by doubts and fears, if I cannot go straight up the shaft
and see the light of my Father's face, there is an old working,
the old-fashioned way by which sinners have gone of old,
by which poor thieves go, by which harlots go.   I will creep
along it, lowly and humbly; I will go flat upon the ground.
I will humble myself till I see my Lord, and cry, "Father, I am
not worthy to be called thy son, make me as one of thy hired
servants, so long as I may but dwell in thy house."   In our
very worst case of despondency we may still come to Jesus as
sinners.   "Jesus Christ came into the world to save sinners."
Call this to mind, and you may have hope.

COMMUNION WITH CHRIST—its Influence on our Views.

WHEN you have been sitting in a well-lighted room and
are suddenly called into the outer darkness, how black it
seems; and thus when a man has dwelt in communion with
God, sin becomes exceeding sinful, and the darkness in
which the world lieth appears like tenfold night.

COMMUNION WITH CHRIST—Joy of.

NO sooner do you pass the brow of the St. Gothard pass,
on your way to Italy, than you perceive that, beyond all
question, you are on the sunny side of the Alps.   The snow
lying there is nothing in comparison to the vast accumulation
upon the Swiss side of the summit, the wind ceases to be
sharp and cutting, and a very few minutes' ride brings you into
a balmy air which makes you forget that you are so greatly
elevated above the sea level. There is a very manifest difference
between the southern side and the bleak northern aspect.
He who climbs above the cares of the world, and turns his
face to his God, has found the sunny side of life.   The world's
side of the hill is chill and freezing to a spiritual mind, but the
Lord's presence gives a warmth of joy which turns winter
into summer.   Some pilgrims to heaven appear never to
have passed the summit of religious difficulty ; they are still

toiling over the Devil's Bridge, or loitering at Andermatt, or plunging into the deep snowdrifts of their own personal unworthiness, ever learning, but never coming to a full knowledge of the truth ; they have not attained to a comfortable perception of the glory, preciousness, and all-sufficiency of the Lord Jesus, and therefore abide amid the winter of their doubts and fears. If they had but faith to surmount their spiritual impediments, how changed would everything become ! It is fair travelling with a sunny land smiling before your eyes, especially when you retain a grateful remembrance of the bleak and wintry road which you have traversed ; but it is sorry work to be always stopping on the Swiss side of the mountain. How is it that so many do this ?

COMMUNION WITH GOD—Power of.

IN driving piles, a machine is used by which a huge weight is lifted up and then made to fall upon the head of the pile. Of course the higher the weight is lifted the more powerful is the blow which it gives when it descends. Now, if we would tell upon our age and come down upon society with ponderous blows, we must see to it that we are uplifted as near to God as possible. All our power will depend upon the elevation of our spirits. Prayer, meditation, devotion, communion, are like a windlass to wind us up aloft ; it is not lost time which we spend in such sacred exercises, for we are thus accumulating force, so that when we come down to our actual labour for God, we shall descend with an energy unknown to those to whom communion is unknown.

COMMUNION OF SAINTS.

COMMUNION is strength, solitude is weakness. Alone, the fine old beech yields to the blast, and lies prone upon the sward : in the forest, supporting each other, the trees laugh at the hurricane. The sheep of Jesus flock together ; the social element is the genius of Christianity.

COMMUNION OF SAINTS.

WHAT the circulation of the blood is to the human body, that the Holy Spirit is to the body of Christ which is the church. Now, by virtue of the one life-flood, every limb of the body holds fellowship with every other, and as long as life lasts that fellowship is inevitable. If the hand be unwashed the eye cannot refuse communion with it on that account ; if the finger be diseased the hand cannot, by binding a cord around it, prevent the life-current from flowing. Nothing but death can break up the fellowship, you must tear away the member, or it must of necessity commune with the rest of the body. It is even thus in the body of Christ ; no laws can prevent one living member of Christ from fellowship with every other, the pulse of living fellowship sends a wave through the whole mystical frame ; where there is but one life, fellow-ship is an inevitable consequence. Yet some talk of restricted communion, and imagine that they can practise it. If they be alive unto God they may in mistaken conscientiousness deny their fellow Christians the outward sign of communion, but communion itself falls not under any rule or regulation of theirs. Tie a red tape round your thumb and let it decree that the whole body is out of fellowship with it ; the thumb's decree is either ridiculously inoperative, or else it proves injurious to itself. God has made us one, one Spirit quickens us, and truly our fellowship is with the Father, and with his Son Jesus ; to deny fellowship with any believer in Jesus is to refuse what you *must* of necessity give, and to deny in symbol what you *must* inevitably render in reality.

CONSCIENCE—Hardening.

IT is a very terrible thing to let conscience begin to grow hard, for it soon chills into northern iron and steel. It is like the freezing of a pond. The first film of ice is scarcely perceptible ; keep the water stirring and you will prevent the frost from hardening it ; but once let it film over and remain quiet, the glaze thickens over the surface, and it thickens still, and at last it is so firm that a waggon might be drawn over the solid ice. So with conscience, it films over gradually, until at last it becomes hard and unfeeling, and is not crushed even with ponderous loads of iniquity.

CONSECRATION.

TRAVELLERS have said that they have discovered gardens of Solomon, which were of old enclosed as private places wherein the king walked in solitude; and they have also found wells of a most deliciously cold water, dexterously covered, so that no person unacquainted with the stone in the wall, which either revolved or slid away with a touch, could have found the entrance to the spring. At the foot of some lofty range of mountains a reservoir received the cooling streams which flowed from melted snows ; this reservoir was carefully guarded and shut out from all common entrance, in order that the king alone might enter there, and might refresh himself during the scorching heats. Such is the Christian's heart. It is a spring shut up, a fountain sealed, a garden reserved for Jesus only. O come, Great King, and enjoy thy possessions.

CONSISTENCY.

MILTON excuses Oliver Cromwell's want of bookish application in his youth thus :—" It did not become that hand to wax soft in literary ease which was to be inured to the use of arms and hardened with asperity ; that right arm to be softly wrapped up among the birds of Athens, by which thunderbolts were soon afterwards to be hurled among the eagles which emulate the sun."

Carnal ease and worldly wisdom are not becoming in the soldier of Jesus Christ. He has to wrestle against principalities and powers, and has need of sterner qualities than those which sparkle in the eyes of fashion or adorn the neck of elegance.

CONSISTENCY.

"I SHALL not attend Sabbath-school any more," said a young girl to one of her class. "Why not?" asked her friend. "Because my mother is going to send me to the dancing-school, and I think it very inconsistent to attend both at the same time." Children are sure to reason, if their parents do not. "Lead us not into temptation," let children pray; for are they not often led there?

CONTENTMENT.'

MAKING a day's excursion from Botzen in the Tyrol, we went along the very narrowest of roads, mere alleys, to which our country lanes would be turnpike roads. Well, you may be sure that we did not engage an ordinary broad carriage, for that would have found the passage as difficult as the needle's eye to the camel; but our landlord had a very narrow chaise for us, just the very thing for threading those four-feet passages. Now, I must make you hear the moral of it, you fretful little gentlemen. When you have a small estate, you must have small wants, and by contentment suit your carriage to your road. "Not so easy," say you? "Very necessary to a Christian," say I.

CONVERSATION.

IN Andrew Fuller's diary is the following entry:—

"Jan. 3, 1782. This afternoon being on a visit, as I stepped aside from the company, I overheard one of them saying, 'I love Mr. Fuller's company, it is so *diverting.* 'This expression moved me much. Oh, wretch that I am! Is this to have my speech seasoned with grace? O Lord, forgive me! Some humbling thoughts for the above in prayer."

"4. Tender this morning in remembering the above circumstance. Lord, make me more spiritual in time to come."

CONVERSATION—Edifying.

THE Spaniards in Chili believed that no water was so

wholesome or of so delicate a flavour as that which flowed
through veins of gold ; certainly no conversation is so edifying
to the hearers as that which pours forth from a heart stored
with sacred knowledge, sanctified experience, devout contem-
plations, and such like precious treasures.

CONVERSION—a Radical Change.

I PASSED by a piece of common which some lord of the
manor or other had been enclosing, as those rascals always
will if they can, to rob the poor of their rights, and filch every
morsel of green grass upon which we may freely plant our
feet ; but I noticed that the enclosers had only railed it round,
but had not dug it up, nor ploughed it, nor planted it ; and
though they had cut down the gorse, it was coming up again;
of course it would, for it was a common still, and a bit of
fence or rail could not alter it ; the furze would come peeping
up, and ere long the enclosure would be as wild as the heath
outside. But this is not God's way of working. When God
encloseth a heart that has laid common with sin, does he cut
down the thorns and the briers and then plant fir trees?
(Isaiah lv. 13.) No, no ; but he so changeth the soil, that
from the ground itself, from its own vitality, there spontaneously starts up the fir tree and the myrtle. This is a
most wonderful result. You take a man and leave him at
heart the same godless man. You mend his habits ; you
make him go to church, or to the meeting-house ; you clothe
him ; you break his wine bottle ; you rinse his mouth out, so
that he does not talk so filthily ; and altogether you say,
" He's now a respectable man." Ah ! but if these outward
respectabilities and rightnesses are only skin deep, you
have done nothing. At least, what you have done is no great
wonder ; there is nothing in it to be proud of. But suppose
this man can be so changed, that just as freely as he was
wont to curse he now delights to pray, and just as heartily as
he hated religion he now finds pleasure in it, and just as

earnestly as he sinned he now delights to be obedient to the
Lord ; ah ! then, this is a wonder, a miracle which man
cannot accomplish, a marvel which only the grace of God can
work, and which gives to God his highest glory.

CONVERSION—a Complete Surrender.

WHEN Henry VIII. had determined to make himself head
of the English Church, he insisted upon it that convocation
should accept his headship without limiting and modifying
clauses. He refused to entertain any compromises, and vowed
that "he would have no *tantums*," as he called them. Thus
when a sinner parleys with his Saviour he would fain have a
little of the honour of his salvation, he would save alive some
favourite sin, he would fain amend the humbling terms of
grace—but there is no help for it, Jesus will be all in all, and
the sinner must be nothing at all. The surrender must be
complete, there must be no *tantums*, but the heart must
without reserve submit to the sovereignty of the Redeemer.

CONVERSIONS (Sudden)—not all Genuine.

FISH sometimes leap out of the water with great energy,
but it would be foolish to conclude that they have left the
liquid element for ever, in a moment they are swimming
again as if they had never forsaken the stream ; indeed, it was
but a fly that tempted them aloft, or a sudden freak, the water is
still their home, sweet home. When we see long-accustomed
sinners making a sudden leap at religion, we may not make
too sure that they are converts ; perhaps some gain allures
them, or sudden excitement stirs them, and if so they will be
back again at their old sins. Let us hope well, but let us not
commend too soon.

CONVICTION—of Sin.

THERE is something to be learned from the conduct of the
Papists to our sires. If any poor wretch recanted and so

escaped the fire, they were accustomed to make him carry a fagot at the next burning, as if to let him see what he had escaped, and make him confess what he had deserved. Depend upon it, conviction of sin is much like this carrying of the fagot. Well do I remember when I felt the sentence of death within me, and trembled lest it should be executed : my conscience was a minor hell, a fagot of the pile of Tophet. But, blessed be God, we are thus judged and sentenced in ourselves that we may not be condemned with the world. We bear the fagot that we may not be burned with it.

CORRUPTIONS—Hard to Die.

A CAT once sprang at my lips while I was talking, and bit me savagely. My friend in whose house it occurred, decreed that the poor creature should die. The sentence he executed personally, to the best of his ability, and threw the carcase away. To his surprise, the cat walked into the house the next day.

Often and often have I vowed death to some evil propensity, and have fondly dreamed that the sentence was fulfilled, but alas ! in weaker moments I have had sad cause to know that the sinful tendency still survived.

CORRUPTIONS—Hated by the Saints.

WHEN Venice was in the hands of the Austrians, those alien tyrants swarmed in every quarter ; but the Venetians hated them to the last degree, and showed their enmity upon all occasions. When the Austrian officers sat down at any of the tables in the square of St. Mark, where the Venetians delight on summer evenings to eat their ices and drink their coffee, the company would immediately rise and retire, showing by their withdrawal that they abhorred their oppressors. After this fashion will every true Christian treat his inbred sins ; he will not be happy under their power, nor tolerate their dominion, nor show them favour. If he cannot expel them, he will not indulge them.

CORRUPTIONS—Indulgence of.

THE man of the world in the olden time bowed to the fallen statue of Jupiter, by way of bespeaking the favour of the god in the event of his being again lifted on his pedestal. What are those provisions for the flesh, which too many Christians so readily make, but a kind of homage to the old man whom they profess to have renounced?

CORRUPTIONS—Overcome by Grace.

MY gardeners were removing a large tree which grew near a wall, and as it would weaken the wall to stub up the roots, it was agreed that the stump should remain in the ground. But how were we to prevent the stump from sprouting, and so disarranging the gravel-walk. The gardener's prescription was, to cover it with a layer of salt. I mused awhile, and thought that the readiest way to keep down my ever-sprouting corruptions in future would be to sow them well with the salt of grace. O Lord, help me so to do.

CORRUPTIONS—Overcome Gradually.

WHEN Sir Christopher Wren was engaged in demolishing the ruins of old St. Paul's in order to make room for his new cathedral, he used a battering-ram with which thirty men continued to beat upon a part of the wall for a whole day. The workmen, not discerning any immediate effect, thought this a waste of time ; but Wren, who knew that the internal motion thus communicated must be operating, encouraged them to persevere. On the second day, the wall began to tremble at the top, and fell in a few hours. If our prayers and repentances do not appear to overcome our corruptions, we must continue still to use these gracious battering-rams, for in due time by faith in Jesus Christ the power of evil shall be overthrown. Lord, enable me to give hearty blows by the power of thy Holy Spirit until the gates of hell in my soul shall be made to totter and fall.

CORRUPTIONS—Strengthened by Habit.

IN preparing places for planting new trees, the diggers
found it needful in certain spots to lay aside the spade and
use the pick-axe. In those positions there had been a well-
gravelled carriage road, and hence it was hard to deal with it.
How often, when we are under sanctifying influences, do we
find certain hard points of our character which are not
touched by ordinary influences ; these are most probably sins
in which we have become hardened, tracks worn by habitual
transgression. We must not wonder if the severest processes
of affliction should be tried upon us, if the pick-axe is used
instead of the spade, that our stony places may yet yield soil
for the plants of grace and holiness.

CORRUPTIONS—Seen even in Solitude.

GEORGE SHADFORD wrote :—" One day a friend took me
to see a hermit in the woods. After some difficulty we found
his hermitage, which was a little place like a hog-sty, built of
several pieces of wood, covered with bark of trees, and his
bed consisted of dry leaves. There was a narrow beaten path
about twenty or thirty yards in length by the side of it, where
he frequently walked to meditate."

" If one offered him food, he would take it, but if money
was offered him, he would be angry. If anything was spoken
which he did not like, he broke out into a violent passion.
He had lived in this cell seven cold winters, and after all his
prayers, counting his beads, and separating from the rest of
mankind, still corrupt nature was all alive within him."

Alas ! alas ! what will it avail us whether we are in England
or Ireland, Scotland or America ; whether we live amongst
mankind, or retire into a hermitage, if we still carry with us
our own hell, our corrupt evil tempers? Without a new
heart and a right spirit, no condition can deliver a man from
the thraldom of his sins. Neither publicity nor solitude
avails anything until grace prevails with us. The devil can

4

tempt in the wilderness as well as in the crowd. We want
not hermitages but heavenly-mindedness.

CORRUPTIONS—Vitality of.

THE yew tree appears to renew itself out of its own decay ;
the decayed wood at the centre of an old yew is gradually
formed into rich vegetable mould, and fresh verdure springs
from it. How like is this to our inward corruptions, which
have a marvellous vitality, so that one sin feeds upon the
death of another. If we are cured of some one fault, we grow
proud of the amendment ; or if we perceive ourselves to be in
the wrong and strive against the evil, we are too apt to despond
and become unbelieving. So pride and unbelief, two master
evils, grow out of the decay of other sins.

COURAGE—Strengthened by past Deliverances.

SIR FRANCIS DRAKE, being in a dangerous storm in the
Thames, was heard to say, "Must I who have escaped the
rage of the ocean, be drowned in a ditch !" Will you,
experienced saints, who have passed through a world of
tribulation lie down and die of despair, or give up your
profession because you are at the present moment passing
through some light affliction ? Let your past preservation
inspire you with courage and constrain you to brave all storms
for Jesus' sake.

COVETOUSNESS.

COVETOUS men must be the sport of Satan, for their grasp-
ing avarice neither lets them enjoy life nor escape from the
second death. They are held by their own greed as surely as
beasts with cords, or fish with nets, or men with chains.
They may be likened to those foolish apes which in some
countries are caught by narrow-necked vessels ; into these
corn is placed, the creatures thrust in their hands, and when
they have filled them they cannot draw out their fists unless

they let go the grain; sooner than do this they submit to be captured. Are covetous men then so like to beasts? Let them ponder and be ashamed.

COVETOUSNESS—its Insidiousness.

BEWARE of growing covetousness, for of all sins this is one of the most insidious. It is like the silting up of a river. As the stream comes down from the land, it brings with it sand and earth, and deposits all these at its mouth, so that by degrees, unless the conservators watch it carefully, it will block itself up, and leave no channel for ships of great burden. By daily deposit it imperceptibly creates a bar which is dangerous to navigation. Many a man when he begins to accumulate wealth commences at the same moment to ruin his soul, and the more he acquires, the more closely he blocks up his liberality, which is, so to speak, the very mouth of spiritual life. Instead of doing more for God he does less ; the more he saves the more he wants, and the more he wants of this world the less he cares for the world to come.

CUTTLE-FISH—Persons who Resemble a.

IT was an old Pythagorean maxim, " Sepiam ne edito," " *never eat the cuttle-fish.*" The cuttle-fish has the power of emitting a black liquid which dyes the water and enables it to conceal itself. Have nothing to do with those who darken all around them that they themselves may be unseen ; honest men love light, and only the evil find darkness to be congenial. When an author is too obscure to be understood, leave him till he knows how to write ; when a preacher is mystical, high-flown, sophistical, shun him, for it is most likely he labours to conceal some latent heresy ; when a man's policy is deep and artful, flee from him, for he means no good. No deceiver or double-tongued man must be admitted within the circle of your confidence. Remember the advice, *never eat a cuttle-fish.*

DANCING.

WHEN I hear of a dancing party I feel an uneasy sensation about the throat, remembering that a far greater preacher had his head danced off in the days of our Lord. However pleasing the polkas of Herodias might be to Herod, they were death to John the Baptist. The caperings and wantonings of the ball-room are death to the solemn influences of our ministry, and many an ill-ended life first received its bent for evil amid the flippancies of gay assemblies met to trip away the hours.

DANGER—of the Christian.

WHEN the instructed Christian sees his surroundings, he finds himself to be like a defenceless dove flying to her nest, while against her tens of thousands of arrows are levelled. The Christian life is like that dove's anxious flight, as it threads its way between the death-bearing shafts of the enemy, and by constant miracle escapes unhurt. The enlightened Christian sees himself to be like a traveller, standing on the narrow summit of a lofty ridge ; on the right hand and on the left are gulfs unfathomable, yawning for his destruction ; if it were not that by divine grace his feet are like hinds' feet, so that he is able to stand upon his high places, he would long ere this have fallen to his eternal destruction.

DAY BY DAY.

A CELEBRATED modern writer says, "Take care of the *minutes*, and the *hours* will take care of themselves." This is an admirable remark, and might be very seasonably recollected when we begin to be "weary in well-doing," from the thought of having much to do. The present moment is all we have to do with in any sense ; the past is irrecoverable ; the future is uncertain ; nor is it fair to burthen one moment with the weight of the next. Sufficient unto the *moment* is the trouble thereof. If we had to walk a hundred miles, we should still have to set but one step at a time, and this process continued would infallibly bring us to our journey's end. Fatigue generally begins, and is always increased, by calculating in a minute the exertion of hours. Thus, in looking forward to future life, let us recollect that we have not to sustain all its toil, to endure all its sufferings, or encounter all its crosses at once. One moment comes laden with its own *little* burthens, then flies, and is succeeded by another no heavier than the last ; if *one* could be borne, so could another, and another. Even in looking forward to a single day, the spirit may sometimes faint from an anticipation of the duties, the labours, the trials to temper and patience, that may be expected. Now, this is unjustly laying the burthen of many thousand moments upon *one.—Youth's Magazine for November*, 1819.

DAY BY DAY.

A PERSON says, " I cannot understand how I am to get along when I leave my father's house." Why should you see it till that time comes ? What if a person going on a journey of five years should undertake to carry provisions, and clothes, and gold enough to last him during the whole time, lugging them as he travelled, like a veritable Englishman, with all creation at his back ! If he is wise he will supply himself at the different points where he stops. When he gets to London, let him buy what he needs there ; when he gets to Paris, let him buy what he needs there ; when he gets to Rome, let him buy what he needs there ; and when he gets to Vienna, Dresden, Munich, St. Petersburg, and Canton, let him buy what he needs at these places ! He will find at each of them, and all the other cities which he visits, whatever things he requires. Why, then, should he undertake to carry them around the globe with him ? It would be the greatest folly imaginable. And as to gold, why should he load down his pockets with that ? Let him take a circular letter of credit, which is good, yet not usable till he arrives at the places where he needs it. When he gets to London, let him present it to Baring Brothers ; when he gets to Paris, let him present it to the Rothschilds. And as he proceeds, let him place it in the hands of the bankers of the various places at which he stops ; and he will get the means for prosecuting his journey. Now God gives every believer a circular letter of credit for life, and says, "Whenever you get to a place where you need assistance, take your letter to the Banker, and the needed assistance will be given you."—*Henry Ward Beecher.*

DEATH.

" PAID *the debt of nature.*" No ; it is not paying a debt ; it is rather like bringing a note to the bank to obtain solid gold in exchange for it. In this case you bring this cumbrous body which is nothing worth, and which you could not wish to retain long ; you lay it down, and receive for it from the eternal treasures—liberty, victory, knowledge, rapture.— *Foster.*

DEATH.

THE hour of death may be fitly likened to that celebrated picture in the National Gallery, of Perseus holding up the head of Medusa. That head turned all persons into stone who looked upon it. There is a warrior represented with a dart in his hand ; he stands stiffened, turned into stone, with the javelin even in his fist. There is another with a poignard beneath his robe, about to stab ; he is now the statue of an assassin, motionless and cold. Another is creeping along stealthily, like a man in ambuscade, and there he stands a consolidated rock ; he has looked only upon that head, and he is frozen into stone. Such is death. What I am when death is held before me, that I must be for ever. When my spirit departs, if God finds me hymning his praise, I shall hymn it in heaven ; if he finds me breathing out oaths, I shall follow up those oaths in hell.

DEATH—of a Believer.

OLD Mr. Lyford being desired, a little before his death, to let his friends know in what condition his soul was, and what his thoughts were about that eternity to which he seemed very near, he answered with a cheerfulness suitable to a believer and a minister, " *I will let you know how it is with me,*" and then, stretching out a hand that was withered and consumed with age and sickness—"*Here is,*" said he "*the grave, the wrath of God, and devouring flames, the just punishment of sin, on the one side; and here am I, a poor sinful soul, on the other side; but this is my comfort, the covenant of grace which is established on so many sure promises, has saved me from all. There is an act of oblivion passed in heaven. I will forgive their iniquities, and their sins will I remember no more. This is the blessed privilege of all within the covenant, among whom I am one.*"—*From T. Rogers, on " Trouble of Mind.*"

DEATH—Desired by few.

BURCKHARDT states, that although the Arabs are strict predestinarians, yet when the plague visited Medina, many of the townsmen fled to the desert, alleging as an excuse that although the distemper was a messenger from heaven sent to call them to a better world, yet being conscious of their own unworthiness, and that they did not merit this special mark of grace, they thought it more advisable to decline it for the present, and make their escape from the town. If it really came to the point with those of us who talk of longing for death as a great deliverance, should we not cling to life? It is a question perhaps more easily asked than answered.

DEATH—Differently Viewed by different Characters.

IT is a blessed thing to know the Saviour, and to feel that your soul is safe. You have been in a ship when it entered the harbour, and you have noticed the different looks of the passengers as they turned their eyes ashore. There was one who, that he might not lose a moment's time, had got everything ready for landing long ago ; and now he smiles and beckons to yonder party on the pier, who in their turn, are so eager to meet him, that they almost press over the margin of the quay ; and no sooner is the gangway thrown across, than he has hold of the arm of one, and another is triumphant on his shoulder, and all the rest are leaping before and after him on their homeward way. But there is another, who showed no alacrity. He gazed with pensive eye on the nearer coast and seemed to grudge that the trip was over. He was a stranger going amongst strangers, and though sometimes during the voyage he had a momentary hope that something unexpected might occur, and that some friendly face might recognise him in regions where he was going an alien and an adventurer, no such welcoming face is there, and with reluctant steps he quits the vessel, and commits himself to the unknown country. And now that everyone else has disembarked, who is this unhappy man whom they have brought on deck, and whom, groaning in his heavy chains, they are conducting to the dreaded shore ? Alas ! he is a felon and a runaway, whom they are bringing back to take his trial there ; and no wonder he is loath to land.

Now, dear brethren, our ship is sailing fast. We shall soon hear the rasping of the shallows, and the commotion overhead, which bespeak the port in view. When it comes to that, how shall you feel ? Are you a stranger, or a convict, or are you going home ? Can you say, " I know whom I have believed " ? Have you a Friend within the veil ? And however much you may enjoy the voyage, and however much you may like your fellow passengers, does your heart sometimes leap up at the prospect of seeing Jesus as he is, and so being ever with the Lord?—*James Hamilton, D.D.*

DEATH—Peace in.

THE late Mr. Young of Jedburgh, was once visiting the death-bed of an aged member of his congregation, who was hourly looking for his last change. "Well, my friend," said the minister, "how do you feel yourself to-day?" "Very weel, sir," was the calm and solemn answer, "Very weel, but just a wee confused wi' the flittin'."—*Children's Missionary Record for* 1857.

DEATH—Realised.

WHEN Bernard Gilpin was privately informed that his enemies had caused thirty-two articles to be drawn up against him in the strongest manner, and presented to Bonner, bishop of London, he said to his favourite domestic, 'At length they have prevailed against me. I am accused to the bishop of London, from whom there will be no escaping. God forgive their malice, and grant me strength to undergo the trial." He then ordered his servant to provide a long garment for him, in which he might go decently to the stake, and desired it might be got ready with all expedition. "For I know not," says he, "how soon I may have occasion for it." As soon as this garment was provided, it is said, he used to put it on every day, till the bishop's messengers apprehended him. It were well if we all thus realised to ourselves the hour of our departure. We ought by anticipation to sleep in our shrouds, and go to bed in our sepulchres. To put on our cerements now is wisdom.

DEATH—its Revealing Power.

TO-DAY the world is like a masquerade. High carnival is being held, and men wear their masks and dominoes, and strut about, and we think that man a king, and this a mighty Oriental prince, and this a haughty Indian chief. But the time is over for the masque; daylight dawns; strip off your garnishings; every one of you put on your ordinary garments.

Who goes out to the unrobing-room with greatest confidence? Why, the man who feels that his next dress will be a far more glorious vestment. Who shall go to that disrobing-room with the greatest tremor? Why, those who feel that the splendid character they once wore will give place to beggary and meanness ; when for robes they shall have rags ; for riches, poverty ; for honour, shame ; and for regal splendour, hissing and reproach. If any of our readers seem to be what they are not, let them be wise enough to think of the spade, the shroud, and the silent dust ; let every one among us now put his soul into the crucible, and as we shall test ourselves in the silence of the dying hour, so let us judge ourselves now.

DECISION FOR CHRIST.

AFTER the disgraceful defeat of the Romans, at the battle of Allia, Rome was sacked, and it seemed as if, at any moment, the Gauls might take the Capitol. Among the garrison was a young man of the Fabian family, and on a certain day the anniversary of a sacrifice returned, when his family had always offered sacrifice upon the Quirinal Hill. This hill was in the possession of the Gauls; but when the morning dawned, the young man took the sacred utensils of his god, went down from the Capitol, passed through the Gallic sentries, through the main body, up the hill, offered sacrifice, and came back unharmed. It was always told as a wonder among Roman legends. This is just how the Christian should act when decision for Christ is called for. Though he be a solitary man in the midst of a thousand opponents, let him, at the precise moment when duty calls, fearless of all danger, go straight to the appointed spot, do his duty, and remember that consequences belong to God, and not to us. I pray God that after this style we may witness for Christ.

DEEP THINGS—Understood by Experienced Men.

THE outlay in opening a mine is usually so great that the Spaniards say, that to prepare a mine one must spend another mine. To open up the hidden preciousness of the promises, we need a mine of experience, and to gain this last a man needs an inexhaustible mine of grace.

DESPONDENCY.

COLTON declares that in moments of despondency Shakespeare thought himself no poet ; and Raphael doubted his right to be called a painter. We call such self-suspicions morbid, and ascribe them to a hypochondriacal fit ; in what other way can we speak of those doubts as to their saintship, which occasionally afflict the most eminently holy of the Lord's people !

DESPONDENCY—its quick Eye for Evils.

MY friend Smith told me, that once on a time he had Mr. Jones to preach in his church. Smith's church holds fifteen hundred people, and is perfectly filled by its congregation, of this circumstance Smith is pardonably proud. When Mr. Jones preached, the church was quite crowded, save that three seats (not pews, seats for a single person each) were vacant in a front gallery. But so keen was Mr. Jones's eye for darks, to the oblivion of lights, that after service he merely said to Smith that he had remarked three seats empty in the gallery. Not one thought or word had he for the fourteen hundred and ninety-seven seats that were filled. Smith was a little mortified. But by-and-by he remembered that the peculiar disposition of Mr. Jones was one that would inflict condign punishment upon itself. Then he was sorry rather than angry. Yes, my friend, let us be glad if we have an eye for the lights of life, rather than for its darks !—*Autumn Holidays of a Country Parson.*

DESTITUTION—of London.

WE have no reason to congratulate ourselves on what we are doing, if we only think of the great work which still

remains undone. The reclaiming of men in this city is like
digging out those noble monuments of the past so long
buried amid the ruins of Nineveh.   In excavating this vast
population you have as it were laid bare the head of a huge
winged bull, until you can observe that it has a human countenance and will well repay you for your toils. Are you
going to congratulate yourselves that you have succeeded
thus far?   Why, there are the colossal feet, and the mighty
wings, and all the rest of the body ; all these are to be un-
covered from the ruins, and the whole mass uplifted from the
depth in which it lies imbedded.   But, because you have done
a little to bless London, and have brought a thousand, three
thousand, ten thousand to hear the word of God, are you to
sit down and say, " It is done."   What is to be done with the
rest of the three millions?   Where are the other tens of
thousands who are not hearing the word?   Where is the
great outlying mass of our leviathan city ?

DIGNITY OF CHRISTIAN CHARACTER—to be Maintained.

ANTISTHENES, the founder of the sect of the Cynics, when
he was told that Ismenias played excellently upon the flute,
answered properly enough, " Then he is good for nothing
else, otherwise he would not have played so well."   Such also
was Philip's saying to his son, when, at a certain entertainment, he sang in a very agreeable and skilful manner, " Are
you not ashamed to sing so well?"   Even so, when one who
professes to be of the seed royal of heaven, is able to
rival the ungodly in their cunning, worldliness, merriment,
scheming, or extravagance, may they not blush to possess
such dangerous capacities?   Heirs of heaven have something better to do than to emulate the children of darkness.

DILIGENCE.

SELECT a large box and place in it as many cannon-balls
as it will hold, it is after a fashion full, but it will hold more if

smaller matters be found. Bring a quantity of marbles, very many of these may be packed in the spaces between the larger globes ; the box is full now, but only full in a sense, it will contain more yet. There are interstices in abundance, into which you may shake a considerable quantity of small shot, and now the chest is filled beyond all question, but yet there is room. You cannot put in another shot or marble, much less another cannon-ball, but you will find that several pounds of sand will slide down between the larger materials, and even then between the granules of sand, if you empty yonder jug there will be space for all the water, and for the same quantity several times repeated. When there is no space for the great, there may be room for the little ; where the little cannot enter, the less can make its way; and where the less is shut out, the least of all may find ample room and verge enough. Now, the diligent preacher may not be able to preach more sermons, his engagement book is crowded. He may not be able to offer more public prayers, or to search the word of God more constantly; there is as much time occupied with these things as could well be given to them. Still there must be stray moments, occasional intervals and snatches, which might hold a vast amount of little usefulnesses in the course of months and years. What a wealth of minor good, as we may think it to be, might be shaken down into the interstices of ten years' work, which might prove to be as precious in result, by the grace of God, as the greater works of the same period. Little fishes are sweet, and these little works might possess in blessing what they lacked in bulk.

DISCONTENT—Chronic with some.

" SOME people are never content with their lot, let what will happen. Clouds and darkness are over their heads, alike whether it rain or shine. To them every incident is an accident, and every accident a calamity. Even when they have their own way, they like it no better than your way, and, indeed, consider their most voluntary acts as matters of compulsion. We saw a striking illustration the other day of the infirmity we speak of in the conduct of a child, about three years old. He was crying because his mother had shut the parlour door. " Poor thing," said a neighbour, compassionately, "you have shut the child *out.*" " It's all the same to him," said the mother; "he would cry if I called him *in* and then shut the door. It is a peculiarity of that boy, that if he is left rather suddenly on either side of a door, he considers himself shut out, and rebels accordingly." There are older children who take the same view of things."

DISPOSITION—Distorting.

HOW terribly bad looking-glasses distort the countenance; the man who looks into one of them sees his hair dishevelled, his forehead smutty, his nose blotched, his eyes out of line, and a dozen other imaginary mischiefs. How like to those morbid, melancholy dispositions which pervert everything into gloom, and compel the most lovely characters to write bitter things against themselves! They may also be likened to depraved judgments, which lead men to impute deformity to perfection, and to censure even innocence itself. It were well if all these good-for-nothing mirrors could be smashed to atoms, and the truth-reflecting glass of the word of God hung up in their places.

DIVINE GOODNESS—Unceasing.

IT is by no means pleasant when reading an interesting article in your magazine to find yourself pulled up short with the ominous words, " *to be continued.*" Yet they are words of good cheer if applied to other matters. What a comfort to remember that the Lord's mercy and lovingkindness is *to be continued!* Much as we have experienced in the long years of our pilgrimage, we have by no means outlived eternal love. Providential goodness is an endless chain, a stream which follows the pilgrim, a wheel perpetually revolving, a star for ever shining, and leading us to the place where he is who was once a babe in Bethlehem. All the volumes which record the doings of divine grace are but part of a series *to be continued.*

DOCTRINES—not for Controversy.

" A HUGE fragment of rock from an adjacent cliff fell upon a horizontal part of the hill below, which was occupied by the gardens and vineyards of two peasants. It covered part of the property of each, nor could it be easily decided to whom the unexpected visitor belonged : but the honest rustics instead of troubling the gentlemen of the long robe with their dispute, wisely resolved to end it by each party excavating the half of the rock on his own grounds, and converting the whole into two useful cottages, with comfortable rooms, and cellars for their little stock of wine, and there they now reside with their families. After such a sort will wise men deal with the great doctrines of the gospel ; they will not make them the themes of angry controversy, but of profitable use. To fight over a doctrine is sorry waste of time, but to live in the quiet enjoyment of it is the truest wisdom."

DOCTRINES—Duplicate Nature of.

FIRST to the right, then to the left, the road was ever ascending but always twisting, and thus, by easy marches, we were able to reach the summit of the pass ; a straight line would have been shorter for the eagle's wing, but no human foot could have followed it. Nobody called us inconsistent for thus facing about ; we kept the road, and no one could complain.

If we honestly desire to gain the heights of divine truth, we shall find many zigzags in the road : here our face will front divine sovereignty with all its lofty grandeur, and anon we shall turn in the opposite direction, towards the frowning peaks of human responsibility. What matters it if we appear to be inconsistent, so long as we keep to the highway of Scripture, which is our only safe road to knowledge ! Angels may, perhaps, be systematic divines ; for men it should be enough to follow the word of God, let its teachings wind as they may.

DOCTRINES—False.

IN "Babbage's Economy of Manufactures," we are told that "some years since, a mode of preparing old clover and trefoil seeds, by a process called 'doctoring,' became so prevalent as to attract the attention of the House of Commons. By this process old and worthless seed was rendered in appearance equal to the best. One witness tried some *doctored* seed, and found that not above one grain in a hundred grew."

Is it not to be feared that a doctored gospel is becoming very common among us, and if so it is no wonder that conversions are but few. Only pure truth is living seed.

DOCTRINES—False.

THERE are no greater foes to sheep than wild dogs. In some regions, sheep were no longer to be found, because these fierce creatures utterly devoured the flocks. The church has never had worse enemies than false teachers ; infidels and persecutors do but mild injury to her, but her heretical preachers have been as evening wolves.

DOCTRINES OF GRACE.

OUR forefathers were very fond of clipping their plants and training their flowers into quaint and grotesque forms ; so that we read of great guns wrought in rosemary and sweet briers. He would have been very foolish who would have trembled at cannons which only shot forth flowers and darted perfume. Let the poor trembler who is sincerely seeking Jesus, rest assured that the seemingly dreadful doctrines of election and predestination are not one whit more terrible, and are far more sweetly fragrant.

DOCTRINES (Mysterious)—to be Believed.

THOSE huge boulders which lie along the valley of Storo in the Tyrol, are of a granite unknown in the neighbourhood ; they must have come from a great distance. Now it might be hard to explain the method by which they arrived in the valley, but it would be absurd to deny that they are there. Most unaccountable is the fact, but a very strong and stubborn fact it is, for there they lie, huge as houses, and yet perfectly alien to the country. There are truths in Scripture which puzzle us, we cannot understand their relation to other portions of revelation, they are mysteries, apparently alien to the spirit of other passages. What then ? Suppose we cannot account for them, that does not alter the fact that there they are, and it would be extreme folly to deny their existence because they puzzle us. Rather let us find room for adoring faith where reason is lost in wonder.

DOCTRINES—Ultra-Calvinistic.

GRIFFITHS says that travellers in Turkey carry with them lozenges of opium, on which is stamped " *mash Allah*," the gift of God. Too many sermons are just such lozenges. Grace is preached but duty denied. Divine predestination is cried up but human responsibility is rejected. Such teaching ought to be shunned as poisonous, but those who by reason of use have grown accustomed to the sedative, condemn all other preaching, and cry up their opium lozenges of high doctrine as *the truth*, the precious gift of God. It is to be feared that this poppy-juice doctrine has sent many souls to sleep who will wake up in hell.

5

DOING GOOD—a Blessing to Ourselves.

IF we view this microcosm, the human body, we shall find that the heart does not receive the blood to store it up, but while it pumps it in at one valve, it sends it forth at another. The blood is always circulating everywhere, and is stagnant nowhere ; the same is true of all the fluids in a healthy body, they are in a constant state of expenditure.   If one cell stores for a few moments its peculiar secretion, it only retains it till it is perfectly fitted for its appointed use in the body ; for if any cell in the body should begin to store up its secretion, its store would soon become the cause of inveterate disease ; nay, the organ would soon lose the power to secrete at all, if it did not give forth its products.   The whole of the human system lives by giving.   The eye cannot say to the foot, I have no need of thee, and will not guide thee ; for if it does not perform its watchful office, the whole man will be in the ditch, and the eye will be covered with mire.   If the members refuse to contribute to the general stock, the whole body will become poverty-stricken, and be given up to the bankruptcy of death.   Let us learn, then, from the analogy of nature, the great lesson, that to get, we must give ; that to accumulate, we must scatter ; that to make ourselves happy, we must make others happy ; and that to get good and become spiritually vigorous, we must do good, and seek the spiritual good of others.

DOUBTS—Foolish.

A CHRISTIAN once, in doubt and discouragement, considered the darkness that overspread her soul as a proof that she was finally cast away.   She stumbled over mole-hills when she should have been removing mountains.   To an old minister who was trying to comfort her, with impassioned emphasis she said, "Oh ! I'm *dead, dead*, twice *dead*, and plucked up by the roots !"   After a pause, he replied, "Well, sitting in my study the other day, I heard a sudden scream—

'John's in the well! John's fallen into the well!' Before I could reach the spot, I heard the sad and mournful cry, 'John's dead—poor little Johnny's dead!' Bending over the curb, I called out, 'John, are you dead?' 'Yes, grandfather,' replied John, 'I'm dead.' I was glad to hear it from his own mouth."

Many doubts are so absurd that the only way to combat them is by gentle ridicule.

DOUBLE-MINDEDNESS.

FARADAY notes that whilst at breakfast at Llangollen, he heard a Welsh harper playing in very excellent style, and he adds, "wishing to gratify myself with a sight of the interesting *bard*, I went to the door and beheld—*the boots!* I must confess I was sadly disappointed and extremely baulked." It is no small stumbling-block to souls when they observe that professors who preach and talk like men inspired, live as meanly as worldlings themselves.

DWARFS—Spiritual.

THERE was once in London a club of small men, whose qualification for membership lay in their not exceeding five feet in height; these dwarfs held, or pretended to hold, the opinion that they were nearer the perfection of manhood than others, for they argued that primeval men had been far more gigantic than the present race, and consequently that the way of progress was to grow less and less, and that the human race as it perfected itself would become as diminutive as themselves. Such a club of Christians might be established in most cities, and without any difficulty might attain to an enormously numerous membership; for the notion is common that our dwarfish Christianity is, after all, the standard, and many even imagine that nobler Christians are enthusiasts, fanatical and hot-blooded, while they themselves are cool because they are wise, and indifferent because they are intelligent.

EARNEST OF THE SPIRIT—the Pledge of Heaven.

IN the early times when land was sold, the owner cut a turf from the greensward and cast it into the cap of the purchaser as a token that it was his ; or he tore off the branch of a tree and put it into the new owner's hand to show that he was entitled to all the products of the soil ; and when the purchaser of a house received seizin or possession, the key of the door, or a bundle of thatch plucked from the roof, signified that the building was yielded up to him.   The God of all grace has given to his people all the perfections of heaven to be their heritage for ever, and the earnest of his Spirit is to them the blessed token that all things are theirs.   The Spirit's work of comfort and sanctification is a part of heaven's covenant blessings, a turf from the soil of Canaan, a twig from the tree of life, the key to mansions in the skies.   Possessing the earnest of the Spirit we have received *seizin* of heaven.

EDIFICATION—the Aim of Christian Speech.

WHEN Handel's oratorio of the " Messiah " had won the admiration of many of the great, Lord Kinnoul took occasion to pay him some compliments on the noble entertainment which he had lately given the town.   " My lord," said Handel, " I should be sorry if I only entertained them ; I wish to make them better."   It is to be feared that many speech-makers at public meetings could not say as much ; and yet how dare any of us waste the time of our fellow immortals in mere amusing talk !   If we have nothing to speak to edification, how much better to hold our tongue !

ELECTION.

ANDREW FULLER remarks, in a letter to two relatives :—" I used to think that the doctrine of election was a reason why we need not pray, and I fear there are many who split upon this rock, who think it is to no purpose to pray, as things will be as they will be.   But I now see that the doctrine of election is the greatest encouragement instead of a discouragement to prayer. He that decreed that any one should be finally saved, decreed that it should be in the way of prayer ; as much as he that has decreed what we shall possess of the things of this life, has decreed that it shall be in the way of industry ; and as we never think of being idle in common business, because God has decreed what we shall possess of this world's good, so neither should we be slothful in the business of our souls, because our final state is decreed."

ENQUIRERS—not to be Discouraged.

AT the Synod of Moscow, held by King Goutran, A.D. 585, bishops were forbidden to keep dogs in their houses, or birds of prey, lest the poor should be bit by these animals instead of being fed. Should not all ministers be equally concerned to chase away all morose habits, angry tempers and repulsive manners, which might discourage the approach of enquiring souls who desire to know of us the way of salvation? Sunday-school teachers may also take the hint.

ETERNAL THINGS AND FLEETING.

AFAR off one can hardly tell which is mountain and which is cloud. The clouds rise with peaks and summits, all apparently as solid, and certainly as glistening, as the snow-clad Alps, so that the clearest eye might readily be deceived. Yet the mountain is unsubstantial as the cloud, and the cloud is never permanent as the mountain. So do the things of time appear to be all-important, far-reaching and enduring, and eternal things are not always of equal weight to the soul with those nearer at hand. Yet, despite all our instinctive judgments may suggest to the contrary, nothing earthly can ever be lasting, nothing in time can be worth considering compared with eternity. The cloudy philosophies of men may assume the shape of eternal truth, but the wind shall scatter them, while the great mountains of the divine word shall stand fast for ever and ever.

EVIDENCE—Experimental.

I HAVE been informed that not long ago a certain infidel lecturer gave an opportunity to persons to reply to him after his oration, and he was of course expecting that one or two rashly zealous young men would rise to advance the common arguments for Christianity, which he was quite prepared, by hook or crook, to battle with or laugh down. Instead of reasoners, an old lady, carrying a basket, wearing an ancient bonnet, and altogether dressed in an antique fashion, which marked both her age and her poverty, came upon the platform. Putting down her basket and umbrella, she began and said, " I paid threepence to hear of something better than Jesus Christ, and I have not heard it. Now, let me tell you what religion has done for me, and then tell me something better, or else you've cheated me out of the threepence which I paid to come in. Now," she said, " I have been a widow thirty years, and I was left with ten children, and I trusted in the Lord Jesus Christ in the depth of poverty, and he appeared for me and comforted me, and helped me to bring up my children so that they have grown up and turned out respectable. None of you can tell what the troubles of a poor lone woman are, but the Lord has made his grace all-sufficient. I was often very sore pressed, but my prayers were heard by my Father in heaven, and I was always delivered. Now, you are going to tell me something better than that—better for a poor woman like me ! I have been to the Lord sometimes when I've been very low indeed, and there's been scarcely anything for us to eat, and I've always found his providence has been good and kind to me. And when I lay very sick, I thought I was dying, and my heart was ready to break at leaving my poor fatherless boys and girls, and there was nothing kept me up but the thought of Jesus and his faithful love to my poor soul ; and you tell me that it was all nonsense. Those who are young and foolish may believe you, but after what I have gone through I know there is a reality in religion and it is no fancy. Tell me something better than what God has done for me, or else, I tell you, you have cheated me out of my threepence. Tell me something better." The lecturer was a good hand at an argument, but such a mode of controversy was novel, and therefore he gave up the contest, and merely said, " Really, the dear old woman was so happy in her delusion he should not like to undeceive her." " No," she said, " that won't do. Truth is truth, and your laughing can't alter it. Jesus Christ has been all this to me, and I could not sit down in the hall and hear you talk against him without speaking up for him, and asking you whether you could tell me something better than what he has done for me. I've tried and proved him, and that's more than you have."

Herein is power, logic invincible, reasoning not to be gainsayed. The testing, and proving of God; getting his love really shed abroad in the heart, this is the great internal evidence of the gospel.

EVILS (Little)—Making Way for Greater.

THE carpenter's gimblet makes but a small hole, but it enables him to drive a great nail. May we not here see a representation of those minor departures from the truth which prepare the minds of men for grievous errors, and of those thoughts of sin which open a way for the worst of crimes ! Beware, then, of Satan's gimblet.

EXAGGERATION.

IN certain ancient Italian frescoes Mary Magdalene is drawn as a woman completely enveloped in her own hair, which reaches to her feet and entirely wraps up her body as in a seamless garment. These queer draughtsmen must needs exaggerate ; granted that the woman had long hair, they must enfold her in it like a silkworm in its own silk. The practice survives among the tribe of talkers, everything with them is on the enlarged scale ; a man with ordinary abilities is a prodigy, another with very pardonable faults is a monster, a third with a few failings is a disgrace to humanity. Truth is as comely and beautiful as a woman with flowing hair, but exaggeration is as grotesque and ugly as the Magdalene, all hair from head to foot.

EXCUSES.

BISHOP W——, we are told, was one day rebuking one of of his clergy for fox-hunting. " My lord," was the clergyman's answer, "every man must have some relaxation. I assure you I never go to balls." " Oh," said the bishop, " I perceive you allude to my having been to the Duchess of S——'s party, but I give you my word that I was never in the same room with the dancers ! " " My lord," responded the clergyman, "my horse and I are getting old, and *we are never in the same field with the hounds.*" Thus each had satisfied his conscience, because of some point beyond which he had not gone. What he had done was to be overlooked on account of what he had not done. The habit of making precisely similar excuses is all but universal ; though we see the absurdity of it in others we continue to practise it ourselves.

EXPERIENCE.

A CHRISTIAN'S experience is like a rainbow, made up of drops of the grief of earth, and beams of the bliss of heaven.

EXPERIENCE—Boasting of its Depth.

IN my house there is a well of extraordinary depth which reminds me of something better than the boasted deep experience of certain censorious professors, who teach that to feel sin within is the main thing, but to be delivered from it of small consequence. When this well was commenced, the owner of the place resolved to have water, cost what it might. The well-sinkers dug through mud, and clay, and stone, but found no water; here was the deep experience of the corruptionist, all earth and no living spring, the filth revealed but not removed, the leper discovered but not healed. Another hundred feet of hard digging deep in the dark, but no water—still deeper experience. Then a third hundred feet, and still dirt, but no crystal—the very finest grade of your deeply experimental professor, who ridicules the joys of faith, as being of the flesh and presumptuous. Still on, on, on went the workers, till one day leaving their tools to go to dinner, upon their return they found that the water was rising fast, and their tools were drowned. Be this last my experience—to go so deep as to reach the springs of everlasting love, and find all my poor doings and efforts totally submerged, because the blessed fountains of grace have broken in upon me, covering all the mire, and rock, and earth of my poor, naturally evil heart.

EXPERIENCE—Necessary to a Minister.

BÜCHSEL says :—" Orthodoxy can be learnt from others ; living faith must be a matter of personal experience. The Lord sent out his disciples, saying, ' Ye shall testify of me, because ye have been with me from the beginning.' He only is a witness who speaks of what he has seen with his own eyes, heard with his own ears, and handled with his own hands. Orthodoxy is merely another form of rationalism, if it be learnt from without."

EXPERIENCE—Teaching the Value of Grace.

IN the olden time when the government of England had resolved to build a wooden bridge over the Thames at Westminster, after they had driven a hundred and forty piles into the river, there occurred one of the most severe frosts in the memory of man, by means of which the piles were torn away from their strong fastenings, and many of them snapped in two. The apparent evil in this case was a great good ; it led the commissioners to reconsider their purpose, and a substantial bridge of stone was erected.

How well it is when the fleshly reformations of unregenerate men are broken to pieces, if thus they are led to fly to the Lord Jesus, and in the strength of his Spirit are brought to build solidly for eternity. Lord, if thou sufferest my resolves and hopes to be carried away by temptations and the force of my corruptions, grant that this blessed calamity may drive me to depend wholly on thy grace, which cannot fail me.

EXPERIENCE—Variety of.

RUSKIN, that most accurate observer, says :—" Break off an elm-bough three feet long, in full leaf, and lay it on the table before you, and try to draw it, leaf for leaf. It is ten to one if in the whole bough (provided you do not twist it about as you work) you find one form of a leaf exactly like another ; perhaps you will not even have *one* complete. Every leaf will be oblique, or foreshortened, or curled, or crossed by another, or shaded by another, or have something or other the matter with it ; and though the whole bough will look graceful and symmetrical, you will scarcely be able to tell how or why it does so, since there is not one line of it like another."

If such infinite variety prevails in creation, we may reasonably expect to find the same in the experience of the saints. Uniformity is no rule of spiritual life. Let us not judge others because their feelings have not been precisely similar to ours. All the saints are led in a right way, but no two of them precisely in the same way. Far be it from us to set up a standard and expect all to be conformed to it ; if we reject all believers who labour under infirmities, or are marred with faults, our fellowship will be scant indeed.

FAITH.

THE stupendous Falls of Niagara have been spoken of
in every part of the world ; but while they are marvellous
to hear of, and wonderful as a spectacle, they have been
very destructive to human life, when by accident any have
been carried down the cataract. Some years ago, two
men, a bargeman and a collier, were in a boat and
found themselves unable to manage it, it being carried so
swiftly down the current that they must both inevitably be
borne down and dashed to pieces. At last, however, one
man was saved by floating a rope to him, which he
grasped. The same instant that the rope came into his hand,
a log floated by the other man. The thoughtless and confused bargeman, instead of seizing the rope, laid hold on the
log. It was a fatal mistake, they were both in imminent
peril, but the one was drawn to shore because he had a connection with the people on the land, whilst the other, clinging
to the loose, floating log, was borne irresistibly along, and
never heard of afterwards. *Faith* has a saving connection
with Christ. Christ is on the shore, so to speak, holding the
rope, and as we lay hold of it with the hand of our confidence, he pulls us to shore ; but our good works having no
connection with Christ are drifted along down to the gulf of
fell despair. Grapple our virtues as tightly as we may, even
with hooks of steel, they cannot avail us in the least degree ;
they are the disconnected log which has no holdfast on the
heavenly shore.

FAITH.

THE Emperor Napoleon I. was reviewing some troops
upon the Place du Carrousel, in Paris ; and, in giving an
order, he thoughtlessly dropped the bridle upon his horse's
neck, which instantly set off on a gallop. The emperor was
obliged to cling to the saddle. At this moment a common
soldier of the line sprang before the horse, seized the bridle,

and handed it respectfully to the emperor. "Much obliged
to you, captain," said the chief, by this one word making the
soldier a captain. The man believed the emperor, and,
saluting him, asked, "Of what regiment, sire?" Napoleon,
charmed with his faith, replied, "Of my guards!" and galloped
off.

Now, what will the soldier do? If he imitates those who
before believing wish to see and feel, and like the apostle
Thomas wait for palpable proof before relying upon testimony, he will say, "a captain of the guard always wears a
captain's uniform, and mine is only that of a common soldier.
I cannot, therefore, believe myself a captain;" and the soldier
would return to the ranks. But if, on the contrary, he believes
fully and implicitly the emperor's word, and that his rank
as captain of the guard depends not upon the uniform he
wears, but that the uniform must be the consequence and
evidence of his rank (and this will be his thought if he honours
the emperor), he will not hesitate because of his dress, nor
will he return to the line. And such, indeed, was the conduct
of the man. As soon as the emperor left, the soldier laid
down his gun, saying, "He may take it who will," and instead
of returning to his comrades, he approached the group of
staff officers. On seeing him, one of the generals scornfully
said, "What does this fellow want here?" "This fellow,"
replied the soldier proudly, "is a captain of the guard." "You?
my poor friend! You are mad to say so!" "*He* said it,"
replied the soldier, pointing to the emperor, who was still in
sight. "I ask your pardon, sir," said the general respectfully,
"I was not aware of it."

Here, then, was exhibited a manifold faith. Since first
the soldier believed the emperor, upon his word, because he
heard him (as the Samaritans said of the Saviour), and afterwards, on the soldier's word, the general believed the emperor.

You now see how a person may be sure that God gives
peace : it is by believing his testimony, just as this soldier

believed that of his emperor. That is to say, as he believed himself to be a captain *before* wearing his uniform; so on the word and promise of God, one believes himself to be a child of Jesus, *before* being sanctified by his Spirit."—*Cæsar Malan, D.D.*

FAITH—Appropriating.

I ONCE heard a father tell, that when he removed his family to a new residence, where the accommodation was much more ample, and the substance much more rich and varied than that to which they had previously been accustomed, his youngest son, yet a lisping infant, ran round every room, and scanned every article with ecstacy, calling out, in childish wonder at every new sight, " Is this ours, father? and is this ours ?" The child did not say "yours," and I observed that the father while he told the story was not offended with the freedom. You could read in his glistening eye that the infant's confidence in appropriating as his own all that his father had, was an important element in his satisfaction.

Such, I suppose, will be the surprise, and joy, and appropriating confidence, with which the child of our Father's family will count all his own, when he is removed from the comparatively mean condition of things present, and enters the infinite of things to come. When the glories of heaven burst upon his view, he does not stand at a distance, like a stranger, saying, " O God, these are thine." He bounds forward to touch and taste every provision which those blessed mansions contain, exclaiming, as he looks in the Father's face, " Father, this and this is ours." The dear child is glad of all the Father's riches, and the Father is gladder of his dear child.—*W. Arnot.*

FAITH—a Death Grip.

A SEA captain related at a prayer-meeting in Boston a short time ago a thrilling incident in his own experi‌nce.

"A few years ago," said he, "I was sailing by the island of Cuba, when the cry ran through the ship, 'Man overboard!' It was impossible to put up the helm of the ship, but I instantly seized a rope and threw it over the ship's stern, crying out to the man to seize it as for his life. The sailor caught the rope just as the ship was passing. I immediately took another rope, and making a slip noose of it, attached it to the other, and slid it down to the struggling sailor, and directed him to pass it over his shoulders and under his arms, and he would be drawn on board. He was rescued; but he had grasped that rope with such firmness, with such a death-grip, that it took hours before his hold relaxed, and his hand could be separated from it. With such eagerness, indeed, had he clutched the object that was to save him, that the strands of the rope became imbedded in the flesh of his hands!"

Reader, has not God let down from heaven a rope to every sinner on the earth, is not every strand a precious promise, and ought we not to lay hold on it as for our very life?—*The Family Treasury for* 1859.

FAITH—God's Regard for it.

A SWALLOW having built its nest upon the tent of Charles V., the emperor generously commanded that the tent should not be taken down when the camp removed, but should remain until the young birds were ready to fly. Was there such gentleness in the heart of a soldier towards a poor bird which was not of his making, and shall the Lord deal hardly with his creatures when they venture to put their trust in him! Be assured he hath a great love to those trembling souls that fly for shelter to his royal courts. He that buildeth his nest upon a divine promise shall find it abide and remain until he shall fly away to the land where promises are lost in fulfilments.

FAITH—God's Trial of.

AT the battle of Crescy, where Edward the Black Prince, then a youth óf eighteen years of age, led the van, the king, his father, drew up a strong party on a rising ground, and there beheld the conflict in readiness to send relief where it should be wanted. The young prince being sharply charged, and in some danger, sent to his father for succour ; and as the king delayed to send it, another messenger was sent to crave immediate assistance. To him the king replied, " Go, tell my son that I am not so inexperienced a commander as not to know when succour is wanted, nor so careless a father as not to send it." He intended the honour of the day should be his son's, and therefore let him with courage stand to it, assured that help should be had when it might conduce most to his renown. God draws forth his servants to fight in the spiritual warfare, where they are engaged, not only against the strongholds of carnal reason, and the exalted imaginations of their own hearts, but also in the pitched field against Satan and his wicked instruments. But they, poor hearts, when the charge is sharp, are ready to despond, and cry with Peter, " Save, Lord, we perish ;" but God is too watchful to overlook their exigencies, and too much a Father to neglect their succour. If help, however, be delayed, it is that the victory may be more glorious by the difficulty of overcoming.

FAITH—Overcoming Temptation.

WHEN a traveller was asked whether he did not admire the admirable structure of some stately building, " *No*," said he, "*for I've been at Rome, where better are to be seen every day.*" O believer, if the world tempt thee with its rare sights and curious prospects, thou mayst well scorn them, having been, by contemplation, in heaven, and being able, by faith, to see infinitely better delights every hour of the day. " This is the victory which overcometh the world, even our faith."

FAITH—Stimulating Endeavour.

SEE the spider casting out her film to the gale, she feels persuaded that somewhere or other it will adhere and form the commencement of her web. She commits the slender filament to the breeze believing that there is a place provided for it to fix itself. In this fashion should we believingly cast forth our endeavours in this life, confident that God will find a place for us. He who bids us pray and work will aid our efforts and guide us in his Providence in a right way. Sit not still in despair, O son of toil, but again cast out the floating thread of hopeful endeavour, and the wind of love will bear it to its resting place.

FAITH—the Summary of Virtue.

THE Jews in the Talmud have the saying, " The whole law was given to Moses at Sinai, in six hundred and thirteen precepts." David, in the fifteenth Psalm, brings them all within the compass of eleven. Isaiah brings them to six, Isaiah xxxiii. 15 ; Micah to three, Micah vi. 8 ; Isaiah, again, to two, Isaiah lvi. ; Habakkuk to this one, " The just shall live by faith." Habakkuk ii. 4.—*Lightfoot.*

FAITH—Triumph of.

DURING an earthquake that occurred a few years since, the inhabitants of a small village were generally very much alarmed, but they were at the same time surprised at the calmness and apparent joy of an old lady whom they all knew. At length one of them, addressing the old lady, said : " Mother, are you not afraid?" " No," said the mother in Israel ; " I rejoice to know that *I have a God that can shake the world.*"

FAITH—and Works.

'TWAS an unhappy division that has been made between faith and works. Though in my intellect I may divide them, just as in the candle I know there is both light and heat, but

yet put out the candle, and they are both gone ; one remains
not without the other : so it is betwixt faith and works. Nay,
in a right conception, *fides est opus :* if I believe a thing
because I am commanded, that is *opus.—The Table Talk of
John Selden.*

FALSE CONFIDENCES.

SOME years ago, there was a bridge at Bath in so crazy a
condition, that cautious persons chose rather to make a long
circuit than run the risk of crossing it.   One day, however,
a very nervous lady, hurrying home to dress for the evening,
came suddenly upon the spot without, till that moment, remembering the danger.   The sight of the bridge reminded
her of its ruinous state, just as she was about to set her foot
upon it.   But what was she to do ? If she went on, the frail arch
might give way under her ; to go round would be fatiguing
and attended with much loss of time.   She stood for some
minutes trembling in anxious hesitation ; but at last a lucky
thought occurred to her, she called for a sedan-chair, and was
carried over in that conveyance ! You may laugh, perhaps,
at this good lady's odd expedient for escaping danger
by shutting out the view of it.   But is not something
of the same kind happening around you every day ? Those
people who are alarmed and perplexed at the danger
of having to judge for themselves in religious matters, think
to escape that danger by choosing to take some guide as an
infallible one, and believe or disbelieve as he bids them.
What is this but crossing the crazy bridge in a sedan-chair ?
In determining to believe whatever their guide affirms, they
are in reality choosing to make every single exercise of faith
which follows that original determination ; and they are
choosing to believe he is infallible into the bargain.   There
are at least as many chances of error as before against every
single article of faith in the creed which they adopt upon
their guide's authority ; and there are also additional chances

6

against that authority itself. Thus, in order to get over more
safely, they put not only their own weight, but that of the
sedan-chair also, upon the tottering arch.—*Excelsior.*

FALSE HOPES—Danger of.

A SAILOR while clinging with others to a waterlogged
vessel, observed great swarms of sharks and other ferocious
fish swimming on all sides, as if waiting for their prey. If
men had eyes might they not clearly see evil spirits gathering
around the sinking hulks of Romanism and self-righteousness,
watching for their expected victims?

FEAR OF SIN.

THE old naturalist, Ulysses Androvaldus, tells us that a
dove is so afraid of a hawk, that she will be frightened at the
sight of one of its feathers. Whether it be so or not, I
cannot tell; but this I know, that when a man has had a
thorough shaking over the jaws of hell, he will be so afraid of
sin, that even one of its feathers—any one sin—will alarm
and send a thrill of fear through his soul. This is a part of
the way by which the Lord turns us when we are turned
indeed.

FOG—a Figure of our Partial Knowledge.

BEING once surrounded by a dense mist on the Styhead
Pass in the Lake District, we felt ourselves to be transported
into a world of mystery where everything was swollen to a
size and appearance more vast, more terrible, than is usual on
this sober planet. A little mountain tarn, scarcely larger than
a farmer's horse-pond, expanded into a great lake whose
distant shores were leagues beyond the reach of our poor
optics ; and as we descended into the valley of Wastwater,
the rocks on one side like the battlements of heaven, and the
descent on the other hand, looked like the dreadful lips of a
yawning abyss ; and yet when one looked back again in the

morning's clear light there was nothing very dangerous in the pathway, or terrible in the rocks. The road was a safe though sharp descent, devoid of terrors to ordinary mountain climbers. In the distance through the fog the shepherd "stalks gigantic," and his sheep are full-grown lions.

Into such blunders do we fall in our life-pilgrimage ; a little trouble in the distance is, through our mistiness, magnified into a crushing adversity. We see a lion in the way, although it is written that no ravenous beast shall go up thereon. A puny foe is swollen into a Goliath, and the river of death widens into a shoreless sea.

Come, heavenly wind, and blow the mist away, and then the foe will be despised, and the bright shores on the other side the river will stand out clear in the light of faith !

FOREBODINGS—Falsified.

JOHN CONDOR, afterwards D.D., was born at Wimple in Cambridgeshire, June 3, 1714. His grandfather, Richard Condor, kissed him, and, with tears in his eyes, said, " Who knows what sad days these little eyes are likely to see?" things wearing at that time a threatening aspect, relative to Dissenters. Dr. Condor remarked upon mentioning the above circumstance, " These eyes have, for more than sixty years, seen nothing but goodness and mercy follow me and the churches of Christ, even to this day."

Thus many a desponding prophecy is falsified by events most blessed. We write bitter things, and God blots them out and writes gracious things in lieu thereof. Many a gloomy vaticinator might save himself his depression of spirit if he would remember that " the Lord reigneth," and " he will speak peace unto his people."

FORMALISM—Tricks of.

IN Mrs. Grant's " Letters from the Mountains" (1806), is the following anecdote of the then Duchess of Gordon. " The duchess said that on Sunday she never saw company, nor played cards, nor went out : in England, indeed, she did so, because every one else did the same, but she would not introduce those manners into this country (Scotland). I stared at these gradations of piety growing warmer as it came northward, but was wise enough to stare silently."

The tricks of formalism and hypocrisy are evermore the same. Man is regarded more than God. What Mrs. Grundy may say has far more influence with many than what the Lord may say. This is miserable meanness and rank impiety.

FORMALITY—Habits of, Worthless.

THAT honoured servant of Christ, Richard Knill, notes in his journal the following amusing incident of the force of habit, as exemplified in his horse. "Mr. and Mrs. Loveless would have me live with them, but they charged me very little for my board, whereby I was enabled, with my salary, to support seven native schools. These were so situated that I could visit them all in one day. My horse and gig were seen constantly on the rounds ; and my horse at last knew where to stop as well as I did. This nearly cost a Bengal officer his life. Captain Page, a godly man, who was staying with us until a ship was ready to take him to the Cape, one morning requested me to lend him my horse and gig to take him to the city. The captain was driving officer-like, when the horse stopped suddenly, and nearly threw him out. He inquired, 'What place is this?' The answer was, 'It's the Sailors' Hospital.' They started again, and soon the horse stopped suddenly, and the captain was nearly out as before. 'What's this?'—'A school, sir,' was the reply. At last he finished his business, and resolved to return another way. By doing this he came near my schools, and again and again the horse stopped. When he got home, he said, 'I am glad that I have returned without broken bones, but never will I drive a religious horse again.'"

Persons who go to places of worship from mere habit and without entering into the devotions of the service, may here see that their religion is only such as a horse may possess, and a horse's religion will never save a man.

FRIENDSHIP OF THE WORLD—Vanity.

THE vanity of all friendship which is not founded in true principle, was never more plainly expressed than in an honest, but heartless, sentence of one of Horace Walpole's letters. "If one of my friends happens to die, I drive down to St. James's Coffee-house, and bring home a new one." The name of "friend" is desecrated in a worldling's mouth— *but there is a friend.*

FRIVOLITIES—Render Men Callous to the Gospel.'

"WHEN Bonaparte put the Duke d'Enghien to death, all Paris felt so much horror at the event that the throne of the tyrant trembled under him. A counter-revolution was expected, and would most probably have taken place, had not Bonaparte ordered a new ballet to be brought out, with the utmost splendour, at the Opera. The subject he pitched on was "*Ossian, or the Bards.*" It is still recollected in Paris, as perhaps the grandest *spectacle* that had ever been exhibited there. The consequence was that the murder of the Duke d'Enghien was totally forgotten, *and nothing but the new ballet* was talked of."

After this fashion Satan takes off men's thoughts from their sins, and drowns the din of their consciences. Lest they should rise in revolt against him, he gives them the lusts of the flesh, the vanities of pride, the cares of this world, or the merriment of fools, to lead away their thoughts. Poor silly men are ready enough for these misleading gaieties, and for the sake of them the solemnities of death and eternity are forgotten.

FRIVOLITY OF MIND.

IF over that little heap of dust you hold a good magnet, should there be present a nail, or a needle, or a few iron filings, they will at once spring up and cling to the attracting bar.   And were there only a magnet strong enough, it might soon become the monopolist of that metal, which, after all, is more precious than silver or gold.

If now, on your coat-sleeve, or on the woollen table-cover you rub a stick of wax or amber, you impart to this substance also an attractive power.   But it is a magnet of a very different sort.   Hold it ever so near that knife or needle, and there is no movement.   Hold it near the carpet, or, better still, insinuate it into some unswept corner, and every loose particle, the thread-clippings and paper-shavings, the stray feathers, and silky fibres, will instantly leap up to it, and convert its bald apex into a little mass of rubbish.

Some minds have a powerful affinity for what is sterling and useful.   Themselves strong like the loadstone, they are constantly acquiring facts, and principles, and maxims of wisdom.   They gain the respect of others.   They become master-spirits, moving and controlling their fellows.   If in business, they turn out successful merchants ; if students, they step forth the chiefs of their profession ; if thrown into public life, they graduate into the highest ranks of states-manship, and become the moulders of an age, the disposers of an empire, the movers of mankind.

But some minds have an attraction quite as intense for what is frivolous.   In early life they do not "take to" tasks and lessons ; and all throughout they retain the intellectual langour, which deprecates instruction and refuses to apply.   Their theory of life is perpetual recreation, and ignoring the commandment which says, "Six days shalt thou labour, and do all thy work," they never know the sweetness of a true Sabbatic repose.   Unused to self-denial, and seldom roused to exertion, if they enter business you soon hear that they have "stopped;" and in a learned profession, if they do not "stop," it is only because they never could get on.—*Excelsior.*

GENEROUS FEELING—towards Brethren.

"ONE incident gives high proof of the native generosity of Turner's nature. He was one of the hanging committee, as the phrase goes, of the Royal Academy. The walls were full when Turner's attention was attracted by a picture sent in by an unknown provincial artist by the name of Bird. 'A good picture,' he exclaimed. 'It must be hung up and exhibited.' 'Impossible!' responded the committee of academicians. 'The arrangement cannot be disturbed. Quite impossible!' 'A good picture,' iterated Turner, 'it must be hung up;' and, finding his colleagues to be as obstinate as himself, he hitched down one of his own pictures, and hung up Bird's in its place." Would to God that in far more instances the like spirit ruled among servants of the Lord Jesus. The desire to honour others and to give others a fair opportunity to rise should lead ministers of distinction to give place to less eminent men to whom it may be of essential service to become better known. We are not to look every man on his own things, but every man also on the things of others.

GIVING.

A WOMAN who was known to be very poor, came to a missionary meeting in Wakefield, and offered to subscribe a penny a-week to the mission fund. "Surely," said one, "you are too poor to afford this?" She replied, "I spin so many hanks of yarn a-week for my living, and *I'll spin one hank more*, and that will be a penny a-week for the society."

GOD—Acting as a Father.

A KING is sitting with his council deliberating on high affairs of state involving the destiny of nations, when

suddenly he hears the sorrowful cry of his little child who has
fallen down, or been frightened by a wasp ; he rises and runs
to his relief, assuages his sorrows and relieves his fears.
Is there anything unkingly here? Is it not most natural?
Does it not even elevate the monarch in your esteem ? Why
then do we think it dishonourable to the King of kings, our
heavenly Father, to consider the small matters of his children?
It is infinitely condescending, but is it not also superlatively
natural that being a Father he should act as such?

GOD—his Benevolence in Creation.

THE benevolence of our great Creator is chanted even by
things unpleasant to the ear. " The nuptial song of reptiles,"
says Kirby, " is not, like that of birds, the delight of every
heart ; but it is rather calculated to disturb and horrify than
to still the soul. The hiss of serpents, the croaking of frogs
and toads, the moaning of turtles, the bellowing of crocodiles
and alligators, form their gamut of discords." Here, also, we
may read beneficent design. Birds are the companions of
man in the lawn and forest, in his solitary walks, amidst his
rural labours, and around the home of his domestic enjoy-
ments. They are, therefore, framed beautiful to the eye, and
pleasing to the ear ; but of the reptile tribes, some are his
formidable enemies, and none were ever intended to be his
associates. They shun cultivation, and inhabit unfrequented
marshes or gloomy wilds. Their harsh notes and ungainly
or disgusting forms, serve therefore to warn him of danger, or
to turn his steps to places more fit for his habitation.—*H.
Duncan's Sacred Philosophy of the Seasons.*

GOD—is Light.

SUPPOSE the case of a cripple who had spent his life in a
room where the sun was never seen. He has heard of its
existence, he believes in it, and indeed, has seen enough of its
light to give him high ideas of its glory. Wishing to see the

sun, he is taken out at night into the streets of an illuminated city. At first he is delighted, dazzled ; but after he has had time to reflect, he finds darkness spread amid the lights, and he asks, " Is this the sun?" He is taken out under the starry sky, and is enraptured ; but, on reflection, finds that night covers the earth, and again asks, " Is this the sun?" He is carried out some bright day at noontide, and no sooner does his eye open on the sky than all question is at an end. There is but one sun. His eye is content : it has seen its highest object, and feels that there is nothing brighter.

So with the soul : it enjoys all lights, yet amid those of art and nature, is still enquiring for something greater. But when it is led by the reconciling Christ into the presence of the Father, and he lifts up upon it the light of his countenance, all thought of anything greater disappears. As there is but one sun, so there is but one God. The soul which once discerns and knows him, feels that greater or brighter there is none, and that the only possibility of ever beholding more glory is by drawing nearer.—*Rev. W. Arthur.*

GOD—Love of.

ALL things that are on earth shall wholly pass away,
Except the love of God, which shall live and last for aye.
The forms of men shall be as they had never been ;
The blasted groves shall lose their fresh and tender green ;
The birds of the thicket shall end their pleasant song,
And the nightingale shall cease to chant the evening long ;
The kine of the pasture shall feel the dart that kills,
And all the fair white flocks shall perish from the hills ;
The goat and antlered stag, the wolf and the fox,
The wild boar of the wood, and the chamois of the rocks,
And the strong and fearless bear, in the trodden dust shall lie ;
And the dolphin of the sea, and the mighty whale shall die ;
And realms shall be dissolved, and empires be no more ;
And they shall bow to death, who ruled from shore to shore ;

And the great globe itself (so the holy writings tell),
With the rolling firmament, where the starry armies dwell,
Shall melt with fervent heat—they shall all pass away,
Except the love of God, which shall live and last for aye.
                                    William Cullen Bryant.

GOD—Vague Conceptions of.

"ONE day, in conversation with the Jungo-kritu, head
pundit of the College of Fort William, on the subject of God,
this man, who is truly learned in his own shastrus, gave me
from one of their books, this parable :—' In a certain country
there existed a village of blind men. These men had heard
that there was an amazing animal called the elephant, but
they knew not how to form an idea of his shape. One day
an elephant happened to pass through the place: the villagers
crowded to the spot where this animal was standing. One
of them got hold of his trunk, another seized his ear, another
his tail, another one of his legs, etc. After thus trying to
gratify their curiosity they returned into the village, and
sitting down together they began to give their ideas on what
the elephant was like : the man who had seized his trunk said
he thought the elephant was like the body of the plantain
tree ; the man who had felt his ear said he thought he was
like the fan with which the Hindoos clean the rice ; the man
who had felt his tail said he thought he must be like a snake,
and the man who had seized his leg, thought he must be like
a pillar. An old blind man of some judgment was present,
who was greatly perplexed how to reconcile these jarring
notions, respecting the form of the elephant ; but he at
length said, " You have all been to examine this animal, it is
true, and what you report cannot be false: I suppose, therefore, that that which was like the plaintain tree must be his
trunk ; that which was like a fan must be his ear ; that which
was like a snake must be his tail, and that which was like a
pillar must be his body." In this way, the old man united all

their notions, and made out something of the form of the elephant. Respecting God,' added the pundit, 'we are all blind; none of us has seen him; those who wrote the shastrus, like the old blind man, have collected all the reasonings and conjectures of mankind together, and have endeavoured to form some idea of the nature of the Divine Being.'"

The pundit's parable may be appropriately applied to the science of theology. Some Christians see one truth and some another, and each one is quite sure that he has beheld the whole. Where is the master-mind who shall gather up the truth out of each creed, and see the theology of the Bible in its completeness?—a sublimer sight than the believers in the *isms* have yet been able to imagine.

GODLINESS—No Burden to True Saints.

THE Princess Elizabeth carried the crown for her sister in the procession at Mary's coronation, and complained to Noailles of its great weight. "Be patient," was the adroit answer, "it will seem lighter when on your own head." The outward forms of godliness are as burdensome to an unregenerate man as was the crown to the princess ; but let him be born again and so made a possessor of the good things of divine grace, and they will sit easily enough upon his head, as his glory and delight.

GOLD—Places of its Abundance Undesirable.

DID the eye ever rest upon a more utter desolation than that which surrounds the gold mines near Goldau in the Hartz mountains? It is worse than a howling wilderness, it is a desert with its bowels torn out, and scattered in horrid confusion. More or less this is true of all gold mining regions, and Humboldt, when writing of the Pearl Coast, says that it presents the same aspect of misery as the countries of gold and diamonds. Is it so then? Are riches so near akin to horror? Lord, let me set my affections on better things, and seek for less dangerous wealth.

GOSPEL—Duty of Spreading it.

HUBER, the great naturalist, tells us, that if a single wasp discovers a deposit of honey or other food, he will return to his nest, and impart the good news to his companions, who will sally forth in great numbers to partake of the fare which has been discovered for them. Shall we who have found honey in the rock Christ Jesus, be less considerate of our fellow men than wasps are of their fellow insects? Ought we not rather like the Samaritan woman to hasten to tell the good news? Common humanity should prevent one of us from concealing the great discovery which grace has enabled us to make.

GOSPEL—Jesus the Sum of.

IN a village church in one of the Tyrolese valleys, we saw upon the pulpit an outstretched arm, carved in wood, the hand of which held forth a cross. We noted the emblem as full of instruction as to what all true ministry should be, and must be—a holding forth of the cross of Christ to the multitude as the only trust of sinners. Jesus Christ must be set forth evidently crucified among them. Lord, make this the aim and habit of all our ministers.

GOSPEL—needs no Meretricious Adornments.

WHEN Dionysius, the tyrant, sent Lysander some rich Sicilian garments for his daughters, he refused them, alleging that "He was afraid these fine clothes would make them look more homely." The truth of God is so comely in itself that the trappings of oratory are far more likely to lessen its glory than to increase it. Paul saith that he preached the gospel "not with wisdom of words, lest the cross of Christ should be made of none effect."

GOSPEL—needs Spiritual Ears to Appreciate it.

ALPHONSE KARR heard a gardener ask his master permission to sleep for the future in the stable ; "for," said he,
"there is no possibility of sleeping in the chamber behind the
greenhouse, sir; there are nightingales there which do nothing
but guggle, and keep up a noise all the night." The sweetest
sounds are but an annoyance to those who have no musical
ear ; doubtless the music of heaven would have no charms to
carnal minds, certainly the joyful sound of the gospel is un-
appreciated so long as men's ears remain uncircumcised.

GOSPEL—Nothing else will Satisfy.

TAKE away a toy from a child, and give him another, and
he is satisfied ; but if he be hungry no toy will do. As new-
born babes, true believers desire the sincere milk of the Word ;
and the desire of grace in this way is grace.—*John Newton.*

GOSPEL—should be Preached Constantly.

WHEN Le Tourneau preached the Lent sermon at St.
Benoit, at Paris, Louis XIV. enquired of Boileau, "if he knew
anything of a preacher called Le Tourneau, whom everybody was running after?" "Sire," replied the poet, "your
Majesty knows that people always run after novelties ; this
man preaches the gospel." Boileau's remark as to the novelty
of preaching the gospel in his time, brings to mind the candid
confession of a Flemish preacher, who, in a sermon delivered
before an audience wholly of his own order, said, "We are
worse than Judas ; he sold and delivered his Master, we sell
him too, but deliver him not."

GOSPEL—to be Preached Simply.

OF the works of a famous alchymist of the thirteenth
century, it is said that, "whoever would read his book to find
out the secret would employ all his labour in vain." All the
gold makers who have written upon their favourite mystery

are in the like predicament, no one can comprehend what
the secret is which they pretend to divulge. May we not
shrewdly guess that if they had any secret to tell they would
put it in intelligible language, and that their pompous and
involved sentences are only a screen for their utter ignorance
of the matter? When we hear preachers talking of divine
things in a style savouring more of metaphysical subtlety
than of gospel plainness ; when the seeking sinner cannot
find out the way of salvation because of their philosophical
jargon, may we not with justice suspect that the preacher
does not know the gospel, and conceals his culpable ignorance
behind the veil of rhetorical magniloquence? Surely if the
man understood a matter so important to all his hearers as
the way of salvation, he would feel constrained to tell it out
in words which all might comprehend.

GOSPEL (Simple)—the Need of the Wisest.

DURING an illness, that illustrious scholar Bengel sent for
a student in the Theological Institution, and requested him
to impart a word of consolation. The youth replied, " Sir, I
am but a pupil, a mere learner; I don't know what to say
to a teacher like *you*." " What!" said Bengel, "a divinity
student, and not able to communicate a word of scriptural
comfort!" The student, abashed, contrived to utter the text,
" The blood of Jesus Christ, the Son of God, cleanseth us from
all sin." " That is the very word I want," said Bengel, " it is
quite enough," and taking him affectionately by the hand
dismissed him.

GRACE.

PAYSON, when dying, expressed himself with great earnestness respecting the grace of God as exercised in saving lost
men, and seemed particularly affected that it should be
bestowed on one so ill-deserving as himself. " Oh, how
sovereign! Oh, how sovereign! Grace is the only thing that

can make us like God. I might be dragged through heaven, earth, and hell, and I should be still the same sinful, polluted wretch, unless God himself should renew and cleanse me."

GRACE—Equal to our Day.

WHENEVER the Lord sets his servants to do extraordinary work he always gives them extraordinary strength; or if he puts them to unusual suffering he gives them unusual patience. When we enter upon war with some petty New Zealand chief, our troops expect to have their charges defrayed, and accordingly we pay them gold by thousands, as their expenses may require; but when an army marches against a grim monarch, in an unknown country, who has insulted the British flag, we pay, as we know to our cost, not by thousands but by millions. And thus, if God calls us to common and ordinary trials, he will defray the charges of our warfare by thousands, but if he commands us to an unusual struggle with some tremendous foe, he will discharge the liabilities of our war by millions, according to the riches of his grace in which he has abounded towards us through Christ Jesus.

GRACE—Maturity in.

MATURITY in grace makes us willing to part with worldly goods; the green apple needs a sharp twist to separate it from the bough; but the ripe fruit parts readily from the wood. Maturity in grace makes it easier to part with life itself; the unripe pear is scarcely beaten down with much labour, while its mellow companion drops readily into the hand with the slightest shake. Rest assured that love to the things of this life, and cleaving to this present state, are sure indications of immaturity in the divine life.

GRACES—should be Seasonable.

IT is said in praise of the tree planted by the rivers of water, that it bringeth forth its fruit *in its season;* good men

should aim to have seasonable virtues. For instance, a for-
giving spirit is golden if it display itself in the moment when
an injury is received ; it is but silver if it show itself upon
speedy reflection, and it is mere lead if it be manifested after
a long time for cooling. The whole matter reminds us of the
Warwickshire estimate of swarms of bees.

> " A swarm of bees in May
> Is worth a load of hay ;
> A swarm of bees in June
> Is worth a silver spune (*spoon*) ;
> A swarm of bees in July
> Is not worth a fly."

GRACE—Triumphant over Trial.

" IN one place near the Hospice of St. Bernard, I met with
a curious natural conservatory. The under surface of the
snow having been melted by the warmth of the soil, which in
Alpine regions is always markedly higher than that of the
air, was not in contact with it. A snowy vault was thus
formed, glazed on the top with thin plates of transparent ice ;
and here grew a most lovely cushion of the *Aretia Helvetica*,
covered with hundreds of its delicate rosy flowers, like a
miniature hydrangea blossom. The dark colour of the soil
favoured the ·absorption of heat ; and, prisoned in its crystal
cave, this little fairy grew and blossomed securely from the
very heart of winter, the unfavourable circumstances around
all seeming so many ministers of good, increasing its strength,
and enhancing its loveliness."

This delightful little sketch of nature by Mr. Hugh
Macmillan may be paralleled in the kingdom of grace ; for in
the cold shade of poverty, protected from a thousand temptations by that very scant, and in the centre of sinful society,
stimulated to a bolder confession by the surrounding opposition, we have met with the rarest specimens of grace.

Where every influence appeared to be deadly, the most vigorous spiritual life has been produced.

GRATITUDE.

THERE is a very touching little story told of a poor woman with two children, who had not a bed for them to lie upon, and scarcely any clothes to cover them. In the depth of winter they were nearly frozen, and the mother took the door of a cellar off the hinges, and set it up before the corner where they crouched down to sleep, that some of the draught and cold might be kept from them. One of the children whispered to her, when she complained of how badly off they were, " Mother, what do those dear little children do who have no cellar door to put up in front of them ? " Even there, you see, the little heart found cause for thankfulness.

GROWTH IN GRACE.

WE have the likenesses of our boys taken on every birthday, and twelve of the annual portraits are now framed in one picture, so that we see them at a glance from their babyhood to their youth. Suppose such photographic memorials of our own spiritual life had been taken and preserved, would there be a regular advance, as in these boys, or should we still have been exhibited in the perambulator? Have not some grown awhile, and then suddenly dwarfed? Have not others gone back to babyhood? Here is a wide field for reflection.

GROWTH IN GRACE.

LETTUCES, radishes, and such like garden crops, are soon out of the ground and ready for the table, a month almost suffices to perfect them ; but an oak requires long centuries to come to the fulness of its growth. Those graces which are most precious and durable will cost us longest to produce ; those good things which spring up hastily may have some

7

transient worth about them, but we cannot look for perman-ence and value in them. There is no need to deplore the slowness of our spiritual growth, if that which comes of it be of a solid character.

GROWTH IN GRACE.

THE vendors of flowers in the streets of London, are wont to commend them to customers by crying, "All a blowing and a growing." It would be no small praise to Christians if we could say as much for them, but, alas ! of too many professors the cry would truthfully be, "All a stunting and a withering."

GRUMBLERS.

A HEAVY waggon was being dragged along a country lane by a team of oxen. The axle-trees groaned and creaked terribly, when the oxen turning round, thus addressed the wheels :—" Halloa, there ! why do you make so much noise ? we bear all the labour, and we, not you, ought to cry out ! " Those complain first in our churches who have least to do. The gift of grumbling is largely dispensed among those who have no other talents, or who keep what they have wrapped up in a napkin.

HABITS—Destructive Power of.

THE surgeon of a regiment in India relates the following incident :—"A soldier rushed into the tent, to inform me that one of his comrades was drowning in a pond close by, and nobody could attempt to save him in consequence of the dense weeds which covered the surface. On repairing to the spot, we found the poor fellow in his last struggle, man-fully attempting to extricate himself from the meshes of rope-like grass that encircled his body; but, to all appearance, the more he laboured to escape, the more firmly they became coiled round his limbs. At last he sank, and the floating plants closed in, and left not a trace of the disaster. After some delay, a raft was made, and we put off to the spot, and sinking a pole some twelve feet, a native dived, holding on by the stake, and brought the body to the surface. I shall never forget the expression of the dead man's face—the clenched teeth, and fearful distortion of the countenance, while coils of long trailing weeds clung round his body and limbs, the muscles of which stood out stiff and rigid, whilst his hands grasped thick masses, showing how bravely he had struggled for life."

This heart-rending picture is a terribly accurate representation of a man with a conscience alarmed by remorse, struggling with his sinful habits, but finding them too strong for him. Divine grace can save the wretch from his unhappy condition, but if he be destitute of that, his remorseful agonies will but make him more hopelessly the slave of his passions. Laocoon, in vain endeavouring to tear off the serpents' coils from himself and children, aptly portrays the long-enslaved sinner contending with sin in his own strength. "Can the Ethiopian change his skin, or the leopard his spots?"

HAPPINESS OF BELIEVERS.

ONE of my hearers had seven children, who had come in rapid succession; he was hard-working and well spoken of. His children were all asleep when I went in, and as I expressed the pleasure the sight of their peaceful little faces gave me, the father said, "Ay, these are fine times for them; they need not to take any thought for themselves." On the Sunday the man was in church. I dwelt much upon the happy state of children, exempt from care as they were, and went on to say that believers were the children of God, that the Lord had commanded them to be careful for nothing, and promised that he would care for them. The man understood me, and it evidently pleased him to hear his expression repeated from the pulpit.—*Büchsel*.

HEAD—Christ.

EVERY one knows that it would be far better to lose our feet than our head. Adam had feet to stand with, but we have lost them by his disobedience ; yet glory be to God, we have found a Head, in whom we abide eternally secure, a Head which we shall never lose.

HEARERS.

JEDEDIAH BUXTON, the famous peasant, who could multiply nine figures by nine in his head, was once taken to see Garrick act. When he went back to his own village, he was asked what he thought of the great actor and his doings. "Oh!" he said, "he did not know, he had only seen a little man strut about the stage, and repeat 7,956 words." Here was a want of the ability to appreciate what he saw, and the exercise of the reigning faculty to the exclusion of every other. Similarly our hearers, if destitute of the spiritual powers by which the gospel is discerned, fix their thoughts on our words, tones, gestures, or countenance, and make remarks upon us which from a spiritual point of view are utterly absurd. How futile are our endeavours without the Holy Spirit !

HEARING.

"I HAVE an ear for other preachers," Sir John Cheke used to say, "but I have a heart for Latimer." Here is a very clear and main distinction. Too often men hear the Word sounding its drums and trumpets outside their walls, and they are filled with admiration of the martial music, but their city gates are fast closed and vigilantly guarded, so that the truth has no admittance, but only the sound of it. Would to God we knew how to reach men's affections, for the heart is the target we aim at, and unless we hit it we miss altogether.

HEARING—Carelessly.

WE crossed and recrossed the river several times by the ferry-boat at Basle. We had no object in the world but merely amusement and curiosity, to watch the simple machinery by which the same current is made to drift the boat in opposite directions from side to side. To other passengers it was a business, to us a sport. Our hearers use our ministry in much the same manner when they come to it out of the idlest curiosity, and listen to us as a means of spending a pleasant hour. That which should ferry them across to a better state of soul, they use as a mere pleasure-boat, to sail up and down in, making no progress after years of hearing. Alas! it may be sport to them, but it is death to us, because we know it will ere long be death to them.

HEARING—for Others.

THE negro preachers are often marked by great shrewdness and mother wit; and will not only point the truth, but barb it, so that if once in it will stick fast. One of these was once descanting with much earnestness on different ways in which men lose their souls. Under one head of remark, he said that men often lose their souls through excessive generosity. "What!" he exclaimed, "you tell me you never heard of that before? You say, ministers often tell us we lose our souls for our stinginess, and for being covetous— but who ever heard of a man that hurt himself by going too far t'other way? I tell you how they do it. They sit down under the sermon, and when the preacher touch upon this sin or that sin, they no take it to themselves, but give this part of the sermon to one brother, and that part to another brother. And so they give away the whole sermon, and it do them no good. And that's the way they lose their souls by being too generous."

There is great truth in this remark. The want of a self-applying conscience causes much of the best of preaching to fall like rain upon a rock, from which it soon runs off ; or if a little is caught in a hollow, it only stagnates, and then dries away, leaving no blessing behind. A sermon, however true and forcible, thus disposed of, does no good to those among whom it is so silently distributed, while it leaves him who squanders its treasures to perish at last in the poverty and emptiness of his soul.

HEARING—Useless Alone.

WHAT a mistake to imagine that, by hearing first one preacher and then another, we can derive benefit to our souls ! More is wanted than such hearing. A raven may fly from cage to cage, but it is not thereby changed into a dove. Go from room to room of the royal feast, and the sight of the tables will never stay thy hunger. Reader, the main thing is to have and hold the truth personally and inwardly ; if this be not seen to, thou wilt die in thy sins, though ten thousand voices should direct thee to the way of salvation. Pity indeed is it that the bulk of hearers are hearers only, and are no more likely to go to heaven than the seats they sit on in the assembly of the saints.

HEART—its Aberrations.

THE compass on board an iron vessel is very subject to aberrations ; yet, for all that, its evident desire is to be true to the pole. True hearts in this wicked world, and in this fleshly body, are all too apt to swerve, but they still show their inward and persistent tendency to point towards heaven and God. On board iron vessels it is a common thing to see a compass placed aloft, to be as much away from the cause of aberration as possible : a wise hint to us to elevate our affections and desires ; the nearer to God the less swayed by worldly influences.

HEART (Broken)—its Prevalence with God.

WHAT man among you can stand against his children's tears? When King Henry II., in the ages gone by, was provoked to take up arms against his ungrateful and rebellious son, he besieged him in one of the French towns, and the son being near to death, desired to see his father, and confess his wrong-doing; but the stern old sire refused to look the rebel in the face. The young man being sorely troubled in his conscience, said to those about him, "I am dying, take me from my bed, and let me lie in sackcloth and ashes, in token of my sorrow for my ingratitude to my father." Thus he died, and when the tidings came to the old man outside the walls, that his boy had died in ashes, repentant for his rebellion, he threw himself upon the earth, like another David, and said, "Would God I had died for him." The thought of his boy's broken heart touched the heart of the father. If ye, being evil, are overcome by your children's tears, how much more shall your Father who is in heaven find in your bemoanings and confessions an argument for the display of his pardoning love through Christ Jesus our Lord? This is the eloquence which God delights in, the broken heart and the contrite spirit.

HEART—Hardness of.

LIGHTFOOT says:—"I have heard it more than once and again, from the sheriffs who took all the gunpowder plotters, and brought them up to London, that every night when they came to their lodging by the way, they had their music and dancing a good part of the night. One would think it strange that men in their case should be so merry." More marvellous still is it that those between whom and death there is but a step, should sport away their time as if they should live on for ages. Though the place of torment is within a short march of all unregenerate men, yet see how they make mirth, grinning and jesting between the jaws of hell!

HEART—must be Renewed.

A MAN may beat down the bitter fruit from an evil tree until he is weary; whilst the root abides in strength and vigour, the beating down of the present fruit will not hinder it from bringing forth more. This is the folly of some men; they set themselves with all earnestness and diligence against the appearing eruption of lust, but leaving the principle and root untouched, perhaps unsearched out, they make but little or no progress in this work of mortification.—*John Owen.*

HEART—Seat of Spiritual Disease.

SOME malady which you do not understand troubles and alarms you. The physician is called. Thinking that the illness proceeds from a certain inflammatory process on a portion of your skin, you anxiously direct his attention to the spot. Silently, but sympathisingly, he looks at the place where you have bidden him look, and because you have bidden him look there, but soon he turns away. He is busy with an instrument on another part of your body. He presses his trumpet tube gently to your breast, and listens for the pulsations which faintly but distinctly pass through. He looks and listens there, and saddens as he looks. You again direct his attention to the cutaneous eruption which annoys you. He sighs and sits silent. When you reiterate your request that something should be done for the external eruption, he gently shakes his head, and answers not a word. From this silence you would learn the truth at last, you would not miss its meaning long.

O miss not the meaning of the Lord when he points to the seat of the soul's disease: "Ye WILL not come." These, his enemies, dwell in your heart.—*W. Arnot.*

HEAVEN.

"WHO," saith an old divine, "chides a servant for taking away the first course at a feast when the second consists of far greater delicacies?" Who then can feel regret that this present world passeth away, when he sees that an eternal world of joy is coming? The first course is grace, but the second is glory, and that is as much better as the fruit is better than the blossom.

HEAVEN—Our Future Condition in.

YOU will very often perceive in your rain-water certain ugly little things, which swim and twist about in it, always trying if they can to reach the surface, and breathe through one end of their bodies. What makes these little things so lively, these innumerable little things like very small tadpoles, why are they so energetic? Possibly they have an idea of what they are going to be. The day will come when all of a sudden there will emerge from the case of the creature which now navigates your bason, a long-legged thing with two bright gauze-like wings, which will mount into the air, and on a summer's evening will dance in the sunlight. It is nothing more nor less than a gnat in one of its earliest stages. Mark in that creature an image of your present self; you are an undeveloped being; you have not your wings as yet, and are earthbound, and yet sometimes in your activity for Christ, when the strong desires for something better are upon you, you leap in foretaste of the bliss to come.

HEAVEN—an Incentive to Diligence.

JULIUS CÆSAR coming towards Rome with his army, and hearing that the senate and people had fled from it, said, "They that will not fight for this city, what city will they fight for?" If we will not take pains for the kingdom of heaven, what kingdom will we take pains for?

HEAVEN—None Admitted but those Like Jesus.

AT heaven's gate there stands an angel with charge to admit none but those who in their countenances bear the

same features as the Lord of the place. Here comes a
monarch with a crown upon his head. The angel pays him
no respect, but reminds him that the diadems of earth have
no value in heaven. A company of eminent men advance
dressed in robes of state, and others adorned with the
gowns of learning, but to these no deference is rendered,
for their faces are very unlike the Crucified. A maiden
comes forward, fair and comely, but the celestial watcher
sees not in that sparkling eye and ruddy cheek the
beauty for which he is looking. A man of renown
cometh up heralded by fame, and preceded by the admiring clamour of mankind; but the angel saith, "Such
applause may pleàse the sons of men, but thou hast no
right to enter here." But free admittance is always given to
those who in holiness are made like their Lord. Poor they
may have been ; illiterate they may have been; but the angel
as he looks at them smiles a welcome as he says, "It is
Christ again ; a transcript of the holy child Jesus. Come in,
come in; eternal glory thou shalt win. Thou shalt sit in
heaven with Christ, for thou art like him."

HEAVEN—to be Shut Out of at Last.

SEVERAL years ago we heard an old minister relate the
following incident:—"He had preached the Word for many
a year in a wood hard by a beautiful village in the Inverness-
shire Highlands, and it was his invariable custom, on dis-
missing his own congregation, to repair to the Baptist Chapel
in this village to partake of the Lord's Supper with his
people assembled there. It was then usual to shut the gates
during this service, in order that communicants might not
be exposed to any disturbance through persons going out or
coming in. On one occasion the burden of the Lord pressed
upon his servant with more than ordinary severity, and
anxious to deliver it and clear his soul, he detained his
hearers a little beyond the time, and consequently had to

hurry to the chapel. As he drew near he noticed the door-keeper retire from the outer gate, after having shut it. He called to him, quickening his pace at the same time, but his cry was not heard, the attendant retreated inside and the minister came up 'just in time' to see the door put to, and hear it fastened from within. He walked round the chapel looking up at the windows, but could gain no admittance ; there was only one door, and that door was shut. He listened and heard the singing, and thought how happy God's people were inside, while he himself was shut out. The circumstance made an impression upon him at the time which he could never afterwards forget, and he was led to ask himself the question, ' Shall it be so at the last? Shall I come up to the gate of heaven only in time to be too late, to find the last ransomed one admitted, and the door everlastingly shut?'"

HEAVEN—a Sustaining Prospect.

ONE Palmer, of Reading, being condemned to die, in Queen Mary's time, was much persuaded to recant, and among other things a friend said to him, " Take pity on thy golden years and pleasant flowers of youth, before it be too late." His reply was as beautiful as it was conclusive—" Sir, I long for those springing flowers which shall never fade away." When he was in the midst of the flames he exhorted his companions to constancy, saying, " We shall not end our lives in the fire, but make a change for a better life ; yea, for coals we shall receive pearls." Thus do we clearly see, that although " if in this life only we have hope in Christ, we are of all men most miserable," yet the prospect of a better and enduring substance enables us to meet all the trials and temptations of this present life with holy boldness and joy.

HEAVEN—its Variety.

WE cannot stay to read the catalogue now, but heavenly joys shall be like the tree of life in the New Jerusalem, which

brings forth twelve manner of fruits, and yields her fruit every
month. Robert Hall used to cry, "O for the everlasting
rest!" but Wilberforce would sigh to dwell in unbroken love.
Hall was a man who suffered—he longed for rest; Wilberforce was a man of amiable spirit, loving society and fellowship—he looked for love. Hall shall have his rest, and
Wilberforce shall have his love. There are joys at God's
right hand, suitable for the spiritual tastes of all those who
shall come thither. The heavenly manna tastes to every
man's peculiar liking.

HEAVENWARD.

My horse invariably comes home in less time than he makes
the journey out. He pulls the carriage with a hearty good
will when his face is towards home. Should not I also both
suffer and labour the more joyously because my way lies
towards heaven, and I am on pilgrimage to my Father's
house, my soul's dear home and resting place?

HOLY WATER.

Holy water, indeed! a vile mixture, neither fit for man
nor beast. You see this liquid virtue at the doors of all the
churches ready for the brows of the faithful, but what is far
more curious, you observe it in little pots placed for use in the
cemeteries; and that the passer-by may give the dead a
showery benediction, there are little sprinkling brushes in the
pots with which to scatter the precious mixture. A mother's
tears over her dead babe are far more in place than such
foolery. Holy water! bah! See how the rain pours down
from yonder black cloud which has passed over the rugged
crags of Pilatus; that sort of holy water is infinitely more
likely to moisten the clay of the defunct, and bring plenteous
blessing to the living, than all the hogsheads of aqueous fluid
that priests ever mumbled over. Holy water, indeed! If
there be such a thing, it trickles from the eye of penitence,

bedews the cheek of gratitude, and falls upon the page of holy Scripture when the word is applied with power. Standing where, when the rain is over, one can see the fair Lake of Lucerne brimming with crystal, and the clouds among the Alpine peaks all charged with moisture, rendered golden by the sun's clear shining, one feels indignant at the idea that the little driblets of nastiness in yonder pots and shells should be venerated, and all nature's reservoirs accounted common or unclean. It needs no small measure of prudence to restrain a man from tumbling pots and pans and holy liquids head-long to the ground. Human folly, how far wilt thou not go when priests lead thee by the nose!

HOPE.

ONCE on a time, certain strong labourers were sent forth by the great King to level a primeval forest, to plough it, to sow it, and to bring to him the harvest. They were stout-hearted and strong, and willing enough for labour, and much they needed all their strength and more. One stalwart labourer was named Industry—consecrated work was his. His brother Patience, with thews of steel, went with him, and tired not in the longest days under the heaviest labours. To help them they had Zeal, clothed with ardent and indomitable energy. Side by side there stood his kinsman Self-denial, and his friend Importunity. These went forth to their labour, and they took with them, to cheer their toils, their well-beloved sister Hope; and well it was they did, for they needed the music of her consolation ere the work was done, for the forest trees were huge, and demanded many sturdy blows of the axe ere they would fall prone upon the ground. One by one the giant forest kings were overthrown, but the labour was immense and incessant. At night when they went to their rest, the day's work always seemed so light, for as they crossed the threshold, Patience, wiping the sweat from his brow, would be encouraged, and Self-denial would be strengthened by hearing the sweet voice of Hope within singing, " God will bless us, God, even our own God, will bless us." They felled the lofty trees to the music of that strain ; they cleared the acres one by one, they tore from their sockets the huge roots, they delved the soil, they sowed the corn, and waited for the harvest, often much discouraged, but still held to their work as by silver chains and golden fetters by the sweet sound of the voice which chanted so constantly, " God, even our own God, will bless us." They never could refrain from service, for Hope never could refrain from song. They were ashamed to be discouraged, they were shocked to be despairing, for still the voice rang clearly out at noon and eventide, " God will bless us, God, even our own God, will bless us." You know the parable, you recognise the voice : may you hear it in your souls to-day !

HOPE.

IT is reported that in the Tamul language there is no word for *hope*. Alas! poor men, if we were all as destitute of the blessed comfort itself as these Tamul speakers are of the word! What must be the misery of souls in hell where they remember the word, but can never know hope itself!

HUMILITY.

WISE men know their own ignorance and are ever ready to learn. Humility is the child of knowledge. Michael Angelo was found by the Cardinal Farnese walking in solitude amid the ruins of the Coliseum, and when he expressed his surprise, the great artist answered, " I go yet to school that I may continue to learn." Who among us can after this talk of finishing our education? We have need to learn of all around us. He must be very foolish who cannot tell us something ; or more likely we must be more foolish not to be able to learn of him.

HUMILITY.

THE whole Roman language, even with all the improvements of the Augustan age, does not afford so much as a name for *humility* (the word from whence we borrow this, as is well known, bearing in Latin a quite different meaning), no, nor was one found in all the copious language of the Greeks, till it was made by the great Apostle.—*John Wesley.*

HUMILITY.

"OF all trees, I observe, God hath chosen the vine, a low plant that creeps upon the helpful wall ; of all beasts, the soft and patient lamb ; of all fowls, the mild and guileless dove. Christ is the rose of the field, and the lily of the valley. When God appeared to Moses, it was not in the lofty cedar, nor the sturdy oak, nor the spreading plane ; but in a bush, a humble, slender, abject shrub ; as if he would, by these elections, check the conceited arrogance of man."—*Owen Feltham.*

HUMILITY AND CHEERFULNESS.

"OBSERVE the peculiar characters of the grass which adapt it especially for the service of man, are its apparent *humility and cheerfulness.* Its humility, in that it seems created only for lowest service, appointed to be trodden on, and fed upon. Its cheerfulness, in that it seems to exult under all kinds of violence and suffering. You roll it, and it is the stronger the next day; you mow it, and it multiplies its shoots, as if it were grateful; you tread upon it, and it only sends up richer perfume. Spring comes, and it rejoices with all the earth, glowing with variegated flame of flowers, waving in soft depth of fruitful strength. Winter comes, and though it will not mock its fellow plants by growing then, it will not pine and mourn, and turn colourless or leafless as they. It is always green, and is only the brighter and gayer for the hoar-frost."

So Ruskin poetically writes of the grass; should it not be thus with believers? Their flesh is like to grass for perishing, it were well if their spirits were like to grass for humility and cheerfulness in service.

HYPOCRISY.

IN the olden times even the best rooms were usually of bare brick or stone, damp, and mouldy, but over these in great houses when the family was resident, were hung up arras or hangings of rich materials, between which and the wall persons might conceal themselves, so that literally walls had ears. It is to be feared that many a brave show of godliness is but an arras to conceal rank hypocrisy; and this accounts for some men's religion being but occasional, since it is folded up or exposed to view as need may demand. Is there no room for conscience to pry between thy feigned profession and thy real ungodliness, and bear witness against thee? Remember, if conscience do it not, certainly "the watcher and the Holy One" will make a thorough search within thee.

HYPOCRISY.

IN the pursuit of pastoral duty, I stood a little while ago in a cheesemonger's shop, and being in a fidgety humour, and having a stick in my hand, I did what most Englishmen are sure to do, I was not content with seeing, but must needs touch as well. My stick came gently upon a fine cheese in the window, and to my surprise a most metallic sound emanated from it. The sound was rather hollow, or one might have surmised that all the tasteholes had been filled up with sovereigns, and thus the cheese had been greatly enriched, and the merchant had been his own banker. There was, however, a sort of crockery jingle in the sound, like the ring of a huge bread or milk pan, such as our country friends use so abundantly; and I came to the very correct conclusion that I had found a very well got-up hypocrite in the shop window. Mark, from this time, when I pass by, I mentally whisper, " Pottery ; " and the shams may even be exchanged for realities, but I shall be long in believing it. In my mind the large stock has dissolved into potsherds, and the fine show in the window only suggests the potter's vessel. The homely illustration is simply introduced because we find people of this sort in our churches, looking extremely like what they should be, yet having no substance in them, so that if, accidentally, one happens to tap them somewhere or other with sudden temptation or stern duty, the baked earth gives forth its own ring, and the pretender is esteemed no longer.

HYPOCRISY.

THE shops in the square of San Marco were all religiously closed, for the day was a high festival : we were much disappointed, for it was our last day, and we desired to take away with us some souvenirs of lovely Venice ; but our regret soon vanished, for on looking at the shop we meant to patronise, we readily discovered signs of traffic within. We stepped to the side door, and found when one or two other customers had been served, that we might purchase to our heart's content, saint or no saint. After this fashion too many keep the laws of God to the eye, but violate them in the heart. The shutters are up as if the man no more dealt with sin and Satan ; but a brisk commerce is going on behind the scenes. From such deceit may the Spirit of truth preserve us.

HYPOCRISY—Easy, but Dangerous.

THE counterfeit will always have some admirers, from its cheapness in the market. One must dig deep in dark mines for gold and silver ; the precious treasure must be brought from far across the seas ; it must be melted down, it must pass through many assays, and the dies must be worked with

8

ponderous engines before the coin can be produced ; all this
to the sluggish many is a heavy disadvantage.   Hush !
hearken ! steal silently upstairs ; the spirit of deceit invites
you to her chamber ; a little plaster of Paris, a fire, a crucible,
molten lead, the mould, and there is your money, sir, without
troubling Peru, Potosi, California, or the Mint. Slink out and
change your fine new shillings, and your fortune's made
without the ignoble waste of sweat and labour.   But be quiet,
for a detective may be near, a coarse-minded minion of
unpoetic law, who may cruelly block up your road, or even
lead you into prison.   Short cuts to wealth have brought
many to the hulks ; and, let me add, there are short cuts to
godliness which have brought many to perdition !

HYPOCRISY—a Fall Fatal.

" THE meteor, if it once fall, cannot be rekindled."   When
those who once flashed before the eyes of the religious public
with the blaze of a vain profession, fall into open and scan-
dalous sin, it is impossible to renew their glory.   Once break
the egg of hypocrisy, and who can repair the damage?

HYPOCRISY—Present Age Suitable to.

THERE was an age of chivalry, when no craven courted
knighthood, for it involved the hard blows, the dangerous
wounds, the rough unhorsings, and the ungentle perils of the
tournament ; nay, these were but child's play : there were
distant eastern fields, where Paynim warriors must be slain
by valiant hands, and blood must flow in rivers from the
Red-cross knights.   Then men who lacked valour preferred
their hawks and their jesters, and left heroes to court death
and glory on the battle-field. This genial time of peace breeds
carpet knights, who flourish their untried weapons, and bear
the insignia of valour, without incurring its inconvenient
toils.   Many are crowding to the seats of the heroes, since

prowess and patience are no more required. The war is
over, and every man is willing to enlist. When Rome commenced her long career of victory, it was no pleasant thing to
be a soldier in the Roman legions. The power which smote
the nations like a rod of iron abroad, was a yoke of iron at
home. There were long forced marches, with hunger and
cold and weariness ; heavy armour was the usual load when
the legionary marched at ease ; but "ease" was a word he
seldom used. Rivers were forded; mountains were scaled ;
barbarians were attacked ; proud nations were assailed ;
kingdoms were subdued. No toil too stern for the scarred
veteran, no odds too heavy, no onslaught too ferocious, no
arms too terrible. Scarcely were his wounds healed, ere
he was called to new fields ; his life was battle ; his home
the tent ; his repast was plunder ; his bed the battle-field;
while the eagle's bloody talons removed all need of sepulchre
for his slaughtered body. But afterwards when Rome was
mistress of the world, and the Prætorian cohorts could sell
the imperial purple to the highest bidder, many would follow
the legions to share their spoils. It is not otherwise to-day.
Into the triumphs of martyrs and confessors few are unwilling to enter; in a national respect to religion, which is
the result of *their* holiness, even ungodly men are willing
to share. *They* have gone before us with true hearts valiant
for truth, and false traitors are willing to divide their
spoils.

HYPOCRISY—of no Service.

COALS of fire cannot be concealed beneath the most sumptuous apparel, they will betray themselves with smoke and
flame ; nor can darling sins be long hidden beneath the most
ostentatious profession, they will sooner or later discover
themselves, and burn sad holes in the man's reputation. Sin
needs quenching in the Saviour's blood, not concealing under
the garb of religion.

HYPOCRITES—Discovered on nearer Inspection.

How many are like that famous painting of the olden time,
in which the artist depicted what seemed at a distance a holy
friar with a book before him, and his hands crossed in devotion, looking like a saint indeed, but when you came close to
the venerable impostor, you found that his hands, though
clasped, enclosed a lemon, and instead of a book there was a
punch-bowl into which he was squeezing the juice. To seem
to be, answers men's purposes so well, that it is little marvel
if pretenders swarm like the flies in Egypt's plague ; yet if
they would remember the last great day, men would abhor
hypocrisy.

HYPOCRITES—Season for.

After a refreshing shower which has made all the flowers
to smile till the teardrops of joy stand in their eyes, you will see
your garden-paths spotted over with slugs and snails. These
creatures lay concealed till the genial rain called them forth
to make their slimy way towards whatsoever they might
devour. After this fashion revivals, of necessity, develop
hypocrites, yet who would deplore the shower because of the
snails, and who would rail at " times of refreshing " because
mere pretenders are excited to make a base profession of a
grace to which they are strangers?

HYPOCRITES—Seeking their own Advantage.

God is in the hypocrite's mouth, but the world is in his
heart, which he expects to gain through his good reputation.
I have read of one that offered his prince a great sum of
money to have leave once or twice a-day to come into his
presence, and only say, " *God save your Majesty!* " The
prince wondering at this large offer for so small a favour,
asked him, " What advantage would this afford him? " " O
sire," saith he, " this, though I have nothing else at your
hands, will get me a name in the country for one who is a

great favourite at court, and such an opinion will help me to more at the year's end, than it costs me for the purchase." Thus some, by the name they get for great saints, advance their worldly interests, which lie at the bottom of all their profession.—*Gurnall.*

HYPOCRITES—their Sinister Motives.

SEE yonder eagle, how it mounts! Does it care for the ethereal blue, or aspire to commune with the stars of heaven ! Not a whit ; such airy considerations have no weight with the ravenous bird ; and yet you will not wonder that it soars aloft when you remember that it thus obtains a broader range of vision, and so becomes the more able to provide for its nest. The bird mounts towards heaven, but it keeps its eye evermore upon the outlook for its prey. No celestial impulse is needed, its love of blood suffices to bear it aloft. It soars only that it may flash downwards with fell swoop upon the object of its desires. Wonder not that men with the hearts of devils yet mount like angels : there is a reason which explains it all.

HYPOCRITICAL CONFESSIONS.

YOU have heard, no doubt, of beggars who tie a leg up when they go a-begging, and then make a hideous lamentation of their lameness. Why, this is just your case, sir, when you go to church a-praying, which is begging, you tie your righteous heart up, and then make woeful outcry for mercy on us miserable sinners. O sir, these tricks may pass a while unnoticed, but Jesus Christ will apprehend such cheats at last, and give them their desert.—*John Berridge.*

IGNORANCE.

PAYSON well says, " Oh ! when we meet in heaven, we shall see how little we knew about it on earth."

IGNORANCE—of One's Own Heart.

" AFTER all, I do not hate God. No, sir ; you will not make

me believe that. I am a sinner, I know, and do many wicked things ; but after all, I have a good heart—I don't hate God." Such was the language of a prosperous worldling. He was sincere, but sadly deceived. A few months afterwards, that God who had given him so many good things, crossed his path in an unexpected manner. A fearful torrent swept down the valley, and threatened destruction to this man's large flour mill. A crowd were watching it, in momentary expectation of seeing it fall, while the owner, standing in the midst of them, was cursing God to his face, and pouring out the most horrid oaths.

He no longer doubted or denied that he hated God. But nothing in that hour of trial came out of his mouth which was not previously in his heart. God's account of the unrenewed heart is true : it is "deceitful above all things," as well as "desperately wicked." He who is wise will believe God's account of the state of his heart by nature, rather than the deceitful heart's account of itself.

IGNORANCE—Possible in Most Constant Hearers.

SAMUEL WESLEY visited one of his parishioners as he was upon his dying bed—a man who had never missed going to church in forty years. " Thomas, where do you think your soul will go ?" " Soul ! soul !" said Thomas. "Yes, sir," said Mr. Wesley, "do you not know what your soul is ?" "Ay, surely," said Thomas ; "why, it is a little bone in the back that lives longer than the body." " So much," says John Wesley, who related it on the authority of Dr. Lupton, who had it from his father, "had Thomas learned from hearing sermons, and exceedingly good sermons, for forty years."— *Anecdotes of the Wesleys. By the Rev. J. B. Wakeley.*

IMITATION—of Good Men, its Limit.

PLUTARCH says that among the Persians those persons were considered most beautiful who were hawk-nosed, for no other reason than that Cyrus had such a nose. In Richard the Third's court humps upon the back were the height of fashion. According as the various potentates who have condescended to rule mankind have lisped, or stuttered, or limped, or squinted, or spoken through their noses, these infirmities have been elevated into graces and commanded the admiration of silly mortals. But is there not more than a possibility that what we ridicule in the kingdoms of earth may have its counterpart in the church? Is there not a tendency among Christians to imitate the spiritual infirmities of their religious leaders, or oftener still of departed saints? We may follow holy men so far as they follow Christ ; the mischief is that we do not readily stop where we should, but rather where we should not. Bunyan, Whitfield, Wesley, Calvin, Luther, yes, by all means imitate them—but not indiscriminately, not slavishly, or you will do so ridiculously. One is your Master, to copy him in every jot and tittle will be safe enough.

INSIGNIFICANT SUBJECTS—Not Fit for the Pulpit.

CARLYLE in narrating an instance of the preservation of etiquette at the court of Louis XVI., while the mob were demanding entrance into his private apartments, and the empire was going to pieces, compares it to the house-cricket still chirping amid the pealing of the trump of doom. When trivial subjects are descanted upon from the pulpit, while souls are perishing for lack of knowledge, the same comparison may be used ; as for instance, when a congregation is collected, and the preacher talks about the drying up of the Euphrates, or ventilates his pet theory for reconciling Moses and geology. Why cannot these things be kept for other assemblies? What can the man be at? Nero fiddling over burning Rome is nothing to it ! Even the women knitting in front of the guillotine were not more coolly cruel. We tolerate the cricket for his incongruous chirp ; but go to, thou silly trifler at the sacred desk, we cannot frame excuse for thee, or have patience with thee.

IMMUTABILITY OF GOD.

THERE be many Christians most like unto young sailors, who think the shore and the whole land doth move when they ship, and they themselves are moved. Just so not a few do imagine that God moveth, and saileth, and changeth places, because their giddy souls are under sail, and subject to alteration, to ebbing and flowing. But the foundation of the Lord abideth sure.—*Samuel Rutherford.*

INACTIVITY—The Evils of.

WHAT a mournful sight the observer may see in some of the outskirts of our huge city ; row after row of houses all untenanted and forlorn. The owners had far better let them at the lowest rent than suffer them to remain empty, for the boys make targets of the windows, enterprising purveyors for the marine store shops rend off all the lead, thieves purloin every movable fitting, damp swells the window frames and doors, and mustiness makes the whole place wretched to all the senses ; into the bargain the district gets a bad name which it probably never loses. Better a poor tenant than a house running to ruin unused. The similitude may well suggest the desirableness of an object and a service to those Christians whose time is wasted in slothful ease. All sorts of mischief happen to unoccupied professors of religion ; there is no evil from which they are secure; better would it be for them to accept the lowest occupation for the Lord Jesus, than remain the victims of inaction.

INCONSISTENCIES.

THE orthodox Greek churchman is scandalised at the image-worship of the Romanist; it is flat idolatry, and he denounces it vehemently. But what are those pictures in the Russian

churches, many of them made to stand out in relief with
solid plates of gold and silver? Why, these are pictures of
the Virgin or of her Son, as the case may be, and your anti-
idolatrous Greek bows before these with voluntary humility.
He hates image-worship, you see, but stands up for
picture-worship. Behold how sinners disagree in name
and unite in spirit! Put Greek and Roman in a sack
together, and let the greatest idolater out first: the
wisest solution would be to keep them both in the sack, for
Solomon himself would be puzzled to select the most guilty. Are
there not such inconsistencies among ourselves? Do we not
condemn in one form what we allow in another? Do we
not censure in our neighbours what we allow in ourselves?
This query need not be answered in a hurry; the reply will
be the more extensive for a little waiting.

INCONSISTENCY.

MARK ANTONY once yoked two lions together, and drove
them through the streets of Rome, but no human skill can
ever yoke together the Lion of the Tribe of Judah and the
Lion of the Pit. I did see a man once trying to walk on both
sides of the street at one time, but he was undoubtedly drunk;
and when we see a man labouring day by day to walk on both
sides of the street, morally—in the shady side of sin and the
sunny side of holiness, or reeling in the evening, at one time
towards the bright lights of virtue, and anon staggering back
to sin in dark places, where no lamp is shining—we say of
him, "He is morally intoxicated," and wisdom adds, "He
is mad, and if the Great Physician heal him not, his madness
will bring him to destruction."

INCONSISTENCY—Glossed Over.

"SILK· is interdicted by Mussulman law as being an excre-
ment. They elude this prohibition by mixing a very little
cotton with it." After the same manner it is growing too

common at what are called Penny Readings, to indulge in
the idlest jesting and absurdity, and then to pass off the
whole entertainment respectably by singing the doxology, or
pronouncing the benediction ; the religion being to the
foolery, in the proportion of the bread to the sack in Fal-
staff's reckoning.   Do men imagine that Christ's laws are to
be as easily evaded as Mahomet's?   Do they dream that
the " very little cotton" will sanctify all the forbidden fabric?
The illustration may be applied in many other ways besides
that which we have here indicated.

INDOLENCE—a Shameful Sickness.

THERE once lived in Ghent a beggar, who was accustomed
to collect alms upon the pretence that he had a secret disease
lying in his bones and weakening his whole body, and that
he dared not for shame mention the name of it.   This appeal
was exceedingly successful, until a person in authority more
curious than the rest, insisted upon following him, and ex-
amining him at home.   At last the beggar confessed as
follows :—" That which pains me you see not ; but I have a
shameful disease in my bones, so that I cannot work ; some
call it sloth, and others term it idleness."   Alas ! that so
many in our churches should be so far gone with THIS SAME
SICKNESS.

INFIRMITIES—Use of.

" SOME of the arable land along the shore on the south-
east coast of Sutherland, is almost covered with shore stones,
from the size of a turkey's egg to eight pounds weight.
Several experiments have been made to collect these off the
land, expecting a better crop ; but in every case the land
proved less productive by removing them ; and on some small
spots of land it was found so evident, that they were spread
on the land again, to ensure their usual crop of oats or
pease."   We would fain be rid of all our infirmities which,

to our superficial conceptions, appear to be great hindrances to our usefulness, and yet it is most questionable if we should bring forth any fruit unto God without them. Much rather, therefore, will I glory in infirmities that the power of Christ may rest upon me.

INFLUENCE.

LORD PETERBOROUGH speaking on one occasion of the celebrated Fénélon, observed:—" He is a delicious creature ; I was forced to get away from him as fast as I possibly could, else he would have made me pious." Would to God that all of us had such an influence over godless men.

INGRATITUDE—to God.

THE Staubach is a fall of remarkable magnificence, seeming to leap from heaven ; its glorious stream reminds one of the abounding mercy which in a mighty torrent descends from above. In the winter, when the cold is severe, the water freezes at the foot of the fall, and rises up in huge icicles like stalagmites, until it reaches the fall itself, as though it sought to bind it in the same icy fetters. How like is this to the common conduct of men ! Divine favours frozen by human ingratitude, are proudly lifted in rebellion against the God who gave them.

INTEREST—in Holy Work to be Maintained.

IT is of the utmost importance to keep up our interest in the holy work in which we are engaged, for the moment our interest flags the work will become wearisome. Humboldt says that the copper-coloured native of central America, far more accustomed than the European traveller to the burning heat of the climate, yet complains more when upon a journey, because he is stimulated by no interest. The same Indian who would complain, when in botanising he was loaded with a box full of plants, would row his canoe fourteen or fifteen

hours together against the current without a murmur, because
he wished to return to his family.   Labours of love are light.
Routine is a hard master.   Love much, and you can do
much.   Impossibilities disappear when zeal is fervent.

INVITATIONS OF THE GOSPEL—the Sinner's Warrant.

IN the courts of law if a man be called as a witness, no
sooner is his name mentioned, though he may be at the end
of the court, than he begins to force his way up to the witness
box.   Nobody says, " Why is this man pushing here?" or, if
they should say, "Who are you?" it would be a sufficient
answer to say, " My name was called."   " But you are not
rich, you have no gold ring upon your finger!"   " No, but
that is not my right of way, but I was called."   " Sir, you are
not a man of repute, or rank, or character!"   " It matters not,
I was called.   Make way."   So make way, ye doubts and
fears, make way, ye devils of the infernal lake, Christ calls
the sinner.   Sinner, come, for though thou hast nought to
recommend thee, yet it is written, " Him that cometh unto
me I will in no wise cast out."

IRASCIBLE PERSONS—Not to be Provoked.

IN the Jardin des Plantes we saw a hooded snake in a
most unamiable condition of temper.   There was a thick
glass and a stout wire between us, and we did nothing but
look at him, yet he persisted in darting at us with the utmost
vehemence of malice, until the keeper requested us to move
away, with the advice that it was not well to irritate such
creatures.   When one meets with an irascible person, on the
look out to pick a quarrel, ill conditioned, and out of elbows
with the whole world, it is best to move on, and let him
alone.   Even if he can do you no harm, and if his irritation
be utterly unreasonable, it is best to remove all exciting causes
of provocation, for it is never wise to irritate vipers.   You
do not on purpose walk heavily across the floor to teach a

gouty man that you have no respect for his tender feelings since he ought not to be so susceptible; neither should you vex those afflicted with a bad temper, and then plead that they have no right to be so excitable. If our neighbours' tempers are gunpowder, let us not play with fire.

JESUITS.

THE cat having a long time preyed upon the mice, the poor creatures at last, for their safety, contained themselves within their holes; but the cat finding his prey to cease, as being known to the mice that he was indeed their enemy and a cat, deviseth this course following, namely, changeth his hue, getting on a religious habit, shaveth his crown, walks gravely by their holes; and yet perceiving that the mice kept their holes, and looking out, suspected the worst, he formally, and father-like, said unto them, " *Quod fueram non sum, frater, caput aspice tonsum*—O brother, I am not as you take me for; I am no more a cat; see my habit and shaven crown." Hereupon some of the more credulous and bold among them were again, by this deceit, snatched up; and therefore when afterwards he came, as before, to entice them forth, they would come out no more, but answered, " Talk what you can, we will never believe you; you bear still a cat's heart within you." And so here the Jesuits, yea, and priests too, for they are all joined in the tails, like Samson's foxes: Ephraim against Manasseh, and Manasseh against Ephraim, and both against Judah.—*Sir E. Coke.*

JOY—at Finding Salvation.

WE are told of some Turks, who have, upon the sight of Mahomet's tomb, put out their eyes, that they might not defile them, forsooth, with any common object, after they had been blessed with seeing one so sacred. I am sure many gracious souls there have been, who, by a prospect of heaven's glory set before the eye of their faith, have been so

ravished by the sight, that they desired God even to seal up
their eyes by death, with Simeon, who would not by his
good-will have lived a day after that blessed hour in which
his eyes had beheld the salvation of God.—*W. Gurnall.*

JOY OF OUR RELIGION—as an Evidence of its Truth.

HOW I long for my bed! Not that I may sleep—I lie
awake often and long! but to hold sweet communion with
my God. What shall I render unto him for all his revelations
and gifts to me? Were there no historical evidence of the
truth of Christianity, were there no well-established miracles,
still I should believe that the religion propagated by the
fishermen of Galilee is divine. The holy joys it brings to me
must be from heaven. Do I write this boastingly, brother?
Nay, it is with tears of humble gratitude that I tell of the
goodness of the Lord."—*Extract from a Private Letter from
Bapa Padmanji, one of the Native Converts in India.*

JUDGMENT—Comparable to Balances.

OUR judgment may be compared to the scales and weights
of the merchant. It should be correct, but it seldom is quite
accurate; even ordinary wear and tear in this world will
suffice to put it out of gear. We had need call in the
Rectifier full often, and entreat him to search out our secret
shortcomings, lest we deviate from equity and know it not.
It would be well if the scales of conscience would turn even
at the finest dust, but how rarely is this the case! False
weights and balances are an abomination unto the Lord, yet
many use them, they weigh their neighbours so as to under-
estimate them, and they use balances far too favourable to
themselves ; they give the Lord a portion sadly too small,
and to their own pleasures a dowry much too great. Trades-
men who have one set of weights to buy with and others to
sell with, are evidently rogues, and we may convict ourselves

of injustice at once if we find ourselves severe to other men and lenient to ourselves. Fraudulent shopkeepers will use a movable piece of metal, by removing which they can lighten the weight or the scale, and we too may have a convenient indignation which we may restrain or indulge according as the person whose fault we judge may be the object of our goodwill or our displeasure. Some of the marine-store dealers, and buyers of kitchen-stuff at the back door, pretend to judge of weight by the feeling of their hand, and herein they are no worse than those who settle everything by prejudice and will not wait for reason. A railway traveller assured me that he had been weighed a dozen times at different stations, and only twice did the machines give the same report, his opinion of their correctness was not very high ; for the same reason, of how little worth are the opinions of the many as to the preachers of the gospel, for scarcely two in a score are of the same mind! There is a great weighing time coming, for which it will be well to be prepared, for woe unto the man whom the infallible balances shall find wanting.

JUDGMENT-DAY—Forgotten.

Is it not foolish to be living in this world without a thought of what you will do at last? A man goes into an inn, and as soon as he sits down he begins to order his wine, his dinner, his bed ; there is no delicacy in season which he forgets to bespeak. He stops at the inn for some time. By-and-by the bill is forthcoming, and it takes him by surprise. " I never thought of that—I never thought of that ! " " Why," says the landlord, " here is a man who is either a born fool or else a knave. What ! never thought of the reckoning— never thought of settling with me ! " After this fashion too many live. They eat, and drink, and sin, but they forget the inevitable hereafter, when for all the deeds done in the body, the Lord will bring us into judgment.

JUDGMENT—Perverted.

WHEN a traveller is newly among the Alps, he is constantly deceived in his reckoning.   One Englishman declared that he could climb the Righi in half-an-hour, but after several panting hours the summit was still a-head of him ; yet when he made the boast, some of us who stood by were much of his mind—the ascent seemed so easy.   This partly accounts for the mistakes men make in estimating eternal things : they have been too much used to molehills to be at home with mountains.   Only familiarity with the sublimities of revelation can educate us to a comprehension of their heights and depths.

JUDGMENTS—Effects of.

IN the province of Quito, after the tremendous earthquake of 1797, a number of marriages were contracted between persons who had neglected for many years to sanction their union by the sacerdotal benediction.   Children found parents by whom they had never till then been acknowledged ; restitutions were promised by persons who had never been accused of fraud ; and families who had long been at enmity were drawn together by the tie of common calamity.   But if this feeling seemed to calm the passions of some, and open the heart to pity, it had a contrary effect on others, rendering them more rigorous and inhuman.—*Alexander Von Humboldt.*

KINGDOM OF CHRIST—its Glories.

THE palace of Versailles with its countless representations of battles, sieges, stormings, surprises, and all other forms of wholesale and retail murder, is dedicated, according to an inscription on its front, " To all the glories of France."   Bah! As well consecrate a shambles to all the glories of a butcher. But what a glorious spiritual palace is the church, and how truly is it dedicated to all the glories of the Lord Jesus! Within its walls hang the memorials of battles far more worthy of the historian's quill than those of Austerlitz or Wagram; victories are there commemorated which put to the blush all the achievements of Charlemagnes or Napoleon; for the contests are with evil principles, and the conquests are triumphs over iniquity and rebellion; there are no garments rolled in blood; fire and vapour of smoke are not there, but the efficacy of atonement, the energy of grace, the Omnipotence of the Holy Ghost, the puissance of eternal love, all these are there, and happy are the eyes that see them. May the life of each one of us contribute a new work of celestial art to those which already represent to angels and heavenly intelligences, " the glories of Christ."

KNOWLEDGE—Lies not in Mere Words.

I HEARD two persons on the Wengern Alp talking by the hour together of the names of ferns; not a word about their characteristics, uses, or habits, but a medley of crack-jaw titles, and nothing more. They evidently felt that they were ventilating their botany, and kept each other in countenance by alternate volleys of nonsense. Well, friend, they were about as sensible as those doctrinalists who for ever talk over the technicalities of religion, but know nothing by experience of its spirit and power. Are we not all too apt to amuse ourselves after the same fashion? He who knows mere Linnæan names, but has never seen a flower, is as reliable in botany, as he is in theology who can descant upon supralapsarianism, but has never known the love of Christ in his heart.

> " True religion's more than doctrine,
> Something must be known and felt."

LETHARGY OF SOUL.

TWO of my hearers perished by a fire in their own house. They were not consumed by the flames, but they were suffocated by the smoke. No blaze was ever visible, nor could

9

any remarkable sign of fire be seen from the street, yet they died as readily as if they had been burned to ashes by raging flames. In this way sin also is deadly. Comparatively few of our hearers are destroyed by outrageous and flaming vices, such as blasphemy, theft, drunkenness, or uncleanness ; but crowds of them are perishing by that deadly smoke of indifference which casts its stifling clouds of carelessness around them, and sends them asleep into everlasting destruction. O that they could be saved from the smoke as well as from the flame !

LIFE.

JOHN MACKINTOSH thus writes to his biographer, Norman Macleod :—" May it not be said that the movement of our age is towards *life ?* I sometimes fancy that I can discern three epochs in the Reformed Churches, corresponding in the main to those three weighty epithets—*via, veritas, vita.* The Reformers themselves, no doubt, laid the stress chiefly upon the first *(via).* It was on this Popery had gone most astray, obscuring the doctrine of justification by faith alone. The epoch following was essentially dogmatic *(veritas),* when the doctors drew up '*systems*' of the truth. It was now, indeed, Christ as *veritas !* but the dogma taken alone led to coldness, dogmatism, sectarianism, and formality. Happy will it be for the church, if, not forgetting the other two, she shall now be found moving on to the third development of Christ as *vita*—the *life,* which will regulate the two former aspects, while it consummates and informs them. This *life* must develop the individual, and on individuals the church depends ; for in God's sight it is no abstraction."

LIFE OF THE BELIEVER—Interesting.

I HEARD a gentleman assert that he could walk almost any number of miles when the scenery was good ; but, he added, "When it is flat and uninteresting, how one tires !"

What scenery enchants the Christian pilgrim; the towering mountains of predestination, the great sea of providence, the rocks of sure promise, the green fields of revelation, the river that makes glad the city of God, all these compose the scenery which surrounds the Christian, and at every step fresh sublimities meet his view.

LIFE—Explains Religion.

ONE of our party greatly needed some elder-flower water for her face upon which the sun was working great mischief. It was in the Italian town of Varallo, and not a word of Italian did I know. I entered a chemist's shop and surveyed his drawers and bottles, but the result was *nil*. Bright thought, I would go down by the river, and walk until I could gather a bunch of elder-flowers, for the tree was then in bloom. Happily the search was successful : the flowers were exhibited to the druggist, the extract was procured. When you cannot tell in so many words what true religion is, exhibit it by your actions. Show by your life what grace can do. There is no language in the world so eloquent as a holy life. Men may doubt what you say, but they will believe what you do.

LIFE—the Need of the Sinner.

WE visited two palaces in Venice, and realised the contrast of life and death. The first was tenanted by a noble family, who delighted to maintain it in good repair, to adorn it with fresh beauties, and to furnish it in the most sumptuous manner. Everything was fresh, fair, bright, and charming. From the paving of mosaics in the hall one looked up to ceilings glowing with the creations of the artist's pencil, and in every chamber paintings, statues, ormolu, tapestry, and all things else of the richest kind surrounded you. The other was a palace, too, with marble pillars, and carved work, but the stones were loosening, and the columns shifting, grass grew in the halls, and the roofs let in the rain, decay was there and desolation, and yet the palace was as noble in its architecture as the first.   Thus when God dwells in a man, all his powers and faculties are bright with a sacred light, and joy and peace and beauty adorn his entire manhood ; but if the Holy Spirit depart, the heart being empty and void becomes a ruin, everywhere decaying, and alas! too often haunted by the demons of vice and iniquity.

LIFE—the Power of an Earnest.

THE upper galleries at Versailles are filled with portraits, many of them extremely valuable and ancient.   These are the likenesses of the greatest men of all lands and ages, drawn by the ablest artists.   Yet most visitors wander through the rooms with little or no interest ; in fact, after noticing one or two of the more prominent pictures, they hasten through the suite of chambers and descend to the other floors.   Notice the change when the sight-seers come to fine paintings like those of Horace Vernet, where the men and women are not inactive portraits but are actively engaged.   There the warrior who was passed by without notice upstairs, is seen hewing his way to glory over heaps of slain, or the statesman is observed delivering himself of weighty words before an assembly of princes and peers.   Not the men but their actions engross attention.   Portraits have no charm when scenes of stirring interest are set in rivalry with them.   After all, then, let us be who or what we may, we must bestir ourselves or be mere nobodies, chips in the porridge, forgotten shells of the shore. If we would impress we must act.   The dignity of standing still will never win the prize, we must run for it.   Our influence over our times will arise mainly from our doing and suffering the will of God, not from our office or person.   Life, life in earnest, life for God, this will tell on the age ; but mere orderliness and propriety, inactive and passionless, will be utterly inoperative.

LIFE—The Hidden.

STANDING by the telegraphic wires one may often hear the mystic wailing and sighing of the winds among them, like the strains of an Æolian harp, but one knows nothing of the message which is flashing along them. Joyous may be the inner language of those wires, swift as the lightning, far-reaching and full of meaning, but a stranger intermeddles not therewith. Fit emblem of the believer's inner life ; men hear our notes of outward sorrow wrung from us by external circumstances, but the message of celestial peace, the divine communings with a better land, the swift heart-throbs of heaven-born desire, they cannot perceive : the carnal see but the outer manhood, but the life hidden with Christ in God, flesh and blood cannot discern.

LIFE—Power of the Inner.

ON a winter's day I have noticed a row of cottages, with a deep load of snow on their several roofs ; but as the day wore on, large fragments began to tumble from the eaves of this one and that other, till, by-and-by, there was a simultaneous avalanche, and the whole heap slid over in powdery ruin on the pavement, and before the sun went down you saw each roof as clear and dry as on a summer's eve. But here and there you would observe one with its snow-mantle unbroken, and a ruff of stiff icicles around it. What made the difference ? The difference was to be found within. Some of these huts were empty, or the lonely inhabitant cowered over a scanty fire ; whilst the peopled hearth and the high-blazing fagots of the rest created such an inward warmth that grim winter melted and relaxed his gripe, and the loosened mass folded off and tumbled over on the trampled street. It is possible by some outside process to push the main volume of snow from the frosty roof, or chip off the icicles one by one. But they will form again, and it needs an inward heat to create a total thaw. And so, by sundry processes, you may

clear off from a man's conduct the dead weight of conspicuous
sins ; but it needs a hidden heat, a vital warmth within, to
produce such a separation between the soul and its besetting
iniquities, that the whole wintry incubus, the entire body of
sin, will come spontaneously away.   That vital warmth is the
love of God abundantly shed abroad—the kindly glow which
the Comforter diffuses in the soul which he makes his home.
His genial inhabitation thaws that soul and its favourite sins
asunder, and makes the indolence and self-indulgence and
indevotion fall off from their old resting-place on that dissolv-
ing heart.   The easiest form of self-mortification is a fervent
spirit.—*James Hamilton, D.D.*

LIFE—Reviewed.

HERE is a good searching question for a man to ask himself as he reviews his past life:—*Have I written in the snow ?*
Will my life-work endure the lapse of years and the fret of
change?   Has there been anything immortal in it, which will
survive the speedy wreck of all sublunary things?   The boys
inscribe their names in capitals in the snow, and in the
morning's thaw the writing disappears ; will it be so with my
work, or will the characters which I have carved outlast the
brazen tablets of history?   *Have I written in the snow?*

LIFE—Spiritual.

HOW like to a Christian a man may be and yet possess no
vital godliness ! Walk through the British Museum, and you
will see all the orders of animals standing in their various
places, and exhibiting themselves with the utmost possible
propriety.   The rhinoceros demurely retains the position in
which he was set at first, the eagle soars not through the
window, the wolf howls not at night ; every creature, whether
bird, beast, or fish, remains in the particular glass case
allotted to it ; but we all know that these are not the creatures,
but only the outward semblances of them.   Yet in what do

they differ? Certainly in nothing which you could readily see, for the well-stuffed animal is precisely like what the living animal would have been; and that eye of glass even appears to have more of brightness in it than the natural eye of the creature itself; there is a secret inward something lacking, which, when it has once departed, you cannot restore. So in the churches of Christ, many professors are not living believers, but stuffed Christians. They possess all the externals of religion, and every outward morality that you could desire; they behave with great propriety, they keep their places, and there is no outward difference between them and the true believer, except upon the vital point, the life which no power on earth can possibly confer. There is this essential distinction, spiritual life is absent.

LIFE—Uncertainty of.

"IT fareth with most men's lives, as with the sand in a deceptive hour-glass; look but upon it in outward appearance, and it seemeth far more than it is, because it riseth up upon the sides, whilst the sand is empty and hollow in the midst thereof, so that when it sinks down in an instant, a quarter of an hour is gone in a moment. Thus many men are mistaken in their own account, reckoning upon threescore and ten years, the age of a man, because their bodies appear strong and lusty. Alas! their health may be hollow, there may be some inward infirmity and imperfection unknown to them, so that death may surprise them on a sudden, and they be cut down like the grass."

LIFE—Uncertain Tenure of.

THERE is a talk of giving *fixity of tenure* in Ireland; can they find it in England, or for the matter of that, in all the world? No, we are all tenants, liable to be ejected without an hour's notice. How death must laugh at our leases and our bonds ! Cobwebs are not more frail. A bubble has as sure a tenure as a man.

> "What boots your houses and your lands?
> In spite of close-drawn deed and fence,
> Like water, 'twixt your cheated hands,
> They slip into the graveyard's sands,
> And mock your ownership's pretence."

LIFE—to be Viewed in Reference to its End.

THE way is good, says Chrysostom, if it be to a feast, though through a dark and miry lane ; if to an execution not good, though through the fairest street of the city. *Non qua sed quo.* Not the way but the end is to be mainly considered.

LIGHT—Detested by the Wicked.

A SLUTTISH housemaid when scolded for the untidiness of the chambers exclaimed, " I'm sure the rooms would be clean enough if it were not for the nasty sun which is always showing the dirty corners." Thus do men revile the gospel because it reveals their own sin. Thus all agitations for reforms in Church and State are opposed, and all manner of mischief attributed to them as if they created the evils which they bring to light. The lover of the right courts anything which may manifest the wrong, but those who love evil have never a good word for those disturbing beams of truth which show up the filthy corners of their hearts and lives.

LITTLE THINGS—Whereunto they may Grow.

WHEN the air balloon was first discovered, a matter-of-fact gentleman contemptuously asked Dr. Franklin what was the use of it. The doctor answered this question by asking another :—" *What is the use of a new-born infant ? It may become a man.*" This anticipation of great things springing from small beginnings should induce us to put into practice those holy promptings which at certain seasons move our

souls. What if we ourselves and our work should be little in
Zion ; cannot the Lord cause the grandest issues to proceed
from insignificant beginnings? Who hath despised the day
of small things?

LIVES—Wrecked.

SAILING down the Thames one occasionally sees a green
flag in tatters, inscribed with the word WRECK, floating in the
breeze over a piece of a mast, or the funnel of a steamer which
is just visible above the water. Alas! how many lives might
thus be marked, and how needful that they should be so
labelled, lest they prove ruinous to others! The debauched,
the self-righteous, the spendthrift, the miserly, the apostate,
the drunken, how wisely might the flag be placed over them,
for they each are a WRECK!

LONGINGS—of the Soul often Painful.

HAVE you never seen a caged eagle with its breast or wing
bleeding from blows received by dashing against the wire of
its cage? The poor creature dreamed of the forest and the
craggy rock, and, filled with aspirations for sublimest flight,
it stretched its wings and flew upward, only to bring itself
into sharp contact with its prison. Even thus the new-born
nature, stirred in its inmost depths with longings suitable to
its celestial origin, aspires after the joys of heaven, stretching
all its wings to soar towards perfection ; but alas! we who are
in this body do groan, we find the flesh to be a prison, and
so the more we long the more we pine, and pining we sigh
and cry, and wound our hearts with insatiable desires and
bleeding discontents. The pangs of strong desire for the
presence of the Lord in glory, who among believers has not
felt them? Who among us has not found our flight upward
brought to a painful pause by the stern facts of flesh and
blood, and earth and sin?

LOVE OF GOD—Shed Abroad by the Holy Ghost.

FREQUENTLY at the great Roman games, the emperors, in order to gratify the citizens of Rome, would cause sweet perfumes to be rained down upon them through the awning which covered the amphitheatre. Behold the vases, the huge vessels of perfume! Yes, but there is nought here to delight you so long as the jars are sealed; but let the vases be opened, and the vessels be poured out, and let the drops of perfumed rain begin to descend, and every one is refreshed and gratified thereby. Such is the love of God. There is a richness and a fulness in it, but it is not perceived till the Spirit of God pours it out like the rain of fragrance over the heads and hearts of all the living children of God. See, then, the need of having the love of God shed abroad in the heart by the Holy Ghost!

LUST.

OUR lusts are cords. Fiery trials are sent to burn and consume them. Who fears the flame which will bring him liberty from bonds intolerable?

MAN—Fallen.

WE saw at Hanover the unfinished palace of the deposed monarch : we were shown his state and private carriages and his stables of cream-coloured horses. A saddening sight to see all the emblems of sovereignty and no king ; the insignia of royalty and the monarch for ever exiled. How like to human nature, which has so much about it prepared for the service of the King of kings, so much of faculty for heavenly occupation, but the king has departed and the house is left desolate, and all the furnishing thereof perverted to alien uses. Thought, imagination, judgment, memory, all fit to be yoked to celestial chariots, become the very hacks of the devil, and the body once a palace now a haunt of thieves. Alas, alas! poor manhood!

MAN (THE GOOD)—Beneficial Influence of.

ALEXANDER VON HUMBOLDT thus writes of the cow-tree :—" On the barren flank of a rock grows a tree with coriaceous and dry leaves. Its large woody roots can scarcely penetrate into the stone. For several months of the year not a single shower moistens its foliage. Its branches appear dead and dried ; but when the trunk is pierced there flows from it a sweet and nourishing milk. It is at the rising of the sun that this vegetable fountain is most abundant. The negroes and natives are then seen hastening from all quarters, furnished with large bowls to receive the milk, which grows yellow, and thickens at its surface. Some empty their bowls under the tree itself, others carry the juice home to their children."

May not the earnest Christian ministering good on all sides be imaged in this marvellous tree? He is in his own esteem full often a withered and dead tree, but there is within him a living sap, which wells up with blessing to all around. His surroundings are all against him, the soil in which he grows is hostile to grace, yet he not only lives on, but luxuriates. He derives nothing from earth, his fountain is from above, but he enriches the sons of earth with untold blessings, and though they often wound him they experimentally know his value. To him full many of the poor and needy look up as to a friend in need, he is full of the milk of human kindness ; where he cannot give in golden coin he distributes comfort in sympathy and words of cheer.

MAN (THE GOOD)—Beneficial Influence of.

IN a hot summer's-day, some years ago, I was sailing with a friend in a tiny boat, on a miniature lake, enclosed like a cup within a circle of steep, bare Scottish hills. On the shoulder of the brown sun-burnt mountain, and full in sight, was a well with a crystal stream trickling over its lip, and making its way down towards the lake. Around the well's

mouth and along the course of the rivulet, a belt of green
stood out in strong contrast with the iron surface of the rocks
all around.   We soon agreed as to what should be made of it.
There it was, a legend clearly printed by the finger of God
on the side of these silent hills, teaching the passer-by how
needful a good man is, and how useful he may be in a desert
world.—*W. Arnot.*

MAN—Natural State of.

A MUSICAL amateur of eminence, who had often observed
Mr. Cadogan's inattention to his performances, said to him
one day, "Come, I am determined to make you feel the
power of music, pay particular attention to this piece." It
was played. "Well, what do you say now?" "Just what I
said before." "What! can you hear this and not be charmed?
I am surprised at your insensibility! Where are your ears?"
"Bear with me, my lord," replied Mr. Cadogan, "since I too
have had my surprise; I have from the pulpit set before you
the most striking and affecting truths; I have found notes
that might have awaked the dead; I have said, Surely he will
feel now; but you never seemed charmed with my music,
though infinitely more interesting than yours. I too might
have said—'Where are his ears?'"

Man, until sovereign grace opens his ears, is deaf to the
heavenly harmonies of the love of God in Christ Jesus,
although these are the ravishment of angels and the wonder
of eternity.

MAN—Perversion of his Faculties.

ACCORDING to the fable, the tail of the snake obtained precedence of the head and led the way in the creature's
journeying. Being altogether blind the new guide dashed
against a stone at one moment, and the next came violently
against a tree, and at last drowned both itself and the head
in the river of death.   Here may be seen the unhappy condition of men in whom their baser nature is dominant, the

animal controlling the intellectual. They invert the order of nature, they rebel against common sense ; their course cannot but be unwise and dangerous, and their end must be fatal. God made man upright, and placed his thoughtful faculties aloft in the place of sovereignty, but man in his folly permits the appetites which he holds in common with the brute creation to reign supreme, while the mind, which ought to rule, is degraded to meanest servitude.

MAN—a Stain on the Universe.

RUSKIN says :—" The Savoyard's cottage, standing in the midst of an inconceivable, inexpressible beauty, set on some sloping bank of golden sward, with clear fountains flowing beside it, and wild flowers, and noble trees, and goodly rocks, gathered round into a perfection as of Paradise, is itself a dark and plague-like stain in the midst of the gentle landscape. Within a certain distance of its threshold the ground is foul and cattle-trampled ; its timbers are black with smoke, its garden choked with weeds and nameless refuse, its chambers empty and joyless, the light and wind gleaming and filtering through the crannies of their stones."

Alas ! too fit an illustration of unregenerate manhood in the midst of divine mercies, surrounded with displays of boundless goodness.

> " Every prospect pleases,
> And only man is vile."

MEANS OF GRACE—their Disuse a Sad Loss.

MY Æolian harp is not sounding and yet a fine fresh wind is blowing in at the window. Why hear I not its soft mystic strains ? I remember, it was put away in the lumber room and some of its strings are broken. There is a gracious revival in the church, and believers are greatly refreshed by the visitations of God's Spirit, but I am in a sadly worldly unbelieving condition. May it not be because I neglect private prayer, and have not been regular at the prayer-meeting ; my family concerns and business cares have kept my heart in the lumber room, and my soul has lost her first love? Yes, these are the reasons. Lord, tune my heart, and I will again seek the places where the heavenly wind of thy Spirit blows graciously and refreshingly. How can I bear to be silent when thy daily mercies are all around me singing of thy love?

MEDITATION—to be Practised.

THOSE who would be in health do not sit still in their houses to breathe such air as may come to them, but they walk abroad and seek out rural and elevated spots that they may inhale the invigorating breezes; and thus those godly souls who would be in a vigorous spiritual state, do not merely think upon such holy doctrines as may come into their minds in the ordinary course of thought, but they give time to meditation, they walk abroad in the fields of truth, and endeavour to climb the heights of gospel promises. It is said that Enoch *walked* with God : here is not an idle but an active communion. The road to bodily health is said to be a footpath, and the way to spiritual health is to exercise one's self in holy contemplation.

MERCIES (TEMPORAL)—an Argument.

IF the Lord has enriched you in temporals, though you have not feared him, have you not every reason to expect that he will do as well for you in spirituals, if you ask him to do so? You call at a friend's house on horseback ; he takes your horse into the stable, and is remarkably attentive to it ; the creature is well groomed, well housed, well fed ; you are not at all afraid that *you* will be shut out, there is surely a warm place in the parlour for the rider, where the horse is so well accommodated in the stable. Now, your body, which we may liken to the horse, has enjoyed temporal prosperity in abundance, and surely the Lord will take care of your soul if you seek his face ! Let your prayer be, " My God, my Father, be my guide. Since thou hast dealt so well with me in these external matters, give me true riches, give me to love thy Son and trust in him, and so be henceforth thy child."

MERCY—Abuse of.

A CERTAIN member of that parliament wherein a statute for the relief of the poor was passed, was an ardent promoter of that Act. He asked his steward when he returned to the country, what the people said of that statute. The steward answered, that he heard a labouring man say, that whereas formerly he worked six days in the week, now he would work but four ; which abuse of that good provision so affected the pious statesman that he could not refrain from weeping. Lord, thou hast made many provisions in thy Word for my support and comfort, and hast promised in my necessities thy supply and protection ; but let not my presumption of help from thee cause my neglect of any of those means for my spiritual and temporal preservation which thou hast enjoined.

MERCY—Continual.

A BENEVOLENT person gave Mr. Rowland Hill a hundred pounds to dispense to a poor minister, and thinking it was too much to send him all at once, Mr. Hill forwarded five pounds in a letter, with simply these words within the envelope, " More to follow." In a few days' time, the good man received another letter by the post—and letters by the post were rarities in those days ; this second messenger contained another five pounds, with the same motto, " And more to follow." A day or two after came a third and a fourth, and still the same promise, " And more to follow." Till the whole sum had been received the astonished minister was made familiar with the cheering words, " And more to follow."

Every blessing that comes from God is sent with the selfsame message, " And more to follow." " I forgive you your sins, but there's more to follow." "I justify you in the righteousness of Christ, but there's more to follow." "I adopt you into my family, but there's more to follow." "I educate you for heaven, but there's more to follow." "I give you grace upon grace, but there's more to follow." "I have helped you even to old age, but there's still more to follow." "I will uphold you in the hour of death, and as you are passing into the world of spirits, my mercy shall still continue with you, and when you land in the world to come there shall still be MORE TO FOLLOW."

MERCY—Dissolves the Heart.

YOU may have heard of some persons condemned to execution, who at the scaffold have been so obdurate and stiff-necked that not a cry or a tear came from them; yet, just as they have been going to lay their necks upon the block, when a pardon has come, and they were at once discharged from guilt, imprisonment, and death, they that could not weep a tear before, no sooner saw the pardon sealed, and themselves acquitted, than they dissolved into tears of joy, thankfulness, and surprise. So it is with believers. The more they see Christ in the pardon of sin, and the love of God in Christ to receive and embrace them, the more they melt.—*Tobias Crisp.*

MERCY—its Effect on the Soul.

A MAN convicted of high treason and condemned to die is not only pardoned, but taken into the favour of his sovereign. He is riding in the royal carriage, and on the road he sees some of his fellow traitors pinioned and manacled, led forth in the midst of officers to die for the offence in which he had as deep a hand as they. What think you, will he not entreat the gracious monarch to extend his clemency to his fellow rebels? Will not the tears stand in his eyes as he admires the difference which his sovereign's free mercy has made? Will he not be moved with emotions impossible to describe, of mingled joy and grief, pity and gratitude, wonder and compassion? Christian, see your likeness-here drawn to the life, you must surely feel ready to fall down on your knees, and cry, "Lord, why dost thou reveal thy mercy to me and not to these? Save them also, O Lord, for thy name's sake."

MERCY—Excellence of.

I REMEMBER well being taken one day to see a gorgeous palace at Venice, where every piece of furniture was made with most exquisite taste, and of the richest material, where statues and pictures of enormous price abounded on all hands, and the floor of each room was paved with mosaics of marvellous art, and extraordinary value. As I was shown from room to room, and allowed to roam amid the treasures by its courteous owner, I felt a considerable timidity, I was afraid to sit anywhere, nor did I hardly dare to put down my foot, or rest my hand to lean. Everything seemed to be too good for ordinary mortals like myself; but when one is introduced into the gorgeous palace of infinite goodness, costlier and fairer far, one gazes wonderingly with reverential awe at the matchless vision. "How excellent is thy lovingkindness, O God!" "I am not worthy of the least of all thy benefits. Oh! the depths of the love and goodness of the Lord."

MERCY—Seen in our Lives.

WHAT a rugged, precipitous, ungainly pass is that Col D'Obbia! It was shrewd common sense, and true humanity which suggested the erection of that poor little hospice at the summit. Never was a shelter more opportune, a refuge more welcome. One could not have expected to find a retreat in so desolate a region, but there it was, and we were received into it with cordiality. The great Lord of pilgrims has taken care that in the hardest parts of our road to the Celestial

10

City there should be blessed resting places, where beneath the shade of promises, weary ones may repose within the shelter of love. God's hospice may be confidently looked for whenever the way is more than ordinarily difficult.

MERITS.

A SHIP on her way to Australia met with a very terrible storm, and sprung a leak. As evils seldom come alone, a little while after another tempest assailed her. There happened to be a gentleman on board, of the most nervous temperament, whose garrulous tongue and important air were calculated to alarm all the passengers. When the storm came on, the captain, who knew what mischief may be done by a suspicious and talkative individual, managed to get near him with a view to rendering him quiet. The gentlemen addressing the captain, said in a tone of alarm, " What an awful storm ; I am afraid we shall go to the bottom, for I hear the leak is very bad." " Well," said the captain, " as you seem to know it, and perhaps the others do not, you had better not mention it to any one, lest you should frighten the passengers or dispirit my men. Perhaps as it is a very bad case, you would lend us your valuable help, and then we may possibly get through it. Would you have the goodness to stand here and hold hard on this rope ; pray do not leave it, but pull as hard as ever you can till I tell you to let it go." So our friend clenched his teeth, and put his feet firmly down, and kept on holding this rope with all his might, till he earnestly wished for a substitute. The storm abated ; the ship was safe, and our friend was released from his rope-holding. He expected a deputation would bring him the thanks of all the passengers, but they were evidently unconscious of his merits ; for it is too often the case that we forget our greatest benefactors. Even the captain did not seem very grateful ; so our hero ventured, in a roundabout style to hint, that such valuable services as his, having saved the vessel, ought to be rewarded at least with some few words of acknowledgment ; when he was shocked to hear the captain say, " What, sir, do *you* think *you* saved the vessel? Why, I gave you that rope to hold to keep you engaged, that you might not be in such a feverish state of alarm." The self-righteous may here see how much men contribute to their own salvation apart from Christ. They think they can certainly save themselves, and there they stand holding the rope with their clenched teeth and their feet tightly fixed, while they are really doing no more than our officious friend, who was thus befooled. If ever you get to heaven, you will find that everything you did towards your own salvation, apart from the Lord Jesus, was about as useful as holding the rope ; that in fact, the safety of the soul lies somewhere else, and not in you ; and that what is wanted with you is just to get out of the way, and let Christ come in and magnify his grace.

MINISTER.

THE sharp shrill cry of "Acqua! Acqua!" constantly pierces the ear of the wanderer in Venice and other towns of sultry Italy. There is the man who thus invites your attention. Look at him. On his back he bears a burden of water, and in his hand a rack of bottles containing essences to flavour the draught if needed, and glasses to hold the cooling liquid. In the streets of London he would find but little patronage, but where fountains are few and the days are hot as an oven, he earns a livelihood and supplies a public need. The present specimen of water-dealers is a poor old man bent sideways, by the weight of his daily burden. He is worn out in all but his voice, which is truly startling in its sharpness and distinctness. At our call he stops immediately, glad to drop his burden on the ground, and smiling in prospect of a customer. He washes out a glass for us, fills it with sparkling water, offers us the tincture which we abhor, puts it back into the rack again when we shake our head, receives half-a-dozen soldi with manifest gratitude, and trudges away across the square, crying still, "Acqua! Acqua!" That cry, shrill as it is, has sounded sweetly in the ears of many a thirsty soul, and will for ages yet to come, if throats and thirst survive so long. How forcibly it calls to our mind the Saviour's favourite imagery, in which he compares the grace which he bestows on all who diligently seek it, to "living water;" and how much that old man is like the faithful preacher of the word, who, having filled his vessel at the well, wears himself out by continually bearing the burden of the Lord, and crying, "Water! water!" amid crowds of sinners, who must drink or die. Instead of the poor Italian water-bearer, we see before us the man of God, whose voice is heard in the chief places of concourse, proclaiming the divine invitation, " Ho, every one that thirsteth, come ye to the waters!" until he grows grey in the service, and men say, "Surely those aged limbs have need of rest;" yet rest he courts not, but pursues his task of mercy; never laying down his charge till he lays down his body, and never ceasing to work until he ceases to live.

At the door of Saint Mark's Cathedral, we bought a glass of what should have been the pure element, but when we began to drink, a pungent flavour of something which had previously been in the cup, made us leave the rest of our purchase, thirsty though we were. The water was good enough, but the vessel which held it imparted an evil taste to it; the like has often happened in the ministry, the gospel preached has been true and divine, but the unhallowed savour of an inconsistent life, or a bitter disposition, has marred the sweetness of the Word. May all of us by whom the Lord hands out the water of life, see that we are clean and pure in conversation, vessels fit for the Master's use. Men who are very thirsty will drink out of any cup, however dirty; but no conceivable advantage can arise from filth, and hundreds will turn away from the water because of it, and thus a very faulty ministry may be useful because of the truth contained in it, but its sinfulness can do no good, and may serve as an excuse to the ungodly for refusing the gospel of Christ.

In the square of the Doge's palace are two wells, from which the sellers of water obtain their stock-in-trade, but we can hardly compare either of them with the overflowing spring from which the preacher of righteousness draws his supplies. One of the wells is filled artificially and is not much used for drinking, since the coldness and freshness of water springing naturally from earth's deep fountains is lacking. It is to be feared that many preachers depend for their matter upon theological systems, books, and mere learning, and hence their teaching is devoid of the living power and refreshing influence which is found in communion with "the spring of all our joys." The other well yields most delicious water, but its flow is scanty. In the morning it is full, but a crowd of eager persons drain it to the bottom, and during the day as it rises by driblets, every drop is contended for and borne away, long before there is enough below to fill a bucket. In its excellence, continuance and naturalness, this well might be a fair picture of the grace of our Lord Jesus, but it fails to set him forth from its poverty of supply. He has a redundance, an overflow, an infinite fulness, and there is no possibility of his being exhausted by the draughts made upon him, even though ten thousand times ten thousand should come with a thirst as deep as the abyss. We could not help saying, "Spring up, O well," as we looked over the margin covered with copper, into which strings and ropes—continually used by the waiting many—had worn deep channels. Very little of the coveted liquid was brought up each time, but the people were patient, and their tin vessels went up and down as fast as there was a cupful to be had. O that men were half as diligent in securing the precious gifts of the Spirit, which are priceless beyond compare! Alas! how few have

David's thirst for the well of Bethlehem. The cans sent down had very broad sides, so that they dropped down flat upon the bottom of the well, and were drawn up less than half full ; larger vessels would have been useless, and so, indeed, would small ones if they had not been made to lie quite down upon their sides, along what we must call the floor of the well, and had they have been erect they would not have received a drop. Humility is always a profitable grace; pride is always as useless as it is foolish. Only by bowing our minds to the utmost before the Lord, can we expect to receive his mercy, for he promises grace unto the humble in that same verse which foretells his resistance of the proud. If there be grace anywhere, contrite hearts will get it. The lower we can fall, the sooner will the springing water of grace reach us, and the more completely shall we be filled with it.

It would be a great misfortune for those who buy their water in the streets, if the itinerant vendors should begin to fill their casks and bottles from muddy streams. At Botzen, in the Tyrol, we saw many fountains running with a liquid of a very brown colour, and a seller of such stuff might cry " ACQUA !" very long and very loudly before we should partake of his dainties. Sundry divines in our age have become weary of the old-fashioned well of which our fathers drank, and would fain have us go to their Abana and Pharpar, but we are still firm in the belief that the water from the rock has no rival, and we shall not, we hope, forsake it for any other. May the Lord send to our happy land more simple gospel, more Christ-exalting doctrine, more free-grace teaching, more distinct testimony to atoning blood and eternal love. In most of the Swiss villages there are streaming fountains by the dozen, and the pure liquid is to be had at every corner; may we yet see the Word of God as abundantly distributed in every town, village, and hamlet in England. Meanwhile, having recorded the prayer, we resolve, by divine grace, to cry more loudly than ever, " Acqua! Acqua!"

MINISTER.

HOWEVER learned, godly, and eloquent a minister may be, he is nothing without the Holy Spirit. The bell in the steeple may be well hung, fairly fashioned, and of soundest metal, but it is dumb until the ringer makes it speak; and in like manner the preacher has no voice of quickening for the dead in sin, or of comfort for living saints until the divine Spirit gives him a gracious pull, and bids him speak with power. Hence the need of prayer from both preacher and hearers.

MINISTER—Need of Personal Tenderness.

SPEAKING of the temper requisite to the right discharge of ministerial duty, Payson said, " I never was fit to say a word to a sinner, except when I had a broken heart myself; when I was subdued and melted into penitency, and felt as though I had just received pardon to my own soul, and when my heart was full of tenderness and pity. No anger, no anger."

MINISTER—Self-dissatisfaction of.

" SWIFT of foot was Hiawatha,
He could shoot an arrow from him,
And run forward with such fleetness,
That the arrow fell behind him ! "

The fable is even less than truth with the fervent preacher: he darts arrows of fire in flaming speech, but his eagerness to win souls far outruns his words. He projects himself far beyond his language. His heart outstrips his utterance. He embraces souls in his love, while his words as yet are but on the wing. Often and often will he weep when his sermon is over, because his words " fell behind him ; " yet has he cause for joy, that he should have received so divine a spirit from his Master's hand : his very dissatisfaction proves his zeal.

MINISTER—Should be a Nursing Father.

IN a church in Verona stands, or rather sits, a wooden image of St. Zeno, an ancient bishop, with knees so ludicrously short that there is no lap on which a babe could be dandled. He was not the first nor the last ecclesiastic who has been utterly incapable of being a nursing father to the church. It were well if all ministers had a heavenly instinct for the nourishing and bringing up of the Lord's little ones. Is there not much lack in this?

MINISTRY—Best Men Needed for it.

"AMONGST the Jesuits they have a rule, that they who are unapt for greater studies, shall study cases of conscience." Is this to be adopted among Protestants, and when a man is too brainless to succeed in any common calling, is he therefore to argue that he is called to the ministry? This mischievous notion fills pulpits, but it empties pews. The fact is, the very pick of our Christian men are wanted for a work

"Which well might fill an angel's heart,
Did fill a Saviour's hands."

MISTAKES—Our Aptness to Make.

WE were riding along in the afternoon of a lovely but blazing day from Varallo to Riva, and to quench our thirst on the road we carried with us some bottles of an excellent lemonade. The empty bottles were of no use to us, and one of them was given to a friend on the box seat of the carriage to throw away. He happened to be the essence of gentleness and liberality, and seeing two very poor peasant women trudging along with huge empty baskets strapped on their backs, he thought it would delight them if he dropped the bottle into one of their receptacles; a bottle being far more a godsend there than in England. Alas, for our friend's happiness during the whole of the next twenty-four hours! The motion of the carriage made him miss his aim, and the bottle fell on the head of the woman instead of into her basket. There was a shrill cry, and a good deal of blood and speedy faintness. Of course, we were all in an instant binding up the wound with silver, and our friend we feel sure used golden ointment, so that the poor old creature would have cheerfully had her head broken ten times to receive such a sum as she obtained by way of solatium; but still the accident saddened us all, and especially our dear tended-hearted friend from whose hand the missile was dropped. How often has his case been ours! We meant to cheer a troubled conscience and instead thereof we wounded it yet more. We intended nothing but love, but our words gave pain ; we had miscalculated, and missed our aim. This has both astonished us and caused us the deepest regret. Yet such a blunder has made us the more careful, and has humbled us under a sense of our readiness to err, and moreover it has led us to be still more liberal in the use of that precious treasure of the gospel, which easily recompenses for all our blundering. Loving reader, be careful with your kindnesses, but be not too much depressed should they fail to comfort. The Lord knows your intentions.

MONEY-MAKING—Nothing but Play.

MR. RUSKIN, in his lecture on "Work,"* says :—" Whatever we do to please ourselves, and only for the sake of the pleasure, not for an ultimate object, is 'play,' the 'pleasing thing,' not the useful thing. .... The first of all English games is making money. That is an all-absorbing game ; and we knock each other down oftener in playing at that than at foot-ball, or any other rougher sport ; and it is absolutely without purpose ; no one who engages heartily in that game ever knows why. Ask a great money-maker what he wants

* In "The Crown of Wild Olive, Three Lectures on Work, Traffic, and War." By John Ruskin, M.A., 1866.

to do with his money—he never knows. He doesn't make it
to do anything with it. He gets it only that he may get it.
'What will you make of what you have got?' you ask.
'Well, I'll get more,' he says. Just as at cricket, you get
more runs. There's no use in the runs, but to get more of
them than other people is the game. And there's no use in
the money, but to have more of it than other people is the
game. So all that great foul city of London there—rattling,
growling, smoking, stinking—a ghastly heap of fermenting
brickwork, pouring out poison at every pore—you fancy it is
a city of work? Not a street of it! It is a great city of
play ; very nasty play, and very hard play, but still play.
It is only Lord's Cricket Ground without the turf—a huge
billiard-table without the cloth, and with pockets as deep as
the bottomless pit, but mainly a billiard table after all."

MONEY-MAKING—No Time for.

A GENTLEMAN of Boston (U. S.), an intimate friend of
Professor Agassiz, once expressed his wonder that a man of
such abilities as he (Agassiz) possessed should remain contented with such a moderate income. " I have enough," was
Agassiz's reply. " I have not *time* to make money. Life is
not sufficiently long to enable a man to get rich, and do his
duty to his fellow men at the same time." Christian, have
you time to serve your God and yet to give your whole soul
to gaining wealth? The question is left for conscience to
answer.

MORALIST.

THE dahlia would surely be a very empress among flowers
if it had but perfume equal to its beauty ; even the rose
might need to look to her sovereignty. Florists have tried
all their arts to scent this lovely child of autumn but in vain,
no fragrance can be developed or produced ; God has denied
the boon, and human skill cannot impart it. The reflecting

mind will be reminded of those admirable characters which are occasionally met with, in which everything of good repute and comely aspect may be seen, but true religion, that sweet ethereal perfume of grace, is wanting ; if they had but love to God, what lovely beings they would be, the best of the saints would not excel them, and yet that fragrant grace they do not seek, and after every effort we may make for their conversion, they remain content without the one thing which is needful for their perfection. O that the Lord would impart to them the mystic sweetness of his grace by the Holy Spirit !

MOTIVES.

THERE are overshot water-wheels and undershot. In the one case the motive power falls from above, in the other the water turns the wheel from below ; the first is the more powerful. Men, like wheels, are turned by forces from various sources, and too many move by the undercurrent—mercenary desires and selfish aims drive them ; but the good man's driving force falls from above ; let him endeavour to prove to all men that this is the most mighty force in existence.

MOTIVES.

STANDING near the remarkable spring at Ewell, in Surrey, and watching the uprising of the waters, one sees at the bottom of the pool innumerable circles with smaller circles within them, from which extremely fine sand is continually being upheaved by the force of the rising water. Tiny geysers upheave their little founts, and from a myriad openings bubble up with the clear crystal. The perpetual motion of the water, and the leaping of the sand are most interesting. It is not like the spring-head in the field, where the cooling liquid pours forth perpetually from a spout, all unseen, till it plunges into its channel ; nor like the river-head where the stream weeps from a mass of mossy rock ; but here are the fountains of earth's hidden deeps all unveiled and laid bare, the very veins of nature opened to the public gaze. How

would it amaze us if we could in this fashion peer into the
springs of human character and see whence words and
actions flow ! What man would wish to have his designs
and aims exposed to every onlooker ? But why this aversion
to being known and read of all men ? The Christian's
motives and springs of action should be so honest and pure
that he might safely defy inspection. He who has nothing
to be ashamed of has nothing to conceal. Sincerity can
afford, like our first parents in Paradise, to be naked and not
ashamed.

If other men cannot read our motives, we ought at least to
examine them carefully for ourselves. Day by day with
extreme rigour must we search into our hearts. Motive is
vital to the goodness of an action. He who should give his
body to be burned might yet lose his soul if his ruling passion
were obstinacy, and not desire for God's glory. Self may be
sought under many disguises, and the man may be utterly
unaware that thus he is losing all acceptance with God. We
must not impute ill motives to others, but we must be equally
clear of another more fascinating habit, namely, that of im-
puting good motives to ourselves. Severity in estimating our
own personal character very seldom becomes excessive ; our
partiality is usually more or less blinding to our judgment. We
will not suspect ourselves if we can help it ; evidence must be
very powerful before it can convince us of being governed by
sordid aims. The stream of generosity does not always
spring from gratitude to God. Zeal is not at all times the
offspring of deep-seated faith. Even devotional habits may
be fostered by other than holy affections. The highest wisdom
suggests that we spend much patient and impartial consideration upon a matter so fundamental as the heart's intent in the
actions which it directs. " If thine eye be single, thine whole
body shall be full of light." Dear reader, stand by thine inner
springs and watch, and make faithful notes of what thou
seest, lest thou be deceived.

NATURE—Need of Renewal.

A VICIOUS horse is none the better tempered because the kicking straps prevent his dashing the carriage to atoms; and so a man is none the better really because the restraints of custom and providence may prevent his following that course of life which he would prefer. Poor fallen human nature behind the bars of laws, and in the cage of fear of punishment, is none the less a sad creature; should its Master unlock the door we should soon see what it would be and do. A young leopard which had been domesticated, and treated as a pet, licked its master's hand while he slept, and it so happened that it drew blood from a recent wound; the first taste of blood transformed the gentle creature into a raging wild beast; yet it wrought no real change, it only awakened the natural ferocity which had always been there. A change of nature is required for our salvation—mere restraints are of small value.

NATURES—the Two in a Christian.

A CHRISTIAN lives in two worlds at one and the same time—the world of flesh and the world of spirit. It is possible to do both. There are certain dangerous gases, which from their weight fall to the lower part of the place where they are, making it destructive for a dog to enter, but safe for a man who holds his head erect. A Christian, as living in the world of flesh, is constantly passing through these. Let him keep his head erect in the spiritual world, and he is safe. He does this so long as the Son of God is the fountain whence he draws his inspiration, his motives, encouragement, and strength.—*George Philip*.

NOVELTY—Influence of.

YES, the people gathered in crowds around the statue, and looked at it again and again. It was not the finest work of

art in the city, nor the most intrinsically attractive. Why,
then, did the citizens of Verona stand in such clusters around
the effigy of Dante on that summer's evening? Do you guess
the reason? It was a fête in honour of the poet? No,
you are mistaken; it was but an ordinary evening, and there
was nothing peculiar in the date or the events of the day.
You shall not be kept in suspense, the reason was very simple,
the statue was new, it had, in fact, only been unveiled the day
before. Every one passes Dante now, having other things to
think of ; the citizens are well used to his solemn visage, and
scarcely care that he stands among them. Is not this the
way of men? I am sure it is their way with us ministers.
New brooms sweep clean. What crowds follow a new man !
how they tread upon one another to hear him, not because he
is so very wise or eloquent, much less because he is eminently
holy, but he is a new man, and curiosity must gratify itself !
In a few short months, the idol of the hour is stale, flat, and
unprofitable ; he is a mediocrity ; there are scores as good as
he ; indeed, another new man, at the end of the town, is far
better. Away go the wonder-hunters ! Folly brought them,
folly removes them : babies must have new toys.

OBEDIENCE.

"SIR," said the Duke of Wellington to an officer of
engineers, who urged the impossibility of executing the
directions he had received, "I did not ask your opinion, I
gave you my orders, and I expect them to be obeyed." Such
should be the obedience of every follower of Jesus. The
words which he has spoken are our law, not our judgments
or fancies. Even if death were in the way it is—

> "Not ours to reason why—
> Ours, but to dare and die ;"

and, at our Master's bidding, advance through flood or
flame.

OBEYING GOD—with Delight.

"I WISH I could mind God as my little dog minds me," said a little boy, looking thoughtfully on his shaggy friend ; " he always looks *so pleased* to mind, and I don't." What a painful truth did this child speak ! Shall the poor little dog thus readily obey his master, and we rebel against God, who is our Creator, our Preserver, our Father, our Saviour, and the bountiful Giver of everything we love?—*Christian Treasury.*

OMNISCIENCE.

A PLATE of sweet cakes was brought in and laid upon the table. Two children played upon the hearthrug before the fire. "Oh, I want one of these cakes!" cried the little boy, jumping up as soon as his mother went out, and going on tiptoe towards the table. "No, no," said his sister, pulling him back ; "no, no ; you must not touch." "Mother won't know it ; she did not count them," he cried, shaking her off, and stretching out his hand. "If *she* didn't, perhaps *God* counted," answered the other. The little boy's hand was stayed. Yes, children, be sure that *God counts!*—*Children's Missionary Record for* 1852.

ORDER IN DUTY—its Beauty.

LINNÆUS, the great Swedish botanist, observing the beautiful order which reigns among flowers, proposed the use of a floral clock, to be composed of plants which open and close their blossoms at particular hours ; as for instance the dandelion which opens its petals at six in the morning, the hawkweed at seven, the succory at eight, the celandine at nine, and so on ; the closing of the flowers being marked with an equal regularity so as to indicate the progress of the afternoon and the evening.

> "Thus has each hour its own rich hue,
> And its graceful cup or bell,
> In whose coloured vase may sleep the dew,
> Like a pearl in an ocean shell."

Would it not be a lovely thing if thus with flowers of grace and blossoms of virtue we bedecked every passing hour ; fulfilling all the duties of each season and honouring him who maketh the outgoings of the morning and the evening to rejoice! Thus with undeviating regularity to obey the influence of the Sun of Righteousness, and give each following moment its due, were to begin the life of heaven beneath the stars.

ORDER—of Gracious Operations.

"A DISCUSSION arose between some members of a Bible class, in reference to the *first* Christian exercise of the converted soul. One contended that it was penitence or *sorrow;* another that it was *fear*, another *love*, another *hope*, another *faith*, for how could one fear or repent without belief? Elder G——, overhearing the discussion, relieved the minds of the disputants with this remark :—'Can you tell which spoke of the wheel moves first? You may be looking at one spoke, and think that it moves first, but they all start together. Thus, when the Spirit of God operates upon the human heart, all the graces begin to affect the penitent soul, though the individual may be more conscious of one than another.'"

PEACE—of a Believer.

THE believer's peace is like a river for *continuance*. Look at it, rising as a little brook among the mosses of the lone green hill ; by-and-by it leaps as a rugged cataract ; anon it flows along that fair valley where the red deer wanders, and the child loves to play. With hum of pleasant music the brook turns the village mill. Hearken to its changeful tune as it ripples over its pebbly bed, or leaps adown the wheel, or sports in eddies where the trees bend down their branches to kiss the current. Anon the streamlet has become a river, and bears upon its flood full many a craft. Then its bosom swells, bridges with noble arches span it, and, grown vaster still, it becomes an estuary, broad enough to be an arm of old Father Ocean, pouring its water-floods into the mighty main. The river abides the lapse of ages, it is no evanescent morning cloud, or transient rain-flood, but in all its stages it is permanent.

"Men may come, and men may go,
But I flow on for ever."

Evermore, throughout all generations, the river speedeth to its destined place. Such is the peace of the Christian. He has always reason for comfort. He has not a consolation like a swollen torrent which is dried up under the hot sun of adversity, but peace is his rightful possession at all times. Do you enquire for the Thames? You shall find it flowing in its own bed in the thick black night, as well as in the clear bright day. You shall discover the noble river when it mirrors the stars or sends back the sheen of the moon, as well as when multitudes of eyes gaze upon the pompous pageantry of civic procession at midday. You may see its waves in the hour of tempest by the lightning's flash, as well as in the day of calm when the sun shineth brightly on them. Ever is the river in its place. And even thus, come night, come day, come sickness, come health, come what will, the peace of God which passeth all understanding will keep the Christian's heart and mind, through Jesus Christ.

Nor must we exclude the idea of *progress*. You can leap the Thames at Cricklade, for the tiny brook is spanned by a narrow plank across which laughing village girls are tripping; but who thinks of laying down a plank at Southend, or at Grays? No, the river has grown—how deep! At the mouth of it, comparable to the sea—how broad! There go the ships, and even leviathan might play therein. Such is the Christian's peace. At the first, little temptations avail to mar it, and the troubles of life threaten to evaporate it. Be not dismayed, but quietly wait. When the Christian is somewhat grown, and has

11

wandered for awhile along the tortuous course of a gracious experience, his peace will gather force like a flowing
stream.   Wait twenty or thirty years, till he has traversed
yonder rich lowlands of fellowship with Christ in his sufferings, and conformity to his death, and you shall mark that the
believer's rest will be like a river deep and broad, for he shall
know the peace which was our Master's precious legacy ; and
he will cast all his care upon God, who careth for him.
True peace will increase till it melts into the eternal rest of
the beatific vision, where

> "Not a wave of trouble rolls
> Across the peaceful breast."

PEACE—False.

YOUR peace, sinner, is that terribly prophetic calm which
the traveller occasionally perceives upon the higher Alps.
Everything is still.   The birds suspend their notes, fly low,
and cower down with fear.   The hum of bees among the
flowers is hushed.   A horrible stillness rules the hour, as if
death had silenced all things by stretching over them his
awful sceptre.   Perceive ye not what is surely at hand ?   The
tempest is preparing ; the lightning will soon cast abroad its
flames of fire.   Earth will rock with thunder-blasts ; granite
peaks will be dissolved ; all nature will tremble beneath the
fury of the storm.   Yours is that solemn calm to-day, sinner.
Rejoice not in it, for the hurricane of wrath is coming, the
whirlwind and the tribulation which shall sweep you away and
utterly destroy you.

PEACE OF PARDON—Not a Mere Forgetfulness.

I HAVE spilled the ink over a bill and so have blotted it
till it can hardly be read, but this is quite another thing from
having the debt blotted out, for that cannot be till payment
is made.   So a man may blot his sins from his memory, and
quiet his mind with false hopes, but the peace which this will

bring him is widely different from that which arises from God's forgiveness of sin through the satisfaction which Jesus made in his atonement. Our blotting is one thing, God's blotting out is something far higher.

PERFECTION—Marred by the World.

THE bloom of the hawthorn or White May looks like snow in Richmond Park, but nearer London or by the road side its virgin whiteness is sadly stained. Too often contact with the world has just such an effect upon our piety; we must away to the far off garden of Paradise to see holiness in its unsullied purity, and meanwhile we must be much alone with God if we would maintain a gracious life below.

PERSECUTION.

THE cold water of persecution is often thrown on the church's face to fetch her to herself when she is in a swoon of indolence or pride.

PERSECUTION—Not to be Feared.

DO not fear the frown of the world. When a blind man comes against you in the street you are not angry at him, you say, He is blind, poor man, or he would not have hurt me. So you may say of the poor worldlings when they speak evil of Christians—they are blind.—*M'Cheyne.*

PERSEVERANCE.

"A POOR woman had a supply of coal laid at her door by a charitable neighbour. A very little girl came out with a small fire-shovel, and began to take up a shovelful at a time, and carry it to a sort of bin in the cellar. I said to the child, 'Do you expect to get all that coal in with that little shovel?' She was quite confused at my question, but her answer was very striking, 'Yes, sir, if I *work long enough.*'"

Humble worker, make up for your want of ability by

abundant continuance in well-doing, and your life-work will not be trivial. The repetition of small efforts will effect more than the occasional use of great talents.

PERSEVERANCE—in Doing Good.

AN old man in Watton, whom Mr. Thornton had in vain urged to come to church, was taken ill and confined to his bed. Mr. Thornton went to the cottage, and asked to see him. The old man, hearing his voice below, answered, in no very courteous tone, " I don't want *you* here, you may go away." The following day the curate was again at the foot of the stairs. " Well, my friend, may I come up to-day, and sit beside you?" Again he received the same reply, " I don't want *you* here." Twenty-one days successively Mr. T. paid his visit to the cottage, and on the twenty-second his perseverance was rewarded. He was permitted to enter the room of the aged sufferer, to read the Bible, and pray by his bedside. The poor man recovered, and became one of the most regular attendants at the house of God.—*Memoirs of Rev. Spencer Thornton.*

PERSEVERANCE—Necessity of.

IN the heathery turf you will often find a plant chiefly remarkable for its peculiar roots ; from the main stem down to the minutest fibre, you will find them all abruptly terminate, as if shorn or bitten off, and the quaint superstition of the country people alleges, that once on a time it was a plant of singular potency for healing all sorts of maladies, and therefore the great enemy of man in his malignity bit off the roots, in which its virtues resided. The plant with this odd history, is a very good emblem of many well-meaning but little-effecting people. They might be defined as *radicibus præmorsis,* or rather *inceptis succisis.* The efficacy of every good work lies in its completion, and all their good works terminate abruptly, and are left off unfinished. The devil

frustrates their efficacy by cutting off their ends ; their unprofitable history is made up of plans and projects, schemes
of usefulness that were never gone about, and magnificent
undertakings that were never carried forward ; societies that
were set agoing, then left to shift for themselves, and forlorn
beings who for a time were taken up and instructed, and just
when they were beginning to show symptoms of improvement
were cast on the world again.—*James Hamilton*, *D.D.*

PERSONAL EFFORT—Needed for Success.

ACCORDING to Christ's law, every Christian is to be
active in spreading the faith, which was delivered, not to
the ministers, but to the saints, to every one of them, that
they might maintain it, and spread it according to the
gift which the Spirit has given them. Shall I venture a
parable ? A certain band of warlike knights had been exceedingly victorious in all their conflicts. They were men of
valour and of indomitable courage ; they had carried everything
before them, and subdued province after province for their
king. But on a sudden they said in the council-chamber,
" We have at our head a most valiant warrior, one whose arm
is stout enough to smite down fifty of his adversaries ; would it
not be better if, leaving a few such as he to go out to the fight,
the mere men-at-arms, who make up the ordinary ranks, were
to rest at home ? We should be much more at our ease ; our
horses would not so often be covered with foam, nor our
armour be bruised, the many would enjoy abundant leisure, and
great things would be done by the valiant few." Now, the foremost champions, with fear and trembling, undertook the task
and went to the conflict, and they fought well, as the rolls of
fame can testify; to the best of their ability they unhorsed
their foes and performed great exploits. But still, from the
very hour in which that scheme was planned and carried out
ho city was taken, no province was conquered. Then the
knights met together, and said, " How is this ? Our former

prestige is departed, our ranks are broken, our pennons are trailed in the dust, what is the cause of it?" When outspoke the champion, and said, " Doubtless it is so, and for a reason clear and plain. How did you think that a slender band could do the work of all the thousands? When you all went to the fight, and every man took his share, we dashed upon the foe like an avalanche, and crushed him beneath our tramp; but now that you stay at home, and put us, who are but a handful, to fight every battle, how can you expect that great things should be done?" So each man resolved to put on his helmet and his armour once again, and hasten to the battle, and lo, the angel of victory returned.

If we are to subdue the earth, every one of us must join in the fight. We must not exempt a single soldier of the cross, neither man nor woman, rich nor poor ; but each must fight for the Lord Jesus according to his ability, that his kingdom may come, and that his will may be done in earth even as it is in heaven. We shall see great things when all agree to this and put it in practice.

PERSONAL WORK.

I ONCE heard a story of an American, who declared he could fight the whole British army, and when he was asked how he could draw so long a bow as that, he said, " Why, this is what I would do : I know I am the best swordsman in the world, so I would go and challenge one Britisher, and kill him ; then take another, and kill him. Thus," said he, "I only want time enough and I would kill the whole British army." It was a ridiculous boast, but there is something in it which I could not bring out so well in any other way. If we want to conquer the world for the Lord Jesus Christ, rest assured we must do it in the Yankee's fashion; we must take men one by one, and these ones must be brought to Christ, or otherwise the great mass must remain untouched. Do not imagine for a moment that you are going to convert a nation at once ; you are to convert the men of that nation, one by one, through the power of God's Holy Spirit. It is not for you to suit your machinery, and arrange your plans for the moving of a mass as such, you must look to the salvation of the units.

POOR—as Hearers.

JOHN WESLEY always preferred the middling and lower classes to the wealthy. He said, " If I might choose, I should still, as I have done hitherto, *preach the gospel to the poor.*" Preaching in Monktown church, a large old, ruinous building, he says, " I suppose it has scarce had such a congregation during this century. Many of them were gay, genteel people, so I spoke on the first elements of the gospel, but I was still out of their depth. Oh, how hard it is to be *shallow* enough for a polite audience!"—*Anecdotes of the Wesleys.*

POPERY.

LIGHTFOOT observes :—"Yoke-fellows, indeed, are the Jew and Romanist above all people of the world, in a deluded fancying their own bravery and privilege above all the world besides. He that comes to read the Jewish writings, especially those that are of the nature of sermons, will find this to be the main stuffing of them, almost in every leaf and page. ' How choice a people is Israel! how dearly God is in love with Israel! what a happy thing it is to be of the seed of Abraham! how blessed the nation of the Jews above all nations!' And such stuff as this all along. And is not the style of the Romanists the very same tune ? ' How holy the Church of Rome! what superiority and pre-eminence hath the church above all churches, and all the men in the world are heretics, and apostates, and cast-aways, if they be not Romanists.' Whereas if both these people would but impartially look upon themselves, they would see that there are such brands upon them as are upon no nation under heaven now extant."

POSITION—No Barrier to Grace.

GRACE makes itself equally at home in the palace and the cottage. No condition necessitates its absence, no position precludes its flourishing. One may compare it in its power to live and blossom in all places to the beautiful blue-bell of Scotland, of which the poetess sings :—

> "No rock is too high, no vale too low,
> For its fragile and tremulous form to grow :
>   It crowns the mountain
>   With azure bells,
>   And decks the fountain
>   In forest dells.
> It wreathes the ruin with clusters grey,
> Bowing and smiling the livelong day."

PRACTICE—Necessary to Perfection.

A NEIGHBOUR near my study persists in practising upon the flute. He bores my ears as with an auger, and renders it almost an impossibility to think. Up and down his scale he runs remorselessly, until even the calamity of temporary deafness would almost be welcome to me. Yet he teaches me that I must practise if I would be perfect ; must exercise myself unto godliness if I would be skilful ; must, in fact, make myself familiar with the word of God, with holy living, and saintly dying. Such practice, moreover, will be as charming as my neighbour's flute is intolerable.

PRAYER—and Activity.

"A SCHOLAR at a boarding-school near London was remarked for repeating her lessons well. A school companion, who was idly inclined, said to her one day, ' How is it that you always say your lessons so perfectly ?' She replied, ' I always *pray* that I may say my lessons well.' ' Do you ?' replied the other, ' then I'll pray too.' But, alas ! next morning she could not repeat one word of her lesson. Very much confounded,

she ran to her friend. 'I prayed,' said she, 'but I could
not repeat a word of my lesson.' 'Perhaps,' rejoined the
other, 'you took no *pains* to learn it.' 'Learn it! learn
it!' answered the first, 'I did not learn it at all. I didn't
know I needed to learn it, when I *prayed* that I might say
it.' She loved her idleness, poor girl ; and her praying was
but a mockery."

PRAYER—Believing.

Is it not a sad thing that we should think it wonderful for
God to hear prayer? Much better faith was that of a little
boy in one of the schools in Edinburgh, who had attended a
prayer-meeting, and at last said to his teacher who conducted
it, " Teacher, I wish my sister could be got to read the Bible;
she never reads it." " Why, Johnny, should your sister read
the Bible ?" " Because if she should once read it, I am sure
it would do her good, and she would be converted and be
saved." "Do you think so, Johnny?" " Yes, I do, sir, and
I wish the next time there's a prayer-meeting, you would ask
the people to pray for my sister that she may begin to read
the Bible." "Well, well, it shall be done, John."
So the teacher gave out that a little boy was very anxious
that prayer should be offered that his sister might begin to
read the Bible. John was observed to get up and go out.
The teacher thought it very rude of the boy to disturb the
people in a crowded room, and so the next day when the lad
came, he said, " John, I thought it was very rude of you to
get up in the prayer-meeting and go out. You ought not to
have done so." " Oh, sir," said the boy, " I did not mean to
be rude ; but I thought I should just like to go home and see
my sister reading her Bible for the first time."
Thus we ought to believe, and watch with expectation for
answers to our prayer. Do not say, " Lord, turn my darkness
into light," and then go out with your candle as though you

expected to find it dark.   After asking the Lord to appear for you, expect him to do so, for according to your faith so be it unto you.

PRAYER—for Help to Pray.

IN Dr. Ryland's memoir of Andrew Fuller is the following anecdote.   At a conference at Soham, a friend of slender abilities being asked to pray, knelt down, and Mr. Fuller and the company with him, when he found himself so embarrassed, that, whispering to Mr. Fuller, he said, " I do not know how to go on." Mr. F. replied in a whisper, " Tell the Lord so." The rest of the company did not hear what passed between them, but the man taking Mr. Fuller's advice began to confess his not knowing how to pray as he ought to pray, begging to be taught to pray, and so proceeded in prayer to the satisfaction of all the company.

PRAYER—Helpful to Study.

IN Payson's diary is the following entry : " Sept. 23.—Was quite dull and lifeless in prayer, and in consequence had no success in study."

PRAYER—its Power Against Satan.

THERE is a huge rock upon the Swiss side of the St. Gothard road, about which an old legend is told by the natives of the neighbouring village.   The devil was whisking this enormous stone along very merrily at early dawn of day, when he was met by a devout old woman, who being somewhat alarmed, uttered a prayer at the sight of the unexpected traveller.   Such was the power of her prayer, that the demon dropped his burden at once, and there it lies, an indisputable proof that the devil is no match for old ladies who know how to invoke the aid of heaven.   Mother Church has sanctioned many a worse legend than this, for a truthful moral lies upon the surface.   Let interceding believers make the fiend tremble always, by praying without ceasing. The weakest saint upon his knees is victorious over all the powers of hell.

PRAYER—its Power to Soften Asperities.

"Two neighbours, a cooper and a farmer, were spending the evening together. Both were professors of religion, but of different communions. Their conversation was first upon topics relating to practical religion, but after a time it diverged to the points of difference between the two denominations to which they belonged. It first became a discussion, and then a dispute. The cooper was the first to perceive its unprofitable and injurious tendency, and remarked, 'We are springing apart from each other, let us put on another hoop—let us pray.' They kneeled down and prayed together, after which they spent the remainder of the evening lovingly together, conversing on the things of the kingdom in which they both felt an equal interest. The suggestion of the cooper was an excellent one, and it were well if it were acted on more frequently by those who, like him, are members of the household of Christ."

PRAYER—Sweet Uses of.

On the first of May in the olden times, according to annual custom, many inhabitants of London went into the fields to bathe their faces with the early dew upon the grass under the idea that it would render them beautiful. Some writers call the custom superstitious ; it may have been so, but this we know, that to bathe one's face every morning in the dew of heaven by prayer and communion, is the sure way to obtain true beauty of life and character.

PRAYER—Simile of.

Prayer pulls the rope below and the great bell rings above in the ears of God. Some scarcely stir the bell, for they pray so languidly ; others give but an occasional pluck at the rope; but he who wins with heaven is the man who grasps the rope boldly and pulls continuously, with all his might.

PRAYER—Success in.

THESE lads to gain the fruit must shake the tree,
Good reader, mark the lesson writ for *thee!*
If from the tree of promis'd mercy thou
Wouldst win the good which loadeth every bough,
Then urge the promise well with pleading cries,
Move heaven itself with vehemence of sighs;
Soon shall celestial fruit thy toil repay—
'Tis ripe, and waits for him who loves to pray.
What if thou fail at first, yet give not o'er,
Bestir thyself to labour more and more ;
Enlist a brother's sympathetic knee,
The tree will drop its fruit when *two* agree :
Entreat the Holy Ghost to give thee power,
Then shall the fruit descend in joyful shower.

PRAYERS—of a Father.

PHILIP JAMES SPENER had a son of eminent talents, but perverse and extremely vicious. All means of love and persuasion were without success. The father could only *pray*, which he continued to do, that the Lord might yet be pleased to save his son at any time and in any way. The son fell sick ; and while lying on his bed in great distress of mind, nearly past the power of speech or motion, he suddenly started up, clasped his hands, and exclaimed : "*My father's prayers, like mountains, surround me!*" Soon after his anxiety ceased a sweet peace spread over his face, his malady came to a crisis, and the son was saved in body and soul. He became another man. Spener lived to see his son a respectable man, in public office, and happily married. Such was the change of his life after his conversion.—*N. E. Puritan.*

PREACHER—Learns by Communion with God.

IT is related that one of his hearers once asked, " How is it that Mr. Bramwell always has something that is new to tell us when he preaches ?" " Why," said the person interrogated, " you see Brother Bramwell lives so near the gates of heaven that he hears a great many things that we don't get near enough to hear anything about."

PREACHER—Must Feed the People.

FROM the deck of an Austrian gunboat we threw into the Lago Garda a succession of little pieces of bread, and presently small fishes came in shoals, till there seemed to be, as the old proverb puts it, more fish than water. They came to feed, and needed no music. Let the preacher give his people food, and they will flock around him, even if the sounding brass of rhetoric, and the tinkling cymbals of oratory are silent.

PREACHER—Must Feed the People.

EVERYBODY knows that large flocks of pigeons assemble at the stroke of the great clock in the square of St. Mark : believe me, it is not the music of the bell which attracts them, they can hear that every hour. They come, Mr. Preacher, for food, and no mere sound will long collect them. This is a hint for filling your meeting-house; it must be done not merely by that fine, bell-like voice of yours, but by all the neighbourhood's being assured that spiritual food is to be had when you open your mouth. Barley for pigeons, good sir; and the gospel for men and women. Try it in earnest and you cannot fail ; you will soon be saying, "Who are these that fly as a cloud, and as doves to their windows?"

PREACHER—to Avoid a Lofty Style.

IN the town of Goslar, in the Hartz mountains, there is in the principal square a fountain evidently of mediæval date, but the peculiarity of its construction is that no one can reach the water so as to fill a bucket or even get a drink to quench his thirst. Both the jets, and the basin into which they fall, are above the reach of any man of ordinary stature ; yet the fountain was intended to supply the public with water, and it fulfils its design by a method which we never saw in use before ; every person brings a spout or trough with him long enough to reach the top of the fountain and bring the water down into his pitcher. We are afraid that all our reverence for antiquity did not prevent the full exercise of our risible faculties ; sixpennyworth of mason's work with a chisel would have made the crystal stream available to all ; but no, every one must bring a trough or go away unsupplied.

When preachers of the gospel talk in so lofty a style that each hearer needs to bring a dictionary, they remind us of the absurd fountain of Goslar. The use of six-syllabled jaw-breaking words is simply a most ludicrous vanity. A little labour on the part of such pedants would save a world of profitless toil to their hearers, and enable those uneducated persons who have no means of reaching the preacher's altitude to derive some measure of instruction from his ministry.

PREACHER—Should be Faithful unto Death.

THE minister of Christ should feel like the old keeper of
Eddystone lighthouse. Life was failing fast, but summoning
all his strength, he crept round once more to trim the lights
before he died. May the Holy Ghost enable his servants
to keep the beacon fire blazing, to warn sinners of the rocks,
shoals, and quicksands which surround them.

PREACHERS—to be Acquainted with Human Nature.

MICHAEL ANGELO, when painting an altar-piece in the
conventual church, in Florence, in order that the figures might
be as death-like as possible, obtained permission of the prior
to have the coffins of the newly-buried opened and placed
beside him during the night;—an appalling expedient, but successful in enabling him to reproduce with terrible effect, not
the mortal pallor only, but the very anatomy of death. If we
would preach well to the souls of men we must acquaint ourselves with their ruined state, must have their case always on
our hearts both by night and day, must know the terrors of
the Lord and the value of the soul, and feel a sacred sympathy
with perishing sinners. There is no masterly, prevailing
preaching without this.

PREACHERS—Different.

THOSE that are all in exhortation, no whit in doctrine, are
like to them that snuff the lamp, but pour not in oil. Again,
those that are all in doctrine, nothing in exhortation, drown
the wick in oil, but light it not ; making it fit for use if it had
fire put to it, but as it is, rather capable of good than profitable for the present. Doctrine without exhortation makes
men all brain, no heart ; exhortation without doctrine makes
the heart full, leaves the brain empty. Both together make a
man. One makes a wise man, the other good ; one serves
that we may know our duty, the other that we may perform
it. I will labour in both, but I know not in whether more.

Men cannot practise unless they know; and they know in vain if they practise not.—*Bishop Hall.*

PREACHERS—How they Gain Perspicuity.

MR. WARBURTON, one of the inspectors of schools, mentions in his report for 1863, that he has nowhere heard such good reading as in a girls' school in Berkshire, than which none in his district bears a better character for instruction in what are called the higher subjects. The clergyman, who is also the acting manager, is rather deaf, and the girls, who are frequently heard by him without book, are obliged to read with unusual clearness and distinctness of tone and articulation, in order that he may not lose a word. The inspector considers the pleasure with which he listened to the girls' reading to be in great measure attributable to the fact of their ordinarily having to make what they read intelligible to one who cannot hear so well as many persons do.

The best of teachers are those who have laboured to be understood by the dullest capacities. Preachers who all along have aimed to suit the educated never become so simple or efficient as those who have made a point of explaining even the elements of faith to the ignorant.

PREACHERS—Too Learned for Real Service.

THE great bell of Moscow is too large to be hung, the question arises, what was the use of making it? Some preachers are so learned that they cannot make themselves understood, or else cannot bring their minds to preach plain gospel sermons; here, too, the same question might be asked.

PREACHERS—Not to Preach Themselves.

WE ascended the Sacro Monte at Orta, expecting to find that its holy hill was like that at Varallo, consecrated to representations of the life of Christ. To our disappointment we found that everything was to the honour and glory of St. Frantis of Assisi, who nevertheless was represented as saying, " God forbid that I should glory, save in the cross of our Lord Jesus Christ." Too often when the preacher should think only of his Master, and labour only to set forth the Redeemer's glories, he is occupied with his own style and oratory, and so honours himself at the expense of his Lord.

PREACHERS—Speak After Death.

THERE are strange legends extant of churches which have been swallowed by earthquakes, or buried beneath fallen mountains. The rustics declare that they have heard the bells still ringing, far down in the bowels of the earth, just as they did when they hung aloft in the tower. Take the bells to be preachers and the legend is true, for being dead they yet speak, and from their graves they sound forth lessons not less powerful than those with which they made their pulpits resound while they were yet with us.

PREACHING—Best Manner of.

THE celebrated actor Garrick having been requested by Dr. Stonehouse to favour him with his opinion as to the manner in which a sermon ought to be delivered, sent him the following judicious answer :—

"MY DEAR PUPIL,—You know how you would feel and speak in a parlour concerning a friend who was in imminent danger of his life, and with what energetic pathos of diction and countenance you would enforce the observance of that which you really thought would be for his preservation. You could not think of playing the orator, of studying your emphases, cadences, and gestures, you would be yourself, and the interesting nature of your subject, impressing your heart, would furnish you with the most natural tone of voice, the most proper language, the most engaging features, and the most suitable and graceful gestures. What you would thus be in

12

the parlour, be in the pulpit, and you will not fail to please, to affect, and to profit. Adieu, my dear friend."

PREACHING—Fruit and Flowers.

AT Hampton Court Palace every one regards with wonder the enormous vine loaded with so vast a multitude of huge clusters : just outside the vine-house is as fine a specimen of the wistaria, and when it is in full bloom, the cluster-like masses of bloom, cause you to think it a flower-bearing vine, as the other is a fruit-bearing vine. Fit emblems these two famous trees of two ministries, both admired, but not equally to be prized ; the ministry of oratory, luxuriant in metaphor and poetry, and the ministry of grace, abounding in sound teaching and soul saving-energy. Gay as are the flower-clusters of the wistaria, no one mistakes them for the luscious bunches of the grape ; yet, there are many simpletons in spiritual things who mistake sound for sense, and seem to satisfy their hunger not on solid meat, but on the jingle of a musical dinner bell.

PREACHING—its Force the Main Consideration.

I HAD tried to drive certain long brass-headed nails into a wall, but had never succeeded except in turning up their points, and rendering them useless. When a tradesman came who understood his work, I noticed that he filed off all the points of the nails, the very points upon whose sharpness I had relied ; and when he had quite blunted them, he drove them in as far as he pleased. With some consciences our fine points in preaching are worse than useless. Our keen distinctions and nice discriminations are thrown away on many ; they need to be encountered with sheer force and blunt honesty. The truth must be hammered into them by main strength, and we know from whom to seek the needed power.

PREACHING—Need of Prayer and Unction.

In a Romish book by Father Faber of the Oratory, we find the following :—" Do you remember the story of that religious, a Jesuit I think, who was a famous preacher, and whose sermons converted men by scores? It was revealed to him that not one of the conversions was owing to his talents or eloquence, but all to the prayers of an illiterate lay-brother who sat on the pulpit steps praying all the time for the success of the sermon. There is another story, a very strange one. I will not vouch for its being true, but I will quote it for the sake of the wise teaching it contains. A certain religious, a very popular preacher, was expected one day in a convent of his order, where he was a stranger. In the afternoon he arrived, or rather an evil spirit who personated him, arrived, to see what mischief he could do. It so happened that there was to be a sermon on hell preached that day by one of the monks, but he was ill and unable to preach. So they asked this devil to preach on hell, which he did; and, as may be supposed from his experience, a most wonderful sermon it was. However, on the arrival of the real preacher, the evil one was discovered, and was obliged to disclose himself, and his malicious designs. Among other things he was asked how it was not against his interests to preach such a frightening sermon about hell, as it would keep people from sin. 'Not at all,' he replied, 'there was no unction with it, so it could do no harm!'"

PREACHING—Personal.

Two Chinese jugglers have been making a public exhibition of their skill. One of them is set up as a target, and the other shows his dexterity by hurling knives which stick into the board at his comrade's back, close to the man's body. These deadly weapons fix themselves between his arms and legs, and between each of his fingers, they fly past his ears, and over his head, and on each side of his neck. The art is *not* to hit him.　Are there not to be found preachers who are remarkably proficient in the same art in the mental and spiritual departments?

PREDESTINATION.

THEY that talk of nothing but predestination, and will not proceed in the way of heaven till they be satisfied on that point, do as a man that would not come to London, unless at his first step he might set his foot upon the top of St. Paul's.—*The Table Talk of John Selden.*

PRESUMPTION—Rebuked by Trial.

" THE Brahmins say that Benares is not a part of this sinful earth; but that it is on the outside of the world.　An earthquake, however, which was lately felt there, has rather nonplussed them, as it proves that what shakes the earth, shakes Benares too."　It is easy enough for those who have been long at ease to imagine themselves protected from the common lot of men, but a shaking trial in their estates or persons soon convinces them that they are as other men are. Spiritual presumption leads many professors to imagine that they are beyond the power of temptation, and are no longer such frail beings as their fellow Christians ; let but the Lord conceal his face, or Satan assail them, and in their sore trouble they will discover that they are men of like passions with the rest.

PRIDE.

When men refuse to hear the gospel from the lips of a gracious but uneducated preacher, they remind us of the Spaniard in South America, who suffered severely from the gout, but refused to be cured by an Indian.　" I know," said he, " that he is a famous man, and would certainly cure me, but he is an Indian, and would expect to be treated with attentions which I cannot pay to a man of colour, and therefore I prefer remaining as I am."

PRIDE—in Dictating to God.

THE petty sovereign of an insignificant tribe in North
America every morning stalks out of his hovel, bids the sun
good-morrow, and points out to him with his finger the
course he is to take for the day. Is this arrogance more
contemptible than ours when we would dictate to God the
course of his providence, and summon him to our bar for his
dealings with us? How ridiculous does man appear when he
attempts to argue with his God!

PRIESTS—Superstitious Reverence of.

A WRITER on the manners and customs of India, says:—
" I was informed that vast numbers of Shoodras drink the
water in which a Brahmin has dipped his foot, and abstain from
food in the morning till this ceremony be over. Some persons
do this every day, and others vow to attend to it for such
a time, in order to obtain the removal of disease. Persons
may be seen carrying a small quantity of water in a cup, and
intreating the first Brahmin they see to put his toe in it.
This person then drinks the water, and bows or prostrates to
the Brahmin, who gives him a blessing. Some persons keep
water thus sanctified in their houses."

How few steps would land Tractarians in the same
degradation ! Their priests are the channels of grace to
them, from them they receive regeneration and absolution,
and from their hands they receive the god of bread whom
they adore and eat. Believing all this of their sacerdotal
fathers, to drink the water in which they wash their feet would
be no humiliation ; their minds have stooped to drink far
fouler puddle, they may well put their bodies on the same level.

PROCRASTINATION.

IT is a snowy day, and some boys have put a few bricks
together, making a sort of square box of them ; they have set
up one on edge on a piece of stick, and have scattered under

it a few crumbs. Here comes a robin, and he picks up a crumb or two, and while he is feeding, down comes the brick! "*I did not wait long,*" says the robin, "*but I am caught! I did not wait long, but I cannot get out! I did not wait long, but I have lost my liberty! I did not wait long, but it may be I shall lose my life!*" Ah! little robin, thou shalt be a preacher to some here. They have gone a little into sin, and they are inclined to-night to wait a little while. Take care that this is not your dolorous note one of these days, "*I did not wait long, but the devil caught me in his trap! I did not wait long, but I waited too long! I did not wait long, but I lost my soul for ever!*" God grant that this may not be your lot.

PROCRASTINATION.

IN Nebuchadnezzar's image, the lower the members, the coarser the metal : the farther off the time, the more unfit. To-day is the golden opportunity, to-morrow will be the silver season, next day but the brazen one, and so on, till at last I shall come to the toes of clay, and be turned to dust.— *Thomas Fuller.*

PROCRASTINATION.

BE not like the foolish drunkard who, staggering home one night, saw his candle lit for him. "Two candles!" said he, for his drunkenness made him see double, "I will blow out one," and as he blew it out, in a moment he was in the dark. Many a man sees double through the drunkenness of sin ; he has one life to sow his wild oats in, and then he half expects another in which to turn to God; so, like a fool, he blows out the only candle that he has, and in the dark he will have to lie down for ever. Haste thee, traveller, thou hast but one sun, and after that sets, thou wilt never reach thy home. God help thee to make haste now !

PROCRASTINATION.

"A Swiss traveller," says a writer in the *Edinburgh Review*, "describes a village, situated on the slope of a great mountain, of which the strata shelve in the direction of the place. Huge crags, directly overhanging the village, and massy enough to sweep the whole of it into the torrent below, have become separated from the main body of the mountain in the course of ages by great fissures, and now scarce adhere to it. When they give way, the village must perish ; it is only a question of time, and the catastrophe may happen any day. For years past engineers have been sent to measure the width of the fissures, and report them constantly increasing. The villagers, for more than one generation, have been aware of their danger ; subscriptions have been once or twice opened to enable them to remove ; yet they live on in their doomed dwellings, from year to year, fortified against the ultimate certainty and daily probablility of destruction by the common sentiment, 'Things may last their time and longer.'"

Like the dwellers in this doomed village, the world's inhabitants have grown careless and secure in sin. The scoffers of the last days are around us, saying, " Where is the promise of his coming? For since the fathers fell asleep, all things continue as they were from the beginning of the creation." But in saying this, they are too confident. Nothing is permanent that has sin about it, nothing secure that has wrath above it, and flames of fire beneath it. Sin has once deluged the world with water, it shall deluge it again with waves of fire. Sodom and Gomorrah are the types that foreshadow the doom of those that live ungodly in these latter times, and he who can walk this reeling world unmoved by all the tokens of its fiery doom, must either have a rock of refuge where his soul may rest secure, or else must have fallen into a strange carelessness, and a sad forgetfulness of God.

PROCRASTINATION—Deprecated.

DO any of you remember the loss of the vessel called the " Central America"? She was in a bad state, had sprung a leak and was going down, and she therefore hoisted a signal of distress. A ship came close to her, the captain of which asked, through the trumpet, " What is amiss?" " We are in bad repair, and are going down : lie by till morning," was the answer. But the captain on board the rescue-ship said, " Let me take your passengers on board now." " Lie by till morning," was the message which came back. Once again the captain cried, " You had better let me take your passengers on board now." " Lie by till morning," was the reply which sounded through the trumpet. About an hour-and-a-half after, the lights were missing, and though no sound was heard, she and all on board had gone down to the fathomless abyss. O unconverted friends, for God's sake, do not say, " Lie by till morning." To-day, even to-day, hear ye the voice of God.

PROFESSION—The Vanity of Mere.

FORGET not that the pretence of religion without the power of it is one of the most comfortless things in the world. It is like a man who should call his servant, and say to him, " Is the larder well stored ?" " There is nothing, sir, not even a mouldy crust." " Let the cloth be laid," saith he ; and it is laid, and all the appurtenances thereof. " And now," he says, " I will sit down to my meal, and you shall wait upon me." The empty dishes are brought in proper course ; from invisible joints he cuts imperceptible slices, and from the empty plates he lifts upon his fork mouthfuls of nothingness and dainty morsels of vacuum. There, the cloth can be removed, the feaster has finished the atmospheric banquet, and rises from the table free from any charge of immoderate eating. Now, this may be a very pleasant operation for once, although its charms require a very poetic and imaginative mind to appreciate them ; but if continued several days, this unsubstantial festival would, I conceive, become somewhat undesirable and cheerless, and in the end the guest might perish amid his empty platters. Yet such must be the life of the man who professes to feed on the bread of heaven and knows not its sustaining virtues, who boasts of drinking the water of life and has never sipped that heavenly stream.

PROFESSORS (MERE)—have no Changes.

Artificial piety, like flowers in wax, droops not in the hour of drought, but the fair lily of true grace hangs its head if the rain of heaven be denied. True faith, like fire, has its attendant smoke of unbelief, but presumption like a painted flame is all brightness. Like ships at sea, true Christians have their storms ; but mere professors, like pictured galleys on the canvas, ride on an unruffled ocean. Life has its changes ; 'tis death that abideth the same. Life has muscle, sinew, brain, spirit, and these vary in physical condition ; but the petrified limbs of death lie still until the worm has devoured the carcase. Life weeps as well as smiles, but the ghastly grin of death relaxes not with anxiety or fear. Moab hath no changes ; he is "settled upon his lees : he has not been emptied from vessel to vessel." "They are not in trouble as other men, neither are they plagued like other men." As no weather can give ague to marble, as no variation of temperature can bring fever to iron, so to some men the events of life, the temptations of prosperity, or the trials of adversity, bring little change. Yet were it better to ebb and flow for ever like the sea, than rot in endless stagnation of false peace. Better to be hunted by the hounds of hell, and so driven to the shelter of the cross, than to dwell at ease and be fattening for the devil's shambles.

PROFESSORS—Too Often Deceptive.

" IN the sweet valley between Chamouni and the Valais, at

every turn of the pleasant pathway, where the scent of the
thyme lies richest upon its rocks, we shall see a little cross
and shrine set under one of them, and go up to it, hoping to
receive some happy thought of the Redeemer, by whom all
these lovely things were made, and still consist. But when
we come near, behold, beneath the cross a rude picture of
souls tormented in red tongues of hell fire, and pierced by
demons."—*Ruskin.*

Too often the house of a fair professor turns out to be
much the same; the beauty at a distance changes into hideous
deformity when near. Oh, to be found, when closest watched,
better than observers would at first sight have conceived us
to be!

PROGRESS—Measure of.

SAILORS would be loath to sail without using their log to
test their pace, and show their progress. The wonder is that
so many Christian professors navigate the sea of life, and are
utterly careless whether they are making headway or drifting
from their course. Should we not all cast overboard our log?
There are various ways by which with readiness we may
measure our progress : our prayers, our labours, our patience,
our faith, our communion with God, our humility, may all
serve as logs by which to measure our sailing pace.

PROMISES.

GOOD old Spurstow says that some of the promises are
like the almond tree—they blossom hastily in the very earliest
spring; but, saith he, there are others which resemble the
mulberry tree—they are very slow in putting forth their leaves.
Then what is a man to do, if he has a mulberry tree promise
which is late in blossoming? Why, he is to wait till it does.
If the vision tarry, wait for it till it come, and the appointed
time shall surely bring it.

PROMPTNESS—in Doing Good.

QUICK must be the hand if an impression is to be made upon the melted wax. Once let the wax cool and you will press the seal in vain. Cold and hard it will be in a few moments, therefore let the work be quickly done. When men's hearts are melted under the preaching of the Word, or by sickness, or the loss of friends, believers should be very eager to stamp the truth upon the prepared mind. Such opportunities are to be seized with holy eagerness. Reader, do you know of such? If you be a lover of the Lord Jesus, hasten with the seal before the wax is cool.

PROPHECY—Too Often Interpreted by Imagination.

ALL along the Oker Thal, in the Hartz, there are huge rocks towering up among the fir-clad hills, to which the peasants have appended names according as they fancy them to bear resemblance to chairs, horses, cobblers, or cocked hats. The likeness in most cases is such as only fancy can make out when she is in her most vigorous mood, nevertheless this rock must needs be called a man, and that a church, and there has no doubt been many a quarrel between rival observers who have discovered each a different image in the one pile of rock; yet the stones are not churches, chairs, or cobblers, and the whole business is childish and nonsensical. Interpreters of prophecy during the last few centuries have been most of them in the same position; one of them sees in the sublimities of the Revelation the form of Louis Napoleon where two or three hundred years ago half Christendom saw the Pope, and the other half Martin Luther. The other day one of the seers saw Sebastopol in the prophecies, and now another detects the Suez Canal, and we feel pretty sure that the Council at Rome will soon be spied out in Daniel or Ezekiel. The fact is, when fancy is their guide men wander as in a maze. Spiritualistic interpreters see, like children gazing into the fire, not what is really before them, but what is in their own heads. Great truths are in the Prophets and in the precious book of Revelation, but your fanciful theologians turn these sublimities of truth into the toys of children, when they give their imagination license to act as an expositor.

PROSPERITY—Evils of.

TOO long a period of fair weather in the Italian valleys creates such a superabundance of dust that the traveller sighs for a shower. He is smothered, his clothes are white, his eyes smart, the grit even grates between his teeth and finds its way down his throat; welcome are the rain clouds, as they promise to abate the nuisance. Prosperity long continued breeds a plague of dust even more injurious, for it almost blinds the spirit and insinuates itself into the soul; a shower or two of grief proves a mighty blessing, for it deprives the things of earth of somewhat of their smothering power. A Christian making money fast is just a man in a cloud of dust, it will fill his eyes if he be not careful. A Christian full of worldly care is in the same condition, and had need look to it lest he be choked with earth. Afflictions might almost be prayed for if we never had them, even as in long stretches of fair weather men beg for rain to lay the dust.

PROVIDENCE.

AN old authority assures us that "the Jews fancy, concerning the cloud that conducted Israel through the wilderness, that it did not only show them the way, but also plane it; that it did not only lead them in the way which they must go, but also fit the way for them to go upon it; that it cleared all the mountains and smoothed all the rocks; that it cleared all the bushes and removed all the rubs."

What is probably a mere legend as to the type is abundantly true of the providence of God, which it so accurately represents. Our gracious God not only leads us in the way of mercy, but he prepares our path before us, providing for all our wants even before they occur.

PROVIDENCE—the Guardian of our Weakness.

THAT image in Lowell's poem of "The Changeling" fascinates me. It is so much what I am and ever wish to be.

"I feel as weak as a violet
Alone 'neath the awful sky."

Unable to defend myself and apparently undefended, yet guarded by omnipotent love, I would fain pour out a perfume of praise to the Great Invisible who watches over me, and would feel that under the care of Providence I may claim the sweetness of the poet's next stanza.

"As weak, yet as trustful also ;
For the whole year long I see
All the wonders of faithful nature
Still worked for the love of me.
Winds wander and dews drip earthward,
Rains fall, suns rise and set,
Earth whirls, and all but to prosper
A poor little violet."

PROVIDENCE—Rightly Places us.

SUPPOSE the mole should cry, "How I could have honoured the Creator had I been allowed to fly!" it would be very foolish, for a mole flying would be a most ridiculous object ; while a mole fashioning its tunnels and casting up its castles, is viewed with admiring wonder by the naturalist, who perceives its remarkable suitability to its sphere. The fish of the sea might say, "How could I display the wisdom of God if I could sing, or mount a tree, like a bird ;" but a dolphin in a tree would be a very grotesque affair, and there would be no wisdom of God to admire in trouts singing in the groves ; but when the fish cuts the wave with agile fin, all who have observed it say how wonderfully it is adapted to its habitat, how exactly its every bone is fitted for its mode of life.   Brother, it is just so with you.   If you begin to say, "I cannot glorify God where I am, and as I am," I answer, neither could you anywhere if not where you are.   Providence, which arranged your surroundings, appointed them so that, all things being considered, you are in the position in which you can best display the wisdom and the grace of God.

PRUDENCE (FALSE)—its Mischief.

JAMES the First once said of armour, that "it was an excellent invention, for it not only saved the life of the wearer, but it hindered him from doing harm to anybody else." Equally destructive to all usefulness is that excessive prudence upon which some professors pride themselves ; not only do they escape all persecution, but they are never able to strike a blow, much less fight a battle for the Lord Jesus.

PUFFERY—Spiritual.

WHEN we read the exaggerated accounts which are so frequently issued, lauding to the skies the successful labours of certain evangelists of doubtful vocation, we are reminded of the battle of Aliwal, of which an officer wrote, "Aliwal was *the battle of the despatch*, for none of us knew we had fought a battle until the particulars appeared in a document which did *more* than justice to every one concerned."   Is there not quite enough religious fiction abroad without filling corners of newspapers and magazines therewith?   We know who they were of old who sounded a trumpet before them.   God's real works of grace are too sublime to need the arts of puffery to publish them.

PULPIT.

CLEMENS BRENTANO, a literary acquaintance of Dr. Krummacher, and a Catholic, once said to the doctor, "Till you Protestants pull down the chatter-box," ("Plapperkasten,") he meant the pulpit, "or, at least, throw it into the corner, where it ought to be, there is no hope of you." I could only reply to him, "It is true indeed, that our 'Plapperkasten' stands greatly in the way of you Catholics."

The pulpit is the Thermopylæ of Protestantism, the tower of the flock, the Palladium of the church of God. Well might Paul magnify his office, for not only Glasgow but the city of our God "flourishes by the preaching of the word."

PURPOSE—Unity of.

IT is said of Thomas Pett, the miser, that his pulse rose and fell with the funds. He never lay down or rose that he did not bless the inventor of compound interest. His one gloomy apartment was never brightened with coal, candle, or the countenance of a visitor, and he never ate a morsel at his own expense. Of course he made money, for he gave himself wholly to it ; and we ought not to forget that the same single-mindedness and self-denial would make Christians rich towards God. What is wanted in the service of Christ, is the same unity of purpose which has ruled all men who have won the object for which they lived. He who makes God's glory the one only aim before which all other things bow themselves, is the man to bring honour to his Lord.

PURPOSE—Unity of.

WHEN Audubon the celebrated American ornithologist was in Paris he grew quite weary of it, and his diary does not contain a cheerful word about that gay city until he writes, "The stock-pigeon roosts in the trees of the garden of the

Tuileries in great numbers ; blackbirds also do the same, and are extremely noisy before dark; some few rooks and magpies are seen there also.   In the Jardin, or walks of the Palais Royal, common sparrows are prodigiously plentiful.   The mountain finch passes in scattered numbers over Paris at this season, going northerly." So also when in London the great naturalist was quite out of his element, and only seemed pleased when a flight of wildfowl passed over the city.   Here was the secret of his success—his complete absorption in his one study—birds alone had charms for him.   We who would attain to eminence in the service of Christ must let the love of souls, in an equal way, master and engross us.   When writing a paper for the Natural History Society upon the habits of the wild pigeon, Audubon says, "So absorbed was my whole soul and spirit in the work, that I felt as if I were in the woods of America, among the pigeons, and my ears were filled with the sound of their rustling wings." We should all write, speak, and preach for our Lord Jesus far more powerfully if our love to the Lord were a passion so dominant as to make the great realities of eternity vividly real and supremely commanding in our minds.

QUARRELS.

IN most quarrels there is a fault on both sides.   A quarrel may be compared to a spark, which cannot be produced without a flint as well as a steel; either of them may hammer on wood for ever, no fire will follow.—*South*.

QUESTIONS—Foolish Theological.

THE follies of the schoolmen should be a warning to all those who would mingle metaphysical speculations or pro- phetical theories with the simple doctrines of the Bible. There was among those learned men such a rage for Aris- totle, that his ethics were frequently read to the people instead of the gospel, and the teachers themselves were

employed either in wresting the words of Scripture to support
the most monstrous opinions, or in discussing the most trivial
questions. Think of men gravely debating whether the angel
Gabriel appeared to the Virgin Mary in the shape of a serpent, of a dove, of a man, or of a woman? Did he seem to
be young or old? In what dress was he? Was his garment
white or of two colours? Was his linen clean or foul? Did
he appear in the morning, noon, or evening? What was the
colour of the Virgin's hair? &c. Think of all this nonsense
veiled in learned terms and obscure phrases! While human
minds were engaged in weaving such cobwebs as these, no
progress was made in real knowledge, and the gloom of the
dark ages deepened into tenfold night. We are much in
danger of the same evil from another quarter. The reign of
obscure nonsense and dogmatic trifling may yet return. An
ultra-spiritual sect has arisen whose theological language is a
jargon, whose interpretations are mystical, whose prophetical
hypotheses are ridiculous, and whose arrogance is superla-
tive. To leave the consideration of well-known and soul-
saving truths to fight over unimportant subtleties, is to turn
our corn fields into poppy gardens. To imagine that the
writers of unintelligible mysticism are men of great depth, is
to find wisdom in the hootings of owls. True spirituality
shuns the obscure and the *dilettanti*, and delights in the plain
and practical; but there is much to fascinate in the superfine
shams of the hour. Quintilian justly observes that the
obscurity of an author is generally in proportion to his incapacity; and we might add, that the ferocity of a bigot is
frequently in proportion to the absurdity of his belief. Some
are zealots for a certain theory of 666, and the two witnesses,
and the little horn, who would be far better employed in
training up their children in the fear of God, or listening for
their instruction to a sober preacher of the word of God. It
is a most fitting thing to be looking for the coming of the
Lord, but a most miserable waste of time to be spinning

13

theories about it, and allowing the millions around us to perish in their sins. Ragged-schools, orphanages, street-preaching, tract distributing, almsgiving, these are the present and pressing questions for the Christian church ; whether the stream of the Euphrates is likely to diminish, or the Dead Sea to flow into the Mediterranean, may be settled in less needy times.

REASON AND FAITH.

An old writer says :—Faith and Reason may be compared to two travellers: Faith is like a man in full health, who can walk his twenty or thirty miles at a time without suffering; Reason is like a little child, who can only, with difficulty, accomplish three or four miles. "Well," says this old writer, "on a given day Reason says to Faith, 'O good Faith, let me walk with thee;' Faith replies, 'O Reason, thou canst never walk with me !' However, to try their paces, they set out together, but they soon find it hard to keep company. When they come to a deep river, Reason says, 'I can never ford this,' but Faith wades through it singing. When they reach a lofty mountain, there is the same exclamation of despair; and in such cases, Faith, in order not to leave Reason behind, is obliged to carry him on his back; and," adds the writer, "oh ! what a luggage is Reason to Faith !"

REGENERATION—Need of.

A raw countryman having brought his gun to the gun-smith for repairs, the latter is reported to have examined it, and finding it to be almost too far gone for repairing, said, "Your gun is in a very worn-out, ruinous, good-for-nothing condition, what sort of repairing do you want for it ?" "Well," said the countryman, "I don't see as I can do with anything short of a new stock, lock, and barrel ; that ought to set it up again." "Why," said the smith, "you had better have a new gun altogether." "Ah !" was the reply, "I never thought of that ; and it strikes me that's just what I do want. A new stock, lock, and barrel ; why that's about equal to a new gun altogether, and that's what I'll have." Just the sort of repairing that man's nature requires. The old nature cast aside as a complete wreck and good for nothing, and a *new* one imparted.

RELIGION—Must be Personal.

" A LITTLE girl, whom we will call Ellen, was some time ago helping to nurse a sick gentleman, whom she loved very dearly. One day he said to her, ' Ellen, it is time for me to take my medicine, I think. Will you pour it out for me? You must measure just a table-spoonful, and then put it in that wine-glass close by.' Ellen quickly did so, and brought it to his bedside ; but, instead of taking it in his own hand, he quietly said, ' Now, dear, will you drink it for me?' ' Me drink it ! What do you mean? I am sure I would, in a minute, if it would cure you all the same ; but you know it won't do you any good, unless you take it yourself.' ' Won't it, really? No, I suppose it will not. But, Ellen, if you can't take my medicine for me, I can't take your salvation for you. You must go to Jesus, and believe in him for yourself.' In this way he tried to teach her that each human being must seek salvation for himself, and repent, and believe, and obey, *for himself.*"

RELIGION—Taken upon Trust.

IT is a preposterous thing that men can venture their souls where they will not venture their money ; for they will take their religion upon trust, but would not trust a synod about the goodness of half-a-crown.— *William Penn.*

RELIGIOUS LIFE—Not mere Imitation.

" AT one of the late grand reviews in Eastern Prussia, says a German paper, a brigade of artillery was ordered to pass at full gallop over a piece of uneven ground, intersected by a ditch full of water. One of the guns, from the horses not making a sufficient spring, got stuck in the ditch. The first gunner, a man of great strength, jumped down into the water and, setting his shoulders to one of the wheels, lifted it out of the mud, and, resuming his seat, the gun crossed the ditch. Prince Augustus, of Prussia, who came up at the moment, cried, ' Bravo, my lad,' and tearing off a strip from his sash, gave it to the artilleryman, telling him to fasten it to his sword-belt in remembrance. In the evening, the soldier, when in his barracks, was surprised by receiving a gratuity of 150 golden crowns. A short time afterwards, another artilleryman having heard this anecdote, wished in his turn to display his strength. Prince Augustus, when one day at the arsenal of Berlin, ordered a 24-pounder to be mounted on its carriage. The man in question immediately raised the piece from the ground, and, unassisted, put it on its carriage. The prince, however, said, ' This man is a fool : he has risked his limbs, and wasted his strength without any necessity. Let him be under arrest for three days.' "

Thus, *Galignani's Messenger* furnishes us with a warning against being mere copyists. An action may from the time and circumstances be noble and praiseworthy in one man, but another would render himself ridiculous who, forgetting the surrounding circumstances, should merely repeat the action itself. True grace, like a truly soldierly spirit, guides its possessor as emergencies arise, but that mimicry of religion which only follows precedents is to be despised.

REMEMBRANCE—How to be Had in.

SIR BERNARD BURKE thus touchingly writes in his *Vicissitudes of Families :*—" In 1850 a pedigree research caused me to pay a visit to the village of Fyndern, about five miles south-west of Derby. I sought for the ancient hall. Not a stone remained to tell where it had stood ! I entered the church. Not a single record of a Finderne was there! I accosted a villager, hoping to glean some stray traditions of the Findernes. 'Findernes!' said he, 'we have no Findernes here, but we have something that once belonged them : we have *Findernes' flowers.*' 'Show them me,' I replied, and the old man led me into a field which still retained faint traces of terraces and foundations. 'There,' said he, pointing to a bank of 'garden flowers grown wild,' 'there are the Findernes' flowers, brought by Sir Geoffrey from the Holy Land, and do what we will, they will never die!'"

So be it with each of us. Should our names perish, may the truths we taught, the virtues we cultivated, the good works we initiated, live on and blossom with undying energy,

> " When time his withering hand hath laid
> On battlement and tower."

REPENTANCE—Must be Real.

THE gondoliers at Venice, when we were sojourning in that queen of the Adriatic, frequently quarrelled with each other, and used such high words and ferocious gestures that we were afraid murder would come of it ; yet they never came to blows, it was only their rough way of disputing. Often and often have we heard men upbraiding themselves for their sins, and crying out against the evil which their follies have wrought them, yet these very people have continued in their transgressions, and have even gone from bad to worse. They barked too much at sin to fall to and destroy it. Their enmity to evil was mere feigning; like the sword-play of the stage, which looks like earnest fight, but no wounds are given or received. Let those who play at repentance remember that they who repent in mimicry shall go to hell in reality.

REPENTANCE—(Thorough)—Searches Out Sin.

WHEN a wound in a soldier's foot refuses to heal, the surgeon examines it very minutely, and manipulates every part. Each bone is there, and in its place; there is no apparent cause for the inflammation, but yet the wound refuses to heal. The surgeon probes and probes again, until his lancet comes into contact with a hard foreign substance. " Here it is," saith he, " a bullet is lodged here ; this must come out, or the wound will never close." Thus may some concealed sin work long disquiet in a seeking soul. May the Lord search us and try us, and see if there be any evil way in us, and lead us in the way everlasting.

REPROOFS—to be Given in Love.

PREACHING on John xiii. 14—the duty of disciples to wash one another's feet—Mr. Finlayson, of Helmsdale, observed, " One way in which disciples wash one another's feet is by reproving one another. But the reproof must not be couched in angry words, so as to destroy the effect ; nor in tame, so as to fail of effect. Just as in washing a brother's feet, you must not use boiling water to scald, nor frozen water to freeze them."

RESIGNATION—Sustained by Faith.

THE habit of resignation is the root of peace. A godly child had a ring given him by his mother, and he greatly prized it, but on a sudden he unhappily lost his ring, and he cried bitterly. Recollecting himself, he stepped aside and prayed ; after which his sister laughingly said to him, " Brother, what is the good of praying about a ring—will praying bring back your ring ?" " No, sister," said he, "perhaps not, but praying has done this for me, it has made me quite willing to do without the ring, if it is God's will ; and is not that almost as good as having it ?" Thus faith quiets us by resignation, as a babe is hushed in his mother's bosom. Faith makes us quite willing to do without the mercy which once we prized ; and when the heart is content to be without the outward blessing, it is as happy as it would be with it ; for it is at rest.

RESIGNATION—Want of, Rebuked.

A LADY who had lost a beloved child, was so oppressed with grief, that she even secluded herself from the society of her own family, and kept herself locked in her chamber, but was at length prevailed on by her husband to come down stairs, and take a walk in the garden. While there, she stooped to pluck a flower; but her husband appeared as though he would hinder her. She plaintively said, "What! deny a flower!" He replied, "You have denied God your flower, and surely you ought not to think it hard in me to deny you mine." The lady suitably felt the gentle reproof, and had reason to say, "A word spoken in season, how good is it!"

RESOLUTION—Overcoming Difficulties.

LOOK at that bare perpendicular mountain side—why, it is worse than perpendicular, it overhangs the lake; yet the bold Tyrolese have carried a road right along the bald face of the rock, by blasting out a gallery, or, as it looks from below, by chiselling out a groove. One would have readily written down that feat as impossible, and yet the road is made, and we have travelled it from Riva into the Tyrol, the Lago Garda lying far below our feet. Henceforth that road shall be to us a cheering memory when our task is more than usually difficult. *If anything ought to be done it shall be done.* With God in front, we shall soon leave difficulties in the rear, transformed into memorials of victory.

RESPONSIBILITY.

JOHN BROWN, of Haddington, said to a young minister, who complained of the smallness of his congregation, "It is as large a one as you will want to give account for in the day of judgment." The admonition is appropriate; not to ministers alone, but to all teachers.

RESURRECTION.

The doctrine of the resurrection is full of joy to the bereaved. It clothes the grave with flowers, and wreathes the tomb with unfading laurel. The sepulchre shines with a light brighter than the sun, and death grows fair, as we say, in full assurance of faith, " I know that my brother shall rise again." Rent from the ignoble shell the pearl is gone to deck the crown of the Prince of Peace ; buried beneath the sod the seed is preparing to bloom in the King's garden. Altering a word or two of Beattie's verse we may even now find ourselves singing :

" 'Tis night and the landscape is lovely no more :
    Yet ye beautiful woodlands I mourn not for you ;
For morn is approaching your charms to restore,
    Perfumed with fresh fragrance, and glittering with dew :
Nor yet for the ravage of winter I mourn ;
    Kind nature the embryo blossom will save ;
The spring shall yet visit the mouldering urn ;
    The day shall yet dawn on the night of the grave."

REVIVAL—Absence and Presence of.

THE decline of a revival is a great testing season. It discovers the true believers by chilling the false. A frosty night or two suffices to nip all the exotic plants of a garden; but the hardy shrubs, the true natives of the soil, live on even in the severest cold. Converts raised in the hot-bed of excitement soon droop and die if the spiritual temperature of the church falls below summer heat : what are these worth compared with the hardy children of divine grace, whose inward life will continue in enduring vigour when all around is dead ! Yet we do not desire to see the revival spirit droop among us, for even the evergreens of our garden delight in a warmer season, for then they send forth their shoots and clothe themselves with new leaves ; and thus it will be seen

that the best of the saints are all the better for the holy glow
of the " times of refreshing."

REWARD—of Benevolence Sometimes Immediate.

OCCASIONALLY a benevolent action wrought in faith brings
with it an instantaneous recompense in kind ; therein Providence is seen as smiling upon the deed. The late John Andrew
Jones, a poor Baptist minister, whilst walking in Cheapside,
was appealed to by some one he knew for help. He had but
a shilling in the world, and poised it in his mind, to give or not
to give ? The greater distress of his acquaintance prevailed,
and he gave his all, walking away with a sweet remembrance of
the promise, " He that hath pity upon the poor, lendeth unto
the Lord, and that which he hath given, will he pay him
again." He had not gone a hundred yards further before he
met a gentleman who said, " Ah, Mr. Jones, I am glad to see
you. I have had this sovereign in my waistcoat pocket this
week past for some poor minister, and you may as well have
it." Mr. Jones was wont to add, when telling the story, " If I
had not stopped to give relief I should have missed the gentleman and the sovereign too."

RICH—Danger of the.

A HOLY woman was wont to say of the rich—" They are
hemmed round with no common misery ; they go down to
hell without thinking of it, because their staircase thither is of
gold and porphyry."

RICHES—Danger of.

CROSSING the Col D'Obbia, the mule laden with our
luggage sank in the snow, nor could it be recovered until its
load was removed ; then, but not till then, it scrambled out
of the hole it had made, and pursued its journey. It reminded
us of mariners casting out the lading into the sea to save the
vessel, and we were led to meditate upon the dangers of

Christians heavily laden with earthly possessions, and the wise way in which the gracious Father unloads them by their losses that they may be enabled to pursue their journey to heaven, and no longer sink in the snow of carnal-mindedness.

RICHES—Ruined by.

Do not be over-anxious about riches. Get as much of true wisdom and goodness as you can ; but be satisfied with a very moderate portion of this world's good. Riches may prove a curse as well as a blessing.

I was walking through an orchard, looking about me, when I saw a low tree laden more heavily with fruit than the rest. On a nearer examination, it appeared that the tree had been dragged to the very earth, and broken by the weight of its treasures. "Oh!" said I, gazing on the tree, "here lies one who has been ruined by his riches."

In another part of my walk, I came up with a shepherd, who was lamenting the loss of a sheep that lay mangled and dead at his feet. On enquiry about the matter, he told me that a strange dog had attacked the flock, that the rest of the sheep had got away through a hole in the hedge, but that the ram now dead had more wool on his back than the rest, and the thorns of the hedge held him fast till the dog had worried him. "Here is another," said I, "ruined by his riches."

At the close of my ramble, I met a man hobbling along on two wooden legs, leaning on two sticks. "Tell me," said I, "my poor fellow, how you came to lose your legs?" "Why, sir," said he, "in my younger days I was a soldier. With a few comrades I attacked a party of the enemy, and overcame them, and we began to load ourselves with spoil. My comrades were satisfied with little, but I burdened myself with as much as I could carry. We were pursued ; my companions escaped, but I was overtaken and so cruelly wounded, that I only saved my life afterwards by losing my legs. . It was a bad affair, sir ; but it is too late to repent of it now." "Ah, friend," thought I, "like the fruit tree, and the mangled sheep, you may date your downfall to your possessions. It was your riches that ruined you."

When I see so many rich people, as I do, caring so much for their bodies, and so little for their souls, I pity them from the bottom of my heart, and sometimes think there are as many ruined by riches as by poverty. "They that will be rich fall into temptation and a snare, and into many foolish and hurtful lusts, which drown men in destruction and perdition." 1 Tim. vi. 9. The prayer will suit you, perhaps, as well as it does me, "Give me neither poverty nor riches ; feed me with food convenient for me : lest I be full, and deny thee, and say, Who is the Lord? or lest I be poor, and steal, and take the name of my God in vain." Prov. xxx. 8, 9.— *Old Humphrey.*

RISING IN THE WORLD—Ambition for.

AMBITION, a good enough thing within reasonable bounds, is a very Apollyon among men, when it gets the mastery over them. Have you ever seen boys climbing a greasy pole to reach a hat or a handkerchief? If so, you will have noticed that the aspiring youths for the most part adopt plans and tricks quite as slimy as the pole ; one covers his hands with sand, another twists a knotted cord, and scarcely one climbs fairly, and he is the one boy whose chance is smallest. How plainly see we the politician's course in these young rascals ; the Right Honourable Member for the town of Corruption vies with the equally Right Honourable representative for the county of Bribery ; the most noble Conservative place-hunter will not be outdone by the Liberal office-lover ; a man must have done a world of planing and shaving, chopping and chiselling, before he can reach the Treasury Bench. Nor less so is it in the path of trade. Small dealers and great contractors eager to rise, are each in their measure to Satan

what a covey of partridges are to a sportsman, fair game if
he can but reach them.   The hasty desire to rise is the cause
of many a fall.   Those who see the glittering heaps of gold
before them are frequently in so much haste to thrust their
arms in up to the elbow among the treasure that they take
short cuts, leave the beaten road of honest labour, break
through hedges, and find themselves ere long in a ditch.   It
is hard to keep great riches without sin, and we have heard that
it is harder still to get them.   Walk warily, successful friend !
Growing wealth will prove no blessing to thee unless thou
gettest growing grace.   Prosperity destroys a fool and en-
dangers a wise man ; be on thy guard, good friend, for
whether thou be the one or the other, thy testing hour is come.

SABBATH—Need to be Awakened for.

AT Harzburg, in the Hartz Mountains, we were awakened
early in the morning, according to an ancient custom, by the
sound of a trumpet, which made us pray that when the last
trumpet sounds it may awaken us to an endless Sabbath.   It
were well if all hearts and minds heard at the dawn of the
Lord's-day, " The sound as of a trumpet," so that every
faculty might be aroused to the highest activity of holy service.
Sleepy hearing, praying, and singing are terrible ; sleepy
preaching and teaching are worse, yet how common they
are, and how needful is the trumpet at the ear of many !

SABBATH—Views of Heaven then Enjoyed.

WHEN a gentleman was inspecting a house in Newcastle,
with a view to hiring it as a residence, the landlord took him
to the upper window, expatiated on the extensive prospect,
and added, " You can see Durham Cathedral from this
window on a Sunday."   " Why on a Sunday above any other
day ?" enquired our friend, with some degree of surprise.
The reply was conclusive enough.   " Because on that day
there is no smoke from those tall chimneys."   Blessed is the

Sabbath to us when the earth-smoke of care and turmoil no longer beclouds our view ; then can our souls full often behold the goodly land, and the city of the New Jerusalem.

SAFETY OF BELIEVERS.

A BRITISH subject may be safe although surrounded by enemies in a distant land—not that he hath strength to contend alone against armed thousands, but because he is a subject of our queen. A despot on his throne, a horde of savages in their desert, have permitted a helpless traveller to pass unharmed, like a lamb among lions—although like lions looking on a lamb, they thirsted for his blood—because they knew his sovereign's watchfulness, and feared his sovereign's power. The feeble stranger has a charmed life in the midst of his enemies, because a royal arm unseen encompasses him as with a shield. The power thus wielded by an earthly throne may suggest and symbolise the perfect protection of Omnipotence. A British subject's confidence in his queen may rebuke the feeble faith of a Christian. " O thou of little faith, wherefore didst thou doubt?" What though there be fears within and fightings without, he who bought his people with his own blood cannot lose his inheritance, and will not permit any enemy to wrest from his hand the satisfaction of his soul. The man with a deceitful heart and a darkened mind, a feeble frame and a slippery way, a fainting heart and a daring foe—the man would stumble and fall : but the member of Christ's body cannot drop off ; the portion of the Redeemer cannot be wrenched from his grasp. " Ye are his." Christ is the safety of a Christian.—*W. Arnot.*

SAFETY OF FEEBLE SAINTS.

YOU can buy complete sets of all the flowers of the Alpine district at the hotel near the foot of the Rosenlaui glacier, very neatly pressed and enclosed in cases. Some of the flowers are very common, but they *must* be included, or the flora would not be completely represented. The botanist is as careful to see that the common ones are there, as he is to note that the rarer specimens are not excluded. Our blessed Lord will be sure to make a perfect collection of all the flowers of his field, and even the ordinary believer, the every-day worker, the common convert, will not be forgotten. To Jesus' eye, there is beauty in all his plants, and each one is needed to perfect the flora of Paradise. May I be found among his flowers, if only as one out of myriad daisies, who with sweet simplicity shall look up and wonder at his love for ever.

SAINTS—Preserve the World.

WE saw in Venice a picture of St. Mark and other holy champions delivering the fair city from the devil, who had resolved to raise a great storm in the Adriatic, flood the lagunes, and drown the inhabitants of the "bride of the sea." All mere legend and lie, but for all that capable of mirroring the truth that the intercession of saints and God's peculiar regard for them have oftentimes delivered the church.

SAINTS—their Real Worth.

A PIECE of plate may become battered and scratched, so that its beauty is hopelessly gone, but it loses not its real worth; put it into the scale, and its weight and not its fashion shall be the estimate of its preciousness; throw it into the melting-pot and its purity will show its actual value. So there are many outward circumstances which may spoil the public repute in which a Christian is held, but his essential preciousness remains unchanged. God values him at as high a rate as ever. His unerring balance and crucible are not guided by appearances. How content may we be to be vile in the sight of men if we are accepted of the Lord!

SAINTS—What they should be.

IN the Cathedral of St. Mark, in Venice—a marvellous building, lustrous with an Oriental splendour far beyond description—there are pillars said to have been brought from Solomon's Temple ; these are of alabaster, a substance firm and durable as granite, and yet transparent, so that the light glows through them. Behold an emblem of what all true pillars of the church should be—firm in their faith, and transparent in their character ; men of simple mould, ignorant of tortuous and deceptive ways, and yet men of strong will, not readily to be led aside, or bent from their uprightness. A few such alabaster men we know ; may the great Master-builder place more of them in his temple !

SALVATION—in Christ.

WE lately read in the papers an illustration of the way of salvation. A man had been condemned in a Spanish court to be shot, but being an American citizen and also of English birth, the consuls of the two countries interposed, and declared that the Spanish authorities had no power to put him to death. What did they do to secure his life, when their protest was not sufficient? They wrapped him up in their flags, they covered him with the Stars and Stripes and the Union Jack, and defied the executioners. " Now fire a shot if you dare, for if you do so, you defy the nations represented by those flags, and you will bring the powers of those two great empires upon you." There stood the man, and before him the soldiery, and though a single shot might have ended his life, yet he was as invulnerable as though encased in triple steel. Even so Jesus Christ has taken my poor guilty soul ever since I believed in him, and has wrapped around me the blood-red flag of his atoning sacrifice, and before God can destroy me or any other soul that is wrapped in the atonement, he must insult his Son and dishonour his sacrifice, and that he will never do, blessed be his name.

SALVATION—Near.

It is said that some years ago a vessel sailing on the
northern coast of the South American continent, was observed
to make signals of distress.   When hailed by another vessel,
they reported themselves as " Dying for water !" " Dip it
up then," was the response, "you are in the mouth of the
Amazon river." There was fresh water all around them, they
had nothing to do but to dip it up, and yet they were dying of
thirst, because they thought themselves to be surrounded by
the salt sea.   How often are men ignorant of their mercies?
How sad that they should perish for lack of knowledge!
Jesus is near the seeker even when he is tossed upon oceans of
doubt.   The sinner has but to stoop down and drink and
live; and yet he is ready to perish, as if salvation were hard to
find.

SALVATION—Theme for Thought.

I have heard of a certain divine, that he used always to
carry about with him a little book.   This tiny volume had
only three leaves in it ; and truth to tell, it contained not a
single word.   The first was a leaf of black paper, black as jet ;
the next was a leaf of red-scarlet; and the last was a leaf of
white, without spot.   Day by day he would look upon this
singular book, and at last he told the secret of what it
meant.   He said, " Here is the black leaf, that is my sin,
and the wrath of God which my sin deserves ; I look, and
look, and think it is not black enough to represent my
guilt, though it is as black as black can be.   The red leaf
reminds me of the atoning sacrifice, and the precious blood;
and I delight to look at it, and weep, and look again.
The white leaf represents my soul, as it is washed in Jesus'
blood and made white as snow." The little book was fuller of
meaning than many a learned folio.

SCEPTICS AND CONTROVERSIAL DIVINES.

THE old fable tells us of a boy who mounted a scavenger's cart with base intent to throw dirt at the moon; whereat another boy, with better intentions, but scarcely less folly, came running with a bason of water to wash the moon, and make its face clean again. Certain sceptics are for ever inventing new infidelities with which they endeavour to defile the fair face of the gospel, and many ministers forsake the preaching of Christ, and him crucified, to answer their endless quibbles : to both of these the ancient fable may be instructive.

SCHOOLS.

BY order of Government the roads in Prussia are lined on each side with fruit trees. Riding once, early in September, from Berlin to Halle, an American traveller noticed that some of the trees had a wisp of straw attached to them. He enquired of the coachman what it meant. He replied that those trees bore choice fruits, and the straw was a notice to the public not to take fruit from those trees without special permission. " I fear," said the traveller, " that in my country such a notice would be but an invitation to roguish boys to attack those very trees." *"Haben Sie keine Schules?"* (" Have you no schools?") was his significant rejoinder. Rest assured, dear reader, that next to godliness, education is the mainstay of order.

SCHOOLS.

RIDING the other day over Westminster Bridge I observed a noble bull quietly walking along, although there was a perfect hurly-burly of cabs, horses, carriages, whips and men all around him. I wondered to see the powerful beast walking so demurely, and only ceased to marvel when I noticed that a herdsman had his hand in a large ring which was inserted in the creature's nose. Here, thought I, is a parable. We ask full often, however it comes to pass that in this age of progress,

14

when all things seem to be in action, John Bull suffers him-self to be duped by priests both Romish and Anglican. It is easy to see that there is a ring in his nose, or he would never be led by the nose so readily. That ring is ignorance. Schools, especially Sabbath schools, are the best means of removing that ring. Catechise the children, let the whole population be taught; especially let the gospel be brought to bear on the rising generation, and by God's grace John Bull will be free, and his first effort will be to toss the priests and make them fly aloft like Sancho Panza in the blanket.

SCOFFER—Silenced.

"A MINISTER of the Presbyterian Church, in America, delivered a series of discourses against Infidelity, in a town in Louisiana, on the Red River, some of the citizens of which were known to be sceptical. A few days afterwards he took passage in a steamer ascending the Mississippi, and found on board several of the citizens of that town, among whom was a disciple of Tom Paine, noted as the ringleader of a band of infidels. So soon as he discovered the minister, he commenced his horrid blasphemies; and when he per-ceived him reading at one of the tables, he proposed to his companions to go with him to the opposite side of the table and listen to some stories that he had to tell upon religion and religious men which he said would annoy the old preacher. Quite a number, prompted by curiosity, gathered around him to listen to his vulgar stories and anecdotes, all of which were pointed against the Bible and its ministers. The preacher did not raise his eyes from the book which he was reading, nor appear to be in the least disconcerted by the presence of the rabble. At length the infidel walked up to him, and rudely slapping him on the shoulder, said, "Old fellow, what do you think of these things?" He calmly pointed out of the door, and said, "Do you see that beautiful landscape spread out in such quiet loveliness before you?" "Yes." "It has a variety of flowers, plants, and shrubs, that are calculated to fill the beholder with delight." " Yes." " Well, if you were to send out a dove, he would pass over that scene and see in it all that was beautiful and lovely, and delight himself in gazing at and admiring it ; but if you were to send out a buzzard over precisely the same scene, he would see in it nothing to fix his attention, unless he could find some rotten carcass that would be loathsome to all other animals, in which case he would alight and gloat upon it with exquisite pleasure." " Do you mean to compare me to a buzzard, sir," said the infidel, colouring very deeply. " I made no allusion to you, sir," said the minister, very quietly. The infidel walked off in confusion, and went by the name of " The Buzzard " during the remainder of the passage."

SCRIPTURES—and Men's Books.

THERE is gold in the rocks which fringe the Pass of the Splugen, gold even in the stones which mend the roads, but there is too little of it to be worth extracting. Alas, how like too many books and sermons ! Not so the Scriptures, they are much fine gold ; their very dust is precious.

SCRIPTURES—Reading of.

LORD BACON tells of a certain bishop who used to bathe regularly twice every day, and on being asked why he bathed thus often, replied, " Because I cannot conveniently do it three times." If those who love the Scriptures were asked why they read the Bible so often, they might honestly reply, " because we cannot find time to read it oftener." The appetite for the Word grows on that which it feeds on. We would say with Thomas à Kempis, " I would be always in a nook with a book."

SCRIPTURE—versus System.

THE late William Jay, in his " Practical Illustrations of Character," says, " What a difference must a Christian and a

minister feel, between the trammels of some systems of
divinity and the advantage of Scripture freedom, the glorious
liberty of the sons of God.   The one is the horse standing in
the street in harness, feeding indeed, but on the contents of a
bag tossed up and down; the other, the same animal in a
large, fine meadow, where he lies down in green pastures, and
feeds beside the still waters.

SELF—Watchfulness over.

AN old writer, speaking of men as stewards of God, urges
upon them as wise traders and servants to look to themselves
carefully, and take care of four houses which are under their
charge.   1.—Their *warehouse*, or heart and memory, wherein
they should store up precious things, holy affections, grateful
remembrances, celestial preparations, etc.   Without a good
stock in the warehouse there can be no good trade.   2.—Their
workhouse, or their actions, wherein they retail to others
for God's glory the grace entrusted to them ; teaching the
ignorant, comforting the poor, visiting the sick, etc.   We
must be active, or we cannot be acceptable servants.   3.—
Their *clock-house*, meaning their speech, which must always,
like a well-timed bell, speak the truth accurately ; and meaning
also their observance of time, redeeming it by promptly
doing the duties of every hour.   We must use time well, or
our spiritual gains will be small.   4.—Their *counting-house*,
or their conscience, which is to be scrupulously watched,
and no false reckonings allowed, lest we deceive our own
souls.   The Master will call for our accounts, let us keep
them honestly.

SELF-CONCEIT—its Danger.

QUINCTILIAN said of some in his time that they might have
become excellent scholars had they not been so persuaded of
their scholarship already.   Grant, most gracious God, that I
may never hold so high an opinion of my own spiritual health
as to prevent my being in very deed full of thy grace and fear!

SELF-DISSATISFACTION—a Spur.

" DURING the nine years that I was his wife," says the widow of the great artist Opie, " I never saw him satisfied with one of his productions, and often, very often, have I seen him enter my sitting-room, and throwing himself in an agony of despondence on the sofa, exclaim, ' I never, never shall be a painter as long as I live !' " It was a noble despair, such as is never felt by the self-complacent daubers of sign-boards, and it bore the panting aspirant up to one of the highest niches in the artistic annals of his country. The selfsame dissatisfaction with present attainments is a potent force to bear the Christian onward to the most eminent degree of spirituality and holiness.

SELF-EXAMINATION—its Right Office.

A HIGHLANDER who purchased a barometer under a mis-taken idea of its purpose, complained that he could not see that it had made any improvement in the weather ; and those who use signs and evidences for an intent which they will never answer, will be sure to complain that their faith is not increased, though they are always practising self-examination. Yet a barometer has its uses, and so have evidences of grace. To feel the pulse is an admirable thing ; the mistake is to put this in the place of strengthening food or tonic medicine.

SELF-RIGHTEOUSNESS—Destroyed by Conviction of Sin.

THE squirrel in his wire cage continually in motion but making no progress, reminds me of my own self-righteous efforts after salvation, but the little creature is never one half so wearied by his exertions as I was by mine. The poor chiffonier in Paris trying to earn a living by picking dirty rags out of the kennel, succeeds far better than I did in my attempts to obtain comfort by my own works. Dickens's cab-horse, which was only able to stand because it was never taken out of the shafts, was strength and beauty itself compared with my starveling hopes propped up with resolutions and regulations. Wretches condemned to the galleys in the days of the old French kings, whose only reward for incessant toils was the lash of the keeper, were in a more happy plight than I when under legal bondage. Slavery in mines where the sun never shines must be preferable to the miseries of a soul goaded by an awakened conscience to seek salvation by its own merits. Some of the martyrs were shut up in a dungeon called Little-ease ; the counterpart of that prison-house I well remember. Iron chains are painful enough, but what is the pain when the iron enters into the soul ! Tell us not of the writhings of the wounded and dying on the battle-field ; some of us, when our heart was riddled by the artillery of the law, would have counted wounds and death a happy exchange. O blessed Saviour, how blissful was the hour when all this horrid midnight of the soul was changed into the day-dawn of pardoning love !

SELF-RIGHTEOUSNESS—Ruin of Many.

"A GENTLEMAN in our late civil wars," says Cowley, "when his quarters were beaten up by the enemy, was taken prisoner, and lost his life afterwards, only by staying to put on a band, and adjust his periwig : he would escape like a person of quality, or not at all, and died the noble martyr of ceremony and gentility." Poor fool, and yet he is as bad who waits till he is dressed in the rags of his own fancied fitness before he will come to Jesus. He will die a martyr to pride and self-righteousness.

SELF-RIGHTEOUSNESS—Vanity of.

WHEN the lofty spire of Old St. Paul's was destroyed by lightning, there were many superstitious persons who were amazed beyond measure at the calamity, for in the cross there had long been deposited relics of certain saints, which were counted fully sufficient to avert all danger of tempests. With what amazement will ignorant, self-righteous sinners see their own destruction come upon them, notwithstanding all the refuges of lies in which they trusted.

SELF-SEEKING.

A CERTAIN king had a minstrel whom he commanded to play before him. It was a day of high feasting ; the cups were flowing and many great guests were assembled. The minstrel laid his fingers among the strings of his harp, and woke them all to the sweetest melody, but the hymn was to the glory of himself. It was a celebration of the exploits of song which the bard had himself performed, and told how he had excelled high-born Hoel's harp, and emulated soft Llewellyn's lay. In high-sounding strains he sang himself and all his glories. When the feast was over, the harper said to the monarch, " O king, give me thy guerdon ; let the minstrel's mede be paid." Then the monarch replied, " Thou hast sung unto thyself, pay thyself ; thine own praises were thy theme ; be thyslf the paymaster." The harper cried, " Did I not sing sweetly ? O king, give me thy gold !" But the king answered, "So much the worse for thy pride, that thou shouldst lavish such sweetness upon thyself. Get thee gone, thou shalt not serve in my train."

If a man should grow grey-headed in the performance of good works, yet when at the last it is known that he has done them all for himself, that he may be honoured thereby, his Lord will say, " Thou hast done well enough in the eyes of man, but so much the worse, because thou didst it only to thyself, that thine own praises might be sung, and that thine own name might be extolled."

SERMONS—Bad, Not to be Listened to.

SOME sermons are not to be listened to at all, just as some meats are not to be eaten. Against the siren's song the only safety was deaf ears. Only a gross simpleton would leap into a pit full of rattlesnakes to see if they would do him any harm ; a wise man is content to leave the experiment untried. Despite the usual fashion of this age, which runs greedily after cleverness even when associated with the most poisonous sentiments, we affirm that it is a participation in other men's sins to assist in furnishing an auditory for deceivers. Mere talent ought not to attract us ; carrion, well dressed and served upon Palissy ware, is still unfit for men. Who thrusts his arm into the fire because its flame is brilliant? Who knowingly drinks from a poisoned cup because the beaded bubbles on the brim reflect the colours of the rainbow? As we would not be fascinated by the azure hues of a serpent, so neither should we be thrown off our guard by the talents of an unsound theologian. To hear or read sufficiently to judge, is allowable to the man who, by reason of use, has had his senses exercised to discern, and whose business it is to warn others ; but where error is manifest upon the surface, to expose our minds to its pernicious influence is as great a madness as to test the strength of the fever by lying in its lair. Godly, scriptural teaching is surely not so rare that we need go down to Egypt for help ; there are streams enough in Israel without our drinking of the polluted water of Sihor.

SERMONS—Brilliant but Useless.

SIR ASTLEY COOPER, on visiting Paris, was asked by the surgeon *en chef* of the empire how many times he had performed a certain wonderful feat of surgery. He replied that he had performed the operation thirteen times. "Ah, but, monsieur, I have done him one hundred and sixty time. How many times did you save his life?" continued the curious Frenchman, after he had looked into the blank amazement of Sir Astley's face. "I," said the Englishman, "saved eleven out of the thirteen. How many did you save out of one hundred and sixty ?" "Ah, monsieur, I lose dem all ; but de operation was very *brilliant.*"

Of how many popular ministries might the same verdict be given ! Souls are not saved, but the preaching is very brilliant. Thousands are attracted and operated on by the rhetorician's art, but what if he should have to say of his admirers, " I lose them all, but the sermons were very brilliant !"

SERMONS—Must be Full of Christ.

"I HAVE had to interline your sermon all through and through with the name of Christ," was the criticism which an aged parishioner once passed upon the discourse of a young pastor. Said the lamented M'Cheyne, " Some speculate on doctrines *about* the gospel, rather than preach the gospel itself." " I see a man cannot be a faithful minister, until he preaches Christ for Christ's sake."—*Christian Treasury.*

SERMONS—Must have the Gospel in them.

A FRIEND called on the Rev. T. Charles, of Bala, on Sunday afternoon, September 11, 1814, after having been in church. "Well," said he, "how did you like Mr. M——? Was there enough of gospel in the sermon to save a sinner? If not, it was of little consequence what was preached. I hope Bala people will never take up with anything short of that."

SERVANTS (GOD'S)—their Ruling Motive.

YOU cannot serve two masters—you *must* serve one or other. If your work is first with you, and your fee second, work is your master, and the Lord of work, who is God. But if your fee is first with you, and your work second, fee is your master, and the lord of fee, who is the devil ; and not only the devil, but the lowest of devils—"the least erected fiend that fell." So there you have it in brief terms—work first, you are God's servants ; fee first, you are the fiend's. And it

makes a difference, now and ever, believe me, whether you
serve him who has on his vesture and thigh written, " King
of kings," and whose service is perfect freedom ; or him on
whose vesture and thigh the name is written, " Slave of
slaves," and whose service is perfect slavery.—*John Ruskin.*

SERVICE—Christian to be ever Ready for.

BRUTUS visiting Ligarius found him ill, and said, " What,
sick, Ligarius?" " No, Brutus," said he, "if thou hast any
noble enterprise in hand, I am well." So should the believer
say of Christ ; what might excuse us from other labour shall
never prevent our engaging in *his* service.

SERVICE—Preparations for.

"METHOUGHT I looked and saw the Master standing,
and at his feet lay an earthen vessel. It was not broken,
not unfitted for service, yet there it lay, powerless and useless,
until he took it up. He held it awhile, and I saw that he
was filling it, and anon, I beheld him walking in his garden,
whither he had 'gone down to gather lilies.' The earthen
vessel was yet again in his hand, and with it he watered his
beauteous plants, and caused their odours to be shed forth
yet more abundantly. Then I said to myself, ' Sorrowing
Christian, hush! hush! peace, be still! thou art this earthen
vessel; powerless, it is true, yet not broken, still fit for the
Master's use. Sometimes thou mayst be laid aside altogether from active service, and the question may arise, what
is the Master doing with me now? Then may a voice speak
to thine inmost heart, ' he is filling the vessel, yes, only filling
it ready for use.' Dost thou ask in what manner? Nay, be
silent. Is it not all too great an honour for thee to be used
by him at all? Be content, whether thou art employed in
watering the lilies, or in washing the feet of the saints.'
Truly, it is a matter of small moment. Enough, surely
enough, for an earthen vessel to be in the Master's hands,
and employed in the Master's service."

SERVICE—the Road to Honour.

WHEN the Spartan king advanced against the enemy, he had always with him some one that had been crowned in the public games of Greece. And they tell us, that a Lacedæmonian, when large sums were offered him on condition that he would not enter the Olympic lists, refused them. Having with much difficulty thrown his antagonists in wrestling, one put this question to him, " Spartan, what will you get by this victory?" He answered with a smile, "*I shall have the honour to fight foremost in the ranks of my prince.*" The honour which appertains to office in the church of God lies mainly in this—that the man who is set apart for such service has the privilege of being first in holiness of example, abundance of liberality, patience of longsuffering, zeal in effort, and self-sacrifice in service. Thou gracious King of kings, if thou hast made me a minister or deacon in thy church, enable me to be foremost in every good word and work, shunning no sacrifice, and shrinking from no suffering.

SERVICE OF GOD—to be Constant.

LOOK at yon miller on the village hill. How does he grind his grist? Does he bargain that he will only grind in the west wind, because its gales are so full of health? No, but the east wind, which searches joints and marrow, makes the millstones revolve, and together with the north and the south it is yoked to his service. Even so should it be with you who are true workers for God ; all your ups and your downs, your successes and your defeats, should be turned to the glory of God.

SERVICE OF GOD—the Honour of.

OF the old hero the minstrel sang—

> " With his Yemen sword for aid ;
> Ornament it carried none,
> But the notches on the blade."

What nobler decoration of honour can any godly man seek after than his scars of service, his losses for the cross, his reproaches for Christ's sake, his being worn out in his Master's service!

SERVING GOD—the Sure Reward of.

WHEN Calvin was banished from ungrateful Geneva, he said, "Most assuredly if I had merely served man, this would have been a poor recompense; but it is my happiness that I have served him who never fails to reward his servants to the full extent of his promise."

SHAMS.

WHAT multitudes of mahogany-handled drawers there are to be met with in daily life labelled in black on a gold ground, with swelling and mysterious names of precious healing drugs; but, alas! they are handles which do not pull out, or drawers that are full of nothing. What myriads of empty bottles make up yonder *enormous stock* in the Universal Emporium so largely advertised! What a noble army of canisters filled with air stand marshalled in shining ranks, as if they were fresh from China, and brimming with the fragrant leaf! Now in mere business such things may answer well enough; but bring them into your moral dealings, and you shall soon become contemptible. One smiles at the busy tradesman arranging the shams in his window, but we are indignant with men who exhibit unreal virtues and excellences; he thinks that he makes a fair show in the flesh, but when we have found him out once, even what may be genuine in him is subjected to suspicion, and the man's honour is hopelessly gone.

SIN.

THOSE who give themselves up to the service of sin, enter the palace of pleasure by wide portals of marble, which conceal the low wicket behind which leads into the fields, where they are in a short time sent to feed swine.—*James D. Burns.*

SIN.

ONE danger of secret sin is that a man cannot commit it without being by-and-by betrayed into a public sin. If a man commit one sin, it is like the melting of the lower glacier upon the Alps, the others must follow in time. As certainly as you heap one stone upon the cairn to-day, the next day you will cast another, until the heap reared stone by stone shall become a very pyramid. See the coral insect at work, you cannot decree where it shall stay its pile. It will not build its rock as high as you please ; it will not stay until an island shall be created. Sin cannot be held in with bit and bridle, it must be mortified.

SIN—Aroused by the Law.

A CONTENTED citizen of Milan, who had never passed beyond its walls during the course of sixty years, being ordered by the governor not to stir beyond its gates, became immediately miserable, and felt so powerful an inclination to do that which he had so long contentedly neglected, that on his application for a release from this restraint being refused, he became quite melancholy, and at last died of grief. How well this illustrates the apostle's confession that he had not known lust, unless the law had said unto him, " Thou shalt not covet !" " Sin," saith he, " taking occasion by the commandment, wrought in me all manner of concupiscence." Evil often sleeps in the soul, until the holy command of God is discovered, and then the enmity of the carnal mind rouses itself to oppose in every way the will of God. " Without the law," says Paul, " sin was dead." How vain to hope for salvation from the law, when through the perversity of sin, it provokes our evil hearts to rebellion, and works in us neither repentance nor love.

SIN—may be Committed by Proxy.

ACCORDING to an old writer, no Capuchin among the Papists may take or touch silver. This metal is as great an anathema to them as the wedge of gold to Achan, at the offer whereof they start back as Moses from the serpent ; yet the monk has a boy behind him who will receive and carry home any quantity, and neither complain of metal nor measure. Such are those who are great sticklers themselves for outward observance in religion, but at the same time compel their servants to sin on their account. They who sin by substitute shall be damned in person.

SIN—its Encroaching Nature.

WHEN a sin is let in as a suppliant, it remains in as a tyrant. The Arabs have a fable of a miller who one day was startled by a camel's nose thrust in the window of the room where he was sleeping. " It is very cold outside," said the camel, " I only want to get my nose in." The nose was let in, then the neck, and finally the whole body. Presently the miller began to be extremely inconvenienced at the ungainly companion he had obtained in a room certainly not big enough for both. " If you are inconvenienced you may leave," said the camel ; " as for myself, I shall stay where I am." There are many such camels knocking at the human heart. Take, for instance, compliance with a single worldly custom—dancing. First, the custom creeps humbly to the door of the heart, and says, " Let me in ; what am I but putting one foot before another ? certainly *you* do not object to music, and *I* would not for the world have a full band." So in comes the nose of the camel, and it is not long before the entire body follows. The Christian then finds his heart occupied in full figure by the very vice which a little while before peeped in so meekly. " Being up," it says to him, " all night at a ball, with the eyes dazzled by lights, and the ears stunned with a full band, interferes, you say, with your private devotions. So it does. But your private devotions will have to go, for I will not."—*Episcopal Recorder.*

SIN—its Hardening Effects.

DR. PRESTON tells us of a professor who on one occasion was found drunk, and when much depressed on account of his folly, the devil said to him, by way of temptation, "Do it again, do it again ; for," said he, "the grief you feel about it now you will never feel any more if you commit the sin again." Dr. Preston says that the man yielded to the temptation, and from that time he never did feel the slightest regret at his drunkenness, and lived and died a confirmed sot, though formerly he had been a very high professor.

SIN—How to Overcome.

Sin is to be overcome, not so much by maintaining a direct opposition to it, as by cultivating opposite principles. Would you kill the weeds in your garden, plant it with good seed: if the ground be well occupied there will be less need of the labour of the hoe. If a man wished to quench fire, he might fight it with his hands till he was burnt to death; the only way is to apply an opposite element.—*Andrew Fuller.*

SIN—Insidious Nature of.

IN the gardens of Hampton Court you will see many trees entirely vanquished and well nigh strangled by huge coils of ivy, which are wound about them like the snakes around the unhappy Laocoon : there is no untwisting the folds, they are too giant-like, and fast fixed, and every hour the rootlets of the climber are sucking the life out of the unhappy tree. Yet there was a day when the ivy was a tiny aspirant, only asking a little aid in climbing ; had it been denied then, the tree had never become its victim, but by degrees the humble weakling grew in strength and arrogance, and at last it assumed the mastery, and the tall tree became the prey of the creeping, insinuating destroyer. The moral is too obvious. Sorrowfully do we remember many noble characters which have been ruined little and little by insinuating habits. Drink has been the ivy in many cases. Reader, see to it, lest some slowly advancing sin overpower you : men who are murdered by slow poisoning die just as surely as those who take arsenic.

SIN—Loathed by a Christian.

AN Arminian arguing with a Calvinist remarked, " If I believed your doctrine, and were sure that I was a converted man, I would take my fill of sin." " How much sin," replied the godly Calvinist, " do you think it would take to fill a true Christian to his own satisfaction?" Here he hit the nail on the head. " How can we that are dead to sin live any longer therein?" A truly converted man hates sin with all his heart, and even if he could sin without suffering for it, it would be misery enough to him to sin at all.

SIN—Man's Readiness to Invent Excuse for.

A TRAVELLER in Venezuela illustrates the readiness of men to lay their faults on the locality, or on anything rather than themselves, by the story of a hard drinker who came home one night in such a condition that he could not for some time find his hammock. When this feat was accomplished, he tried in vain to get off his big riding-boots. After many fruitless efforts he lay down in his hammock, and soliloquised aloud, " Well, I have travelled all the world over ; I lived five years in Cuba, four in Jamaica, five in Brazil, I have travelled through Spain and Portugal, and been in Africa, but I never yet was in such an abominable country as this, where a man is obliged to go to bed with his boots on."

Commonly enough are we told by evildoers in excuse for their sins that no man could do otherwise were he in their position, that there is no living at their trade honestly, that in such a street shops must be open on a Sunday, that their health required an excursion to Brighton on the Sabbath because their labours were so severe, that nobody could be religious in the house in which they were engaged, and so on, all to the same effect, and about as truthful as the soliloquy of the drunkard of Venezuela.

SIN—One, the Soul's Ruin.

THERE was but one crack in the lanthorn, and the wind has found it out and blown out the candle. How great a mischief one unguarded point of character may cause us! One spark blew up the magazine and shook the whole country for miles around. One leak sank the vessel and drowned all on board. One wound may kill the body ; one sin destroy the soul.

SIN—One, the Soul's Ruin.

WHILE I was walking in the garden one bright morning, a breeze came through and set all the flowers and leaves a fluttering. Now that is the way flowers talk, so I pricked up my ears and listened.

Presently, an old elder tree said, Flowers, shake off your caterpillars !"

" Why ?" said a dozen altogether—for they were like some children, who always say " Why," when they are told to do anything—bad children those!

The elder said, " If you don't, tney'll eat you up alive."

So the flowers set themselves a shaking till the caterpillars were shaken off.

In one of the middle beds there was a beautiful rose, who shook off all but one, and she said to herself, " Oh, that's a beauty ! I'll keep that one."

The elder overheard her, and called out, " One caterpillar is enough to spoil you."

15

" But," said the rose, " look at his brown and crimson fur, and his beautiful black eyes, and scores of little feet ; I want to keep *him;* surely *one* won't hurt me."

A few mornings after, I passed the rose again ; there was not a whole leaf on her ; her beauty was gone ; she was all but killed, and had only life enough to weep over her folly, while the tears stood like dew-drops on her tattered leaves. " Alas! I didn't think one caterpillar would ruin me."—*C. A. Davis.*

SIN—Power over the Unregenerate.

So long as a man is dead in trespasses and sin, there is no iniquity which may not get the mastery of him. Where the body is, thither will the vultures of hell be gathered together. The devil finding him dead, calls up his hosts of temptations and his bands of evils to feed on him. The great destroyer, who at other times is as a lion, often plays the part of a jackal, whose cry, when it finds its prey, is said to sound exactly like the words—

> "Dead Hindōō, dead Hindōō !
> Whĕre, whĕre, whĕre, whĕre ?
> Here, here, here, here !"

Nothing but the new life can secure a man from the worst fiends in the Pandemonium of vice, for they gather like a scattered pack to a feast when they hear their master cry—

> Dead sinner, dead sinner !
> Where, where, where, where ?
> Here, here, here, here!

Vices seldom come alone ; where there is room for one devil, seven other spirits more wicked than himself will find a lodging. We may say of sins as Longfellow of birds of prey, in his song of Hiawatha :—

> " Never stoops the soaring vulture
> On his quarry in the desert,

On the sick or wounded bison,
But another vulture watching,
From his high aërial look-out
Sees the downward plunge and follows ;
And a third pursues the second,
Coming from the invisible ether,
First a speck, and then a vulture
Till the air is dark with pinions."

SIN—Punishment of.

WHAT a diabolical invention was the " Virgin's kiss," once used by the fathers of the Inquisition ! The victim was pushed forward to kiss the image, when, lo, its arms enclosed him in a deadly embrace, piercing his body with a hundred hidden knives. The tempting pleasures of sin offer to the unwary just such a virgin's kiss. The sinful joys of the flesh lead, even in this world, to results most terrible, while in the world to come the daggers of remorse and despair will cut and wound beyond all remedy.

SIN—the Toil of it.

HENRY WARD BEECHER says, " There was a man in the town where I was born who used to steal all his firewood. He would get up on cold nights and go and take it from his neighbours' wood-piles. A computation was made, and it was ascertained that he spent more time and worked harder to get his fuel, than he would have been obliged to if he had earned it in an honest way, and at ordinary wages. And this thief is a type of thousands of men who work a great deal harder to please the devil than they would have to work to please God."

SIN—its Wide Consequences.

SAGES of old contended that no sin was ever committed whose consequences rested on the head of the sinner alone ;

that no man could do ill and his fellows not suffer. They
illustrated it thus :—"A vessel sailing from Joppa, carried a
passenger, who, beneath his berth, cut a hole through the
ship's side.   When the men of the watch expostulated with
him, "What doest thou, O miserable man?" the offender
calmly replied, "What matters it to you?   The hole I have
made lies under my own berth."

This ancient parable is worthy of the utmost consideration.
No man perishes alone in his iniquity ; no man can guess the
full consequences of his transgressions.

SINS—the most Attractive, the most Deadly.

IT is notable that nearly all the poisonous fungi are
scarlet or speckled, and the wholesome ones brown or grey, as
if to show us that things rising out of darkness and decay are
always most deadly when they are well dressed.—*Ruskin.*

SINS—Home-born, our Worst Foes.

THE old proverb hath it, "Here's talk of the Turk and
the Pope, but 'tis my next neighbour that does me the most
harm."   It is neither popery nor infidelity that we have half
so much cause to dread as our own besetting sins.   We want
more Protestants against sin, more Dissenters from carnal
maxims, and more Nonconformists to the world.   Our own
besetting sins require far more of our watchfulness than State
blunders or ecclesiastical abuses.

SINS—How Men Treat them.

WHAT swarms of rabbits the traveller sees on the commons
and fields near Leatherhead (in Surrey), and yet a few miles
further on at Wootton one scarcely sees a single specimen of
that prolific race.   The creature is indigenous to both places,
but at Leatherhead he is tolerated and therefore multiplies,
while at the other places the gamekeepers diligently shoot
down all they see.   Sins are natural to all men, but it makes

all the difference whether they are fostered or kept under; the carnal mind makes itself a warren for evil, but a gracious spirit wages constant war with every transgression.

SINNERS—their Company to be Avoided.

WHEN a man is known to suffer from a sadly contagious disease, none of his friends will come near the house. There is little need to warn them off, they are all too alarmed to come near. Why is it men are not as much afraid of the contagion of vice? How dare they run risks for themselves and children by allowing evil companions to frequent their house? Sin is as infectious and far more deadly than the small-pox or fever. Flee, then, from every one who might lead you into it.

SINNERS—Madness of.

A RECENT traveller, relating the incidents of his voyage to India, writes :—" Flocks of greedy albatrosses, petrels, and Cape pigeons, crowded around the ship's stern.. A hook was baited with fat, when upwards of a dozen albatrosses instantly rushed at it, and as one after another was being hauled on deck, the remainder, regardless of the struggles of the captured, and the vociferations of the crew, kept swimming about the stern. Not even did those birds which were indifferently hooked and made their escape, desist from seizing the bait a second time." Thus to the letter do ungodly men rush at the baits of Satan; they see others perish, but remain careless, and even when they are all but destroyed themselves they persist in their infatuation.

SLANDER.

WE saw in the Museum at Venice an instrument with which one of the old Italian tyrants was accustomed to shoot poisoned needles at the objects of his wanton malignity : we thought of gossips, backbiters, and secret slanderers, and

wished that their mischievous devices might come to a speedy
end.   Their weapons of innuendo, shrug, and whisper, appear
to be as insignificant as needles, but the venom which they
instil is deadly to many a reputation.

SLANDER—to be Despised.

ONE of our ancient nobility had inscribed over his castle
gate these words, which we commend to all persons who are
thin-skinned in the matter of private gossip or public opinion.

> THEY SAY.
> WHAT DO THEY SAY?
> LET THEM SAY.

SLANDER—How to Overcome it.

SOME person reported to the amiable poet Tasso that a
malicious enemy spoke ill of him to all the world.   " Let him
persevere," said Tasso, " his rancour gives me no pain. How
much better is it that he should speak ill of me to all the
world, than that all the world should speak ill of me to him."

SLANDER—Rebuked.

THE Rev. B. Jacobs, of Cambridgeport, could, when
necessary, administer reproof very forcibly, though the gentleness of his character was always seen in the manner in
which it was done.   Some young ladies at his house were one
day talking about one of their female friends.   As he entered
the room, he heard the epithets " odd," " singular," &c.,
applied.   He asked and was told the name of the young lady
in question, and then said, very gravely, " Yes, she is an odd
young lady ; she is a *very* odd young lady ; I consider her
extremely singular."   He then added very impressively, " She
was never heard to speak ill of an absent friend."   The
rebuke was not forgotten by those who heard it.

SMOOTH PLACES—Peril of.

After crossing the Grimsel, on the way down towards Handeck, the traveller traverses a road cut in red marble, so smoothly polished that, even when it is divested of its usual thin coating of snow, it is dangerous in the extreme. Notwithstanding that steps are hewn, and rough marks made across the granite, he would be foolhardy who should try to ride along the slippery way, which is called Helle Platte, or Hell Place, for reasons which glisten on its surface. " Dismount," is the word, and none are slow to obey it. There are many such Hell Places on the road to the celestial city— smooth places of pleasure, ease, flattery, self-content, and the like ; and it will be the wisest course if any pilgrim has been fond of riding the high horse, for him to dismount at once and walk humbly with his God. That enchanted ground of which Bunyan tells us that the air naturally tended to make one drowsy, is just the spot to which we refer ; men had need be watchful whose path lies through that deceitful country.

It has been said that in a calm sea every man is a pilot, but we take leave to doubt it ; calms have dangers quite unknown to storms, and rocks and quicksands are none the less perilous because the deceitful sea which covers them smiles softly on the mariner. Not to be tempted is a great temptation. Safety breeds carelessness, and carelessness is the mother of ruin. When Mansoul was at peace, Mr. Carnal-security invited her citizens to his fatal feasts, and the Prince Immanuel withdrew himself ; let the result warn us against a repetition of the evil.

80—"God so Loved," etc.

PLINY declares that Cicero once saw the Iliad of Homer written in so small a character that it could be contained in a nutshell. Peter Bales a celebrated caligrapher, in the days of Queen Elizabeth, wrote the whole Bible so that it was shut

up in a common walnut as its casket. In these days of
advanced mechanism even greater marvels in miniature have
been achieved, but never has so much meaning been com-
pressed into so small a space as in that famous little word
" So," in the text which tells us that " God so loved the
world, that he gave his only begotten Son, that whosoever
believeth in him should not perish, but have everlasting life."

SORROW—Benefit of.

TWO seeds lie before us—the one is warmed in the sun, the
other falls from the sower's hand into the cold dark earth, and
there it lies buried beneath the soil.   That seed which suns
itself in the noontide beam may rejoice in the light in which
it basks, but it is liable to be devoured by the bird ; and
certainly nought can come of it, however long it may linger
above ground ; but the other seed, hidden beneath the clods
in a damp, dark sepulchre, soon swells, germinates, bursts its
sheath, upheaves the mould, springs up a green blade, buds,
blossoms, becomes a flower, exhales perfume, and loads the
wings of every wind.   Better far for the seed to pass into the
earth and die, than to lie in the sunshine and produce no
fruit ; and even thus for thee the future in its sorrow shall be
as a sowing in a fertile land ; tears shall moisten thee, grace
shall increase within thee, and thou shalt grow up in the likeness of thy Lord unto perfection of holiness, to be such a
flower of God's own planting as even angels shall delight
to gaze upon in the day of thy transplanting to celestial soil.

SORROW—for Sin, Absorbing.

WHEN that famous statesman Mirabeau died, all France
bewailed his loss, and men for some hours could think or
speak of little else.   A waiter in one of the Restaurants of
the Palais Royal, after the manner of his race, saluted a
customer with the usual remark, " Fine weather, Monsieur,"

" Yes, my friend," replied the other, " very fine; but Mirabeau
is dead."

If one absorbing thought can thus take precedence of every
other in the affairs of life, is it so very wonderful that men
aroused to care for the life to come should be altogether
swallowed up with grief at the dread discovery that they are
by reason of sin condemned of God? Fine or foul may the
weather be, but if the soul be under the wrath of God its
woeful condition will make it careless of surroundings. If his
former security be dead, and the fear of coming judgment be
alive in the man's heart, it is little wonder if eating and drinking be forgotten, if sleep forsake his eyelids and even household joys become insipid. Let but the one emotion be great
enough, and it will push out every other. The bitterness of
spiritual grief will destroy both the honey of earthly bliss and
the quassia of bodily pain.

SORROWS—Leading to Conversion.

AUGUSTINE says that his God was "mercifully rigorous"
to him, besprinkling with most bitter alloy all his unlawful
pleasures, " that he might seek pleasures without alloy."

SOUL—Needing Something to Cling to.

THE soul of man is a clasping, clinging soul, seeking to
something over which it can spread itself, and by means of
which it can support itself. And just as in a neglected garden
you may see the poor creepers making shift to sustain themselves as. best they can ; one convolvulus twisting round
another, and both draggling on the ground ; a clematis
leaning on the door, which will by-and-by open and let the
whole mass fall down ; a vine or a passion-flower wreathing
round a prop which all the while chafes and cuts it ; so in
this fallen world it is mournful to see the efforts which human
souls are making to get some sufficient object to lean upon
and twine around.—*James Hamilton, D.D.*

SOULS—Care for.

IN Switzerland, where land is very precious because rock abounds and the rugged soil is chary in its yieldings, you see the husbandman looking after a little tuft of grass growing on one of the edges of a lofty cliff. From the valley he had caught a sight of it and thought of clambering up to where it grew, but the rock was all too steep. From a ledge nearer the top of the precipitous wall he looked down, but could see no pathway to the coveted morsel of green. That armful of grass would feed his goat, or help to fill the cottage loft with winter fodder for the cow. Every armful is an item, and he cannot forego that tempting clump. He looks, and looks, and looks again, but looks in vain. By-and-by, he fetches his bold boy who can follow wherever a chamois can climb, but the boy after a hard scramble comes back with the tidings, "Father, it cannot be done." Father's answer is, "Boy, it must be done." It is only an armful, and would not be worth a farthing to us, but to the poor mountaineer even a farthing or a farthing's worth is precious. The grass waves its flowers in the breeze and scorns the daring climbers from below ; but where there is a will, there is a way ; and what cannot be reached from below may be gained from above. With a rope slung round him, or firmly grasped in his accustomed hand, with a stout stake or tree to hold it up above, the Switzer is let down till he gets to the jutting crag, there he stands with his sickle, reaps the grass, ties it into a bundle, puts it under his arm, and climbing back again, joyfully returns with his little harvest. Poor pay, you think, for such dangerous toil ; but, fellow worker for Jesus, I wish we were as venturesome for souls, and as careful of them, as these poor peasants are concerning miserable bundles of grass. I wish that we sometimes looked up or down upon apparently inaccessible spots, and resolved to reach immortal souls who are to be found there, and pined to bring them to Christ.

SOULS—the Crisis of.

OFTEN, when travelling among the Alps, one sees a small black cross planted upon a rock, or on the brink of a torrent, or on the verge of the highway, to mark the spot where men have met with sudden death by accident. Solemn reminders these of our mortality! but they led our mind still further; for we said within us, if the places where men seal themselves for the second death could be thus manifestly indicated, what a scene would this world present! Here the memorial of a soul undone by yielding to a foul temptation, there a conscience seared by the rejection of a final warning, and yonder a heart for ever turned into stone by resisting the last tender appeal of love. Our places of worship would scarce hold the sorrowful monuments which might be erected over spots where spirits were for ever lost—spirits that date their ruin from sinning against the gospel while under the sound of it.

SOULS—Love of.

THOMAS FULLER, in his "Worthies," gives the following interesting account of one Gervase Scroop, Knight :—" He engaged with his majesty in Edgehill fight, where he received twenty-six wounds, and was left on the ground amongst the dead. Next day his son Adrian obtained leave from the king to find and fetch off his father's corpse: and his hopes pretended no higher than to a decent interment thereof.

Hearty seeking makes happy finding. Indeed, some more commended the affection than the judgment of the young gentleman, concerning such a search in vain amongst many naked bodies, with wounds disguised from themselves, and where pale death had confounded all complexions together.

However, he having some general hint of the place where his father fell, did light upon his body, which had some heat left therein. This heat was, with rubbing, within a few minutes, improved into motion; within some hours, into sense; that

sense, within a day, into speech; that speech, within certain
weeks, into a perfect recovery; living more than ten years
after, a monument of God's mercy and his son's affection."
True love to souls will seek them out with all the eagerness
of this heroic son, and, finding them, will be as persevering in
attempts to save. Not all at once shall we see all we could
wish in the objects of our holy care, but no difficulties must
daunt us; we must continue by God's grace to agonise for
their souls till we see them safe in Christ. The little awakened
interest which cheers us must be nursed into anxiety, and
through the Holy Spirit we must labour to see anxiety turned
into hope, and hope to faith and salvation. None are too far
gone for zeal and prayer. Love is ever hopeful and God is
ever gracious. Let us renew our search, and the Lord send
us good-speed to-day.

SPECULATIONS—their Folly.

WHILE a minister of my acquaintance was riding in a railway carriage, he was saluted by a member of an exceedingly
litigious and speculative sect. "Pray, sir," said the sectary,
"what is your opinion of the seven trumpets?" "I am not
sure," said the preacher, "that I understand your question,
but I hope you will comprehend mine: What think you of
the fact that your seven children are growing up without God
and without hope? You have a Bible-reading in your house
for your neighbours, but no family prayer for your children."
The nail was fastened in a sure place, enough candour of
mind remained in the professor to enable him to profit by
the timely rebuke. It were greatly to be desired that
Christians who are so much given to speculate upon the
prophecies, would turn their thoughts and leisure to the
perishing myriads by whom we are surrounded, and sow in
the fields of evangelisation rather than in the cloudland of
guess-work interpretation.

SPIRIT OF GOD—the Fire from Heaven.

SUPPOSE we saw an army sitting down before a granite fort, and they told us that they intended to batter it down, we might ask them, "How!" They point to a cannon ball. Well, but there is no power in that ; it is heavy, but not more than half-a-hundred or perhaps a hundredweight ; if all the men in the army hurled it against the fort they would make no impression. They say, "No, but look at the cannon!" Well, but there is no power in that. A child may ride upon it ; a bird may perch in its mouth. It is a machine, and nothing more. "But look at the powder." Well, there is no power in that ; a child may spill it ; a sparrow may peck it. Yet this powerless powder and powerless ball are put in the powerless cannon : one spark of fire enters it, and then, in the twinkling of an eye, that powder is a flash of lightning, and that cannon ball is a thunderbolt which smites as if it had been sent from heaven.

So is it with our church or school machinery of this day ; we have the instruments necessary for pulling down strongholds, but O for the fire from heaven !

SPIRITUAL WARMTH—How to Maintain it.

PHILIP HENRY'S advice to his daughter : "If you would keep warm in this cold season (January, 1692), take these four directions : 1. Get into the sun ; under his blessed beams ·there are warmth and comfort. 2. Go near the fire. 'Is not my word like a fire?' How many cheering passages are there ! 3. Keep in motion and action—stirring up the grace and gift of God that is in you. 4. Seek Christian communion. 'How can one be warm alone?'"

STERNNESS.

IT is said of that eminent saint and martyr, Bishop Hooper, that on one occasion a man in deep distress was allowed to go into his prison to tell his tale of conscience, but Bishop

Hooper looked so sternly upon him, and addressed him so severely at first, that the poor soul ran away, and could not get comfort until he had sought out another minister of a gentler aspect. Hooper really was a gracious and loving soul, but the sternness of his manner kept the penitent off.

SUBMISSION—to the Divine Will.

PAYSON was asked, when under great bodily affliction, if he could see any particular reason for this dispensation. "No," replied he, "but I am as well satisfied as if I could see ten thousand ; God's will is the very perfection of all reason."

SUFFERING—True Service.

OLD BETTY was converted late in life, and though very poor, was very active. She visited the sick ; out of her own poverty she gave to those who were still poorer ; collected a little money from others when she could give none of her own, and told many a one of the love of the Saviour. At last she caught cold and rheumatism, and lay in bed month after month, pain-worn and helpless. A good minister went to see her, and asked, if after her active habits she did not find the change very hard to bear. "No, sir, not at all. When I was well, I used to hear the Lord say day by day, 'Betty, go here ; Betty, go there ; Betty, do this ; Betty, do that ;' and I used to do it as well as I could; and now I hear him say every day, 'Betty, lie still and cough.'"—*James Hamilton, D.D.*

SYMPATHY—Fruit of Experience.

HONE in his "Year Book," has the following anecdote of Charles Pratt, Earl Camden, when Chief Justice of the Common Pleas. "Being on a visit to Lord Dacre, at Alveley, in Essex, he walked out with a gentleman, a very absent man, to a hill, at no great distance from the house, upon the top of which stood the stocks of the village. The Chief

Justice sat down upon them, and after awhile, having a mind to know what the punishment was, he asked his companion to open them and put him in. This being done, his friend took a book from his pocket, sauntered on, and so completely forgot the judge and his situation that he returned to Lord Dacre's. In the meantime, the Chief Justice being tired of the stocks, tried in vain to release himself. Seeing a countryman pass by, he endeavoured to move him to let him out, but obtained nothing by his motion. 'No, no, old gentleman,' said the countryman, 'you was not set there for nothing,' and left him until he was released by a servant of the house despatched in quest of him. Some time after he presided at a trial in which a charge was brought against a magistrate for false imprisonment, and for setting in the stocks. The counsel for the magistrate in his reply, made light of the whole charge, and more especially setting in the stocks, which he said everybody knew was no punishment at all. The Chief Justice rose, and, leaning over the bench, said, in a half-whisper, 'Brother, have you ever been in the stocks?' 'Really, my lord, never.' 'Then I have,' said the judge, 'and I assure you, brother, it is no such trifle as you represent.' " A little experience of the real trials of life, as endured by the poor, the sick, and the desponding, would be of essential service to many professors, and especially to those religious teachers whose path in life has been smooth and prosperous. Nothing promotes true sympathy like a kindred experience.

SYMPATHY—How Learned.

THE story goes that Harry the Eighth wandering one night in the streets of London in disguise, was met at the bridge-foot by some of the watch, and not giving a good account of himself was carried off to the Poultry Compter, and shut up for the night without fire or candle. On his liberation he made a grant of thirty chaldrons of coals and a quantity of bread for the solace of night prisoners in the Compter.

Experience brings sympathy. Those who have felt sharp afflictions, terrible convictions, racking doubts and violent temptations, will be zealous in consoling those in a similar condition. It were well if the great Head of the church would put unsympathising pastors into the Compter of trouble for a season until they could weep with those that weep.

TASTE—Spiritual, Needful for Heavenly Joys

THE unfitness of unrenewed souls for heaven, may be illustrated by the incapacity of certain uneducated and coarse-minded persons for elevated thoughts and intellectual pursuits. When a little child, I lived some years in my grandfather's house. In his garden there was a fine old hedge of yew of considerable length, which was clipped and trimmed till it made quite a wall of verdure. Behind it was a wide grass walk, which looked upon the fields, and afforded a quiet outlook. The grass was kept mown, so as to make pleasant walking. Here, ever since the old Puritanic chapel was built, godly divines had walked, and prayed, and meditated. My grandfather was wont to use it as his study. Up and down it he would walk when preparing his sermons, and always on Sabbath-days when it was fair, he had half-an-hour there before preaching. To me it seemed to be a perfect paradise, and being forbidden to stay there when grandfather was meditating, I viewed it with no small degree of awe. I love to think of the green and quiet walk at this moment, and could wish for just such a study. But I was once shocked and even horrified by hearing a farming man remark concerning this *sanctum sanctorum*, "It' ud grow a many 'taturs if it wor ploughed up." What cared he for holy memories? What were meditation and contemplation to him? Is it not the chief end of man to grow potatoes and eat them? Such, on a larger scale, would be an unconverted man's estimate of joys so elevated and refined as those of heaven, could he by any possibility be permitted to gaze upon them.

TEMPER—Important.

THE Adige at Verona appears to be a river quite broad and deep enough for navigation, but its current is so rapid as to make it quite unserviceable. Many men are so rash, and impetuous, and at the same time so suddenly angry and excited, that their otherwise most valuable abilities are rendered useless for any good purpose.

TEMPTATION.

MANY horses fall at the bottom of a hill because the driver thinks the danger past and the need to hold the reins with firm grip less pressing. So it is often with us when we are not specially tempted to overt sin, we are the more in danger through slothful ease. I think it was Ralph Erskine who said, "There is no devil so bad as no devil." The worst temptation that ever overtakes us, is, in some respects, preferable to our becoming carnally secure and neglecting to watch and pray.

More the treacherous calm I dread
Than tempests rolling overhead."

TEMPTATIONS.

NOTICE the invention used by country people to catch wasps. They will put a little sweet liquor into a long and narrow-necked phial. The do-nothing wasp comes by, smells the sweet liquor, plunges in and is drowned. But the bee comes by, and if she does stop for a moment to smell, yet she enters not, because she has honey of her own to make; she is too busy in the work of the commonwealth to indulge herself with the tempting sweets. Master Greenham, a Puritan divine, was once waited upon by a woman who was greatly tempted. Upon making enquiries into her way of life, he found she had little to do, and Greenham said, "That is the secret of your being so much tempted. Sister, if you

16

are very busy, Satan may tempt you, but he will not easily prevail, and he will soon give up the attempt." Idle Christians are not tempted of the devil so much as they tempt the devil to tempt them.

TEMPTATIONS.

ONE of the ancient fathers, we are told, had, before his conversion, lived with an ill woman, and some little time after, she accosted him as usual. Knowing how likely he was to fall into sin, he ran away with all his might, and she ran after him, crying, "Wherefore runnest thou away? It is I." He answered, "I run away because I am not I. I am a new man."

TEMPTATIONS—from Friends, to be watchfully Resisted.

THE lady in Millais' famous picture would fain save her lover's life from the massacre of Bartholomew, by binding the popish badge around his arm ; he kisses her for her love, but firmly removes the badge. So when the dearest friends we have, out of mistaken tenderness would persuade us to avoid persecution by relinquishing principle, and doing as others do, we should thank them for their love, but with unbending decision refuse to be numbered with the world. Moses must have loved Pharaoh's daughter for her kindness, but he refused to be called her son.

TERROR—of Convicted Consciences.

IN certain places on Alpine summits the way is peculiarly dangerous on account of the frequent falling of avalanches, and the traveller walks in dread of instant destruction. Samuel Rogers puts it thus :—

> "Then my guide
> Lowering his voice addressed me : ' Through this gap
> On and say nothing ; lest a word, a breath,
> Bring down the winter's snow, enough to whelm
>   An army."

Thus when alarmed by an awakened conscience men walk in fear from hour to hour, trembling lest a thought or word of sin should bring down upon them the impending wrath of God. Thrice happy is he who has traversed that awful gap of terror and now breathes freely because sin is pardoned, and therefore every apprehension is removed.

TEXTS—Memorable.

ONE looks with interest on that ancient stone at Kingston-upon-Thames, upon which so many Saxon kings were crowned, but far more reverent is the gaze we fix upon those texts of Scripture whereby (through God's grace) many have been made kings unto our God. We rail them off in a special enclosure and place them where the highways meet, that others may look on them and find their coronations at the selfsame spot.

THEOLOGY—Ought Not to be Petrified Scripture.

PETRARCH'S works are said to have laid so long in the roof of St. Mark's, at Venice, that they became turned into stone ; by what process deponent sayeth not. To many men it might well seem that the Word of God had become petrified, for they receive it as a hard, lifeless creed, a stone upon which to sharpen the daggers of controversy, a stumbling-block for young beginners, a millstone with which to break opponents' heads, after the manner experienced by Abimelech at Thebez. A man must have a stout digestion to feed upon some men's theology; no sap, no sweetness, no life, but all stern accuracy, and fleshless definition. Proclaimed without tenderness, and argued without affection, the gospel from such men rather resembles a missile from a catapult than bread from a Father's table. Teeth are needlessly broken over the grit of systematic theology, while souls are famishing. To turn stones into bread was a temptation of our Master, but how many of his servants yield readily to the far worse temptation to turn bread into stone ! Go thy way, metaphysical divine, to the stone-yard, and break granite for McAdam, but stand not in the way of loving spirits who would feed the family of God with living bread. The inspired Word is to us spirit and life, and we cannot afford to have it hardened into a huge monolith, or a spiritual Stonehenge—sublime, but cold, majestic, but lifeless ; far rather would we have it as our own household book, our bosom companion, the poor man's counsellor and friend.

THREE WHATS.

" NEVER forget the three Whats. First, What from? Secondly, What by ? And, thirdly, What to ? What from ? Believers are redeemed from hell and destruction. What by? By the precious blood of Christ. What to ? To an inheritance incorruptible, undefiled, and that fadeth not away."

TITHES.

'TIS ridiculous to say the tithes are God's part, and therefore the clergy must have them ; why, so they are if the layman has them. 'Tis as if one of my Lady Kent's maids should be sweeping this room, and another of them should come and take away the broom, and tell for a reason why she should part with it, 'tis my lady's broom ; as if it were not my lady's broom which of them soever had it.—*Table-Talk of John Selden.*

TO-DAY.

" IT is not after the storm has arisen, or the telegraph has reported that his ship has struck, that the merchant runs to insure his goods. He effects the insurance while the sun is shining and the air calm ; he effects the insurance before the ship has cleared from the dock, or at all events before the ship has left the river. Go and do likewise, living, but dying men ! Now is the accepted time; to-day, according to the true testimony of his adversaries, ' This man receiveth sinners.' God with us is waiting ; still his terms are, ' Whosoever will.' To-day you may enter into life ; to-morrow the door may be shut."

TONGUE—the.

I SAW a terrible fire some time ago, or rather I saw the reflection of it in the sky, the heavens were crimsoned with it. It burned a large manufactory to the ground, and the firemen had hard work to save the buildings which surrounded it. They poured streams of water on it from fifteen engines, but it licked it up, and would have its course till the walls gave way. That terrible fire was kindled *by a farthing rush-light!* Some years ago, I saw the black ashes of what the night before was a cheerful farm-yard, with its hay-ricks, corn-stacks, stables, and cow-sheds ; and lying about upon them were the carcases of a number of miserable horses and bullocks, which had perished in the flames. All that was done *by a lucifer-match!* In America the Indians strike a *spark* from a flint and steel, and set fire to the dry grass, and the flames spread and spread until they sweep like a roaring torrent over prairies as large as England, and men and cattle have to flee for their lives. " Behold, how great a matter a little fire kindleth !" *And the tongue is a fire!* A few rash *words* will set a family, a neighbourhood, a nation, by the ears; they have often done so. Half the law-suits, and half the wars have been brought about by the tongue.—*James Bolton.*

TRANSFORMATIONS OF GRACE.

A SHORT time ago the manufacturers of lighting gas were puzzled to know how to dispose of the coal-tar left in the retorts. A more useless, nauseous substance was hardly known to exist. Chemistry came to the rescue, and to-day not less than thirty-six marketable articles are produced from this black, vile, sticky slime—solvents, oils, salts, colours, flavours. You eat a bit of delicious confectionery, happily unconscious that the exquisite taste which you enjoy so keenly comes from coal-tar ; you buy at the druggist's a tiny phial of what is labelled " Otto of Roses," little dreaming that the delicious perfume is wafted, not from " the fields of Araby," but from the foul gas retort.

Christianity is a moral chemistry. Well were it for nations if it held a higher place among their social economics. Tar-saving is all well enough, but soul-saving is better. Grace transforms a villain into an honest man, a harlot into a holy woman, a thief into a saint. Where fœtid exhalations of vice alone ascended, prayer and praise are to be found ; where moral miasmata had their lair, righteousness and tem-perance pitch their tent. Every sort of good thing is produced by godliness, and that too in hearts once reeking with all manner of foulness. Should not this stay every persecuting hand, hush every railing tongue, and incite every sanctified spirit to continued and increasing energy.

TRIALS—of Young Believers.

DUNCAN in his Sacred Philosophy of the Seasons, tells us, —There is an insect (*musca pumilionis*), which is accustomed to deposit its eggs in the very core of the *plumula*, or primary shoot of wheat, so that this shoot is completely destroyed by the larvæ. Did the plant possess no means within itself, no means of repairing this injury, the whole previous labour of the husbandman would, in this case, have been in vain. But this destruction occurring in the spring of the year, when the vegetable power of the plant is in its greatest vigour, an effect is produced somewhat analogous to that of heading down a fruit tree. Shoots immediately spring up from the knots, the plant becomes more firmly rooted, and produces probably a dozen stems and ears, when but for the temporary mischief it might have sent forth one only. Thus may it often occur that those early trials which appear almost to destroy the faith of young believers are their best friends, since they never would have been so useful had they been left to flourish as their heart desired.

TRINITY—its Mystery.

IT was reported of Alanus, when he promised his auditory to discourse the next Sunday more clearly of the Trinity, and to make plain that mystery, while he was studying the point by the sea-side, he spied a boy very busy with a little spoon trudging often between the sea and a small hole he had digged in the ground. Alanus asked him what he meant. The boy answers, "I intend to bring all the sea into this pit." Alanus replies, "Why dost thou attempt such impossibilities, and misspend thy time?" The boy answers, "So dost thou, Alanus: I shall as soon bring all the sea into this hole, as thou bring all the knowledge of the Trinity into thy head. All is equally possible; we have begun together, we shall finish together; saving of the two, my labour hath more hope and possibility of taking effect."—*Thomas Adams.*

TROUBLE—Needed.

SPEAKING of a Norwegian summer, the Rev. H. Macmillan says :—" The long daylight is very favourable to the growth of vegetation, plants growing in the night as well as in the day in the short but ardent summer. But the stimulus of perpetual solar light is peculiarly trying to the nervous system of those who are not accustomed to it. It prevents proper repose and banishes sleep. I never felt before how needful darkness is for the welfare of our bodies and minds. I longed for night, but the farther north we went, the farther we were fleeing from it, until at last, when we reached the most northern point of our tour, the sun set for one hour and a half. Consequently, the heat of the day never cooled down, and accumulated until it became almost unendurable at last. Truly for a most wise and beneficent purpose did God make light and create darkness. ' Light is sweet, and it is a pleasant thing to the eyes to behold the sun.' But darkness is also sweet, it is the nurse of nature's kind restorer, balmy sleep, and without the tender drawing round us of its curtains the weary eyelid will not close, and the jaded nerves will not be soothed to refreshing rest. Not till the everlasting day break, and the shadows flee away, and the Lord himself shall be our light, and our God our glory, can we do without the cloud in the sunshine, the shade of sorrow in the bright light of joy, and the curtain of night for the deepening of the sleep which God gives his beloved."—*Rev. Hugh Macmillan's "Holidays on High Lands."*

TRUTH.

"HE will guide you into all truth." John xvi. 13. Truth may be compared to some cave or grotto, with wondrous stalactites hanging from the roof, and others starting from the floor ; a cavern glittering with spar and abounding in marvels. Before entering the cavern you enquire for a guide, who comes with his lighted flambeau. He conducts you down to a considerable depth, and you find yourself in the midst of the cave. He leads you through different chambers. Here he points you to a little stream rushing from amid the rocks, and indicates its rise and progress ; there he points to some peculiar rock and tells you its name, then takes you into a large natural hall, tells you how many persons once feasted in it, and so on. Truth is a grand series of caverns, it is our glory to have so great and wise a conductor as the Holy Spirit. Imagine that we are coming to the darkness of it. He is a light shining in the midst of us to guide us. And by the light he shows us wondrous things. He teaches us by suggestion, direction, and illumination.

TRUTH—Qualifications for Learning.

RUSKIN, in reference to painters, declares, that "A person false at heart may, when it suits his purposes, seize a stray truth here or there ; but the relations of truth, its perfectness, that which makes it wholesome truth, he can never perceive. As wholeness and wholesomeness go together, so also sight with sincerity ; it is only the constant desire of, and sub-missiveness to truth, which can measure its strange angles, and mark its infinite aspects, and fit them and knit them into the strength of sacred invention."

The like remark, with keener edge, applies to those who would be disciples in Christ's school, or aspire to be teachers in his church.

TRY.

No man is likely to accomplish much who moodily indulges a desponding view of his own capacities. By God's help the weakest of us may be strong, and it is the way to become so, to resolve never to give up a good work till we have tried our best to achieve it. To think nothing impossible is the privilege of faith. We deprecate the indolent cowardice of the man who always felt assured that every new enterprise would be too much for him, and therefore declined it ; but we admire the pluck of the ploughman who was asked on his cross-examination if he could read Greek, and replied he did not know, because he had never tried. Those Suffolk horses which will pull at a post till they drop are worth a thousand times as much as jibbing animals that run back as soon as ever the collar begins to press them.

UNBELIEF—Wickedness of.

THE late Dr. Heugh, of Glasgow, a short time before he breathed his last, said, " There is nothing I feel more than the criminality of not trusting Christ without doubt—without doubt. Oh, to think what Christ is, what he did, and whom he did it for, and *then* not to believe him, not to trust him ! There is no wickedness like the wickedness of unbelief !"

UNDERSTANDING—No Time for.

"How is it, my dear," inquired a schoolmistress of a little girl, "that you do not understand this simple thing?" "I do not know, indeed," she answered, with a perplexed look; "but I sometimes think I have so many things to learn that I have not the time to understand."

Alas! there may be much hearing, much reading, much attendance at public services, and very small result, and all because the word was not the subject of thought, and was never embraced by the understanding. What is not understood is like meat undigested, more likely to be injurious than nourishing.

UNGODLY MEN—Much Alike.

In the Aosta Valley we were tormented by the recklessness of a driver who was drunk. Glad enough were we to change him for a sober man—sober as we thought ; but, alas ! we had only seen him in the morning, and before the afternoon had much advanced his sobriety was gone, and we would willingly have taken back the discarded sot of yesterday. Ungodly men are very much alike when the time of temptation has fully come. The difference between one sinner and another is rather created by outward than by inward causes. Put them in like circumstances, and they would be much the same. All swine are not in the mire, but they all love it.

UNION TO CHRIST.

Two friends are said to come into Vulcan's shop, and to beg a boon of him : it was granted. What was it? that he would either beat them on his anvil, or melt them in his furnace, both into one. But without fiction, here is a far greater love in Christ ; for he would be melted in the furnace of wrath, and beaten on the anvil of death, to be made one with us. And to declare the exceeding love, here were not both to be beaten on the anvil, or melted in the furnace ; but without us, he alone would be beaten on the anvil, he alone melted that we might be spared.—*Thomas Adams.*

UNITY—Among Christians to be Desired.

MELANCTHON mourned in his day the divisions among Protestants, and sought to bring the Protestants together by the parable of the war between the wolves and the dogs. The wolves were somewhat afraid, for the dogs were many and strong, and therefore they sent out a spy to observe them. On his return, the scout said, " It is true the dogs are many, but there are not many mastiffs among them. There are dogs of so many sorts one can hardly count them ; and as for the worst of them," said he, " they are little dogs, which bark loudly, but cannot bite. However, this did not cheer me so much," said the wolf, " as this, that as they came marching on, I observed they were all snapping right and left at one another, and I could see clearly that though they all hate the wolf, yet each dog hates every other dog with all his heart." I fear it is true still ; for there are many professors who snap right and left at their own brethren, when they had better save their teeth for the wolves. If our enemies are to be put to confusion, it must be by the united efforts of all the people of God : unity is strength.

UNTRUTH—in Religious Giving.

LOUIS XI. made a donation to the Virgin Mary of the whole county of Boulogne, *retaining, however, for his own use, the revenues thereof!* A solemn deed was drawn up, signed, sealed, and delivered, and it bears date 1478. What a ridiculous farce ! The instrument gives away just nothing at all. But are there no such farces among us ? When men of mean and miserly dispositions sing certain of our hymns, are they not guilty of just such a pretence of generosity ?

With abundance of goods in their power, they fumble for a threepenny-piece in their pockets, singing, meanwhile,

> " Were the whole realm of nature mine,
>   That were a present far too small ;
> Love so amazing, so divine
>   Demands my soul, my life, my all."

USEFULNESS—Better than Mere Capacity.

A MONSTROUS vat, certainly, is the great tun of Heidelberg. It might hold eight hundred hogsheads of wine at the least ; but what is the use of such wasted capacity, since, for nearly a hundred years, there has not been a drop of liquor in it ! Hollow and sounding, empty and void and waste ; vintages come and go, and find it perishing of dry rot. An empty cask is not so great a spectacle after all, let its size be what it may, though old travellers called this monster one of the wonders of the world. What a thousand pities it is that many men of genius and of learning are, in respect of usefulness, no better than this huge but empty tun of Heidelberg ! Very capacious are their minds, but very unpractical. Better be a poor household kilderkin, and give forth one's little freely, than exist as a useless prodigy, capable of much and available for nothing.

USEFULNESS—the Least Christian to Aim at.

MANY true saints are unable to render much service to the cause of God. See, then, the gardeners going down to the pond, and dipping in their watering-pots to carry the refreshing liquid to the flowers. A child comes into the garden and wishes to help, and yonder is a little watering-pot for him. Note well the little water-pot, though it does not hold so much, yet carries the same water to the plants ; and it does not make any difference to the flowers which receive that water, whether it came out of the big pot or the little pot, so long as it is the same water, and they get it. You who are as little children in God's church, you who do not know much, but try to tell to others what little you know ; if it be the same gospel truth, and be blessed by the same Spirit, it will not matter to the souls who are blessed by you whether they were converted or comforted under a man of one or ten talents.

USEFULNESS—Wisdom Needed for.

IN order to reach their hearts on sacred and divine things, he strove to cultivate the art of conciliating even the careless and indifferent, by talking to them, in the first instance, on subjects in which they would be interested ; and in this taught a precious lesson, which all who are engaged in evangelistic labour would do well to learn and exemplify. When acting as a regular district visitor in Whitechapel, London, he happened to visit a currier, to whom he was unknown, and his knowledge of the various processes of tanning and the preparation of leather, elicited the remark, " Ah, I see you are in the trade yourself, sir."—*From Dr. Duff's " Life of Lord Haddo, fifth Earl of Aberdeen."*

WANTS.

ON a tradesman's table I noticed a book labelled WANT BOOK. What a practical suggestion for a man of prayer ! He should put down all his needs on the tablets of his heart, and then present his *want book* to his God. If we knew all our need, what a large want book we should require ! How comforting to know that Jesus has a supply book, which exactly meets our want book! Promises, providences, and divine visitations, combine to meet the necessities of all the faithful.

WARFARE—Spiritual.

IN the road from Bellinzona to Lugano, on the Monte Cenere, we met with a detachment of carbineers, who had a

station in the forest upon the mountain ; we learned that
they had been placed there by the Italian government
because a party of bandits had been impudent enough to rob
the mail.   We felt all the safer from knowing that protectors
were so near at hand.   Soldiers are needed where brigands
are abroad ; nobody advises the letting of freebooters alone.
We are occasionally asked by lovers of quietude why we
draw our swords so frequently against the Ritualists and
other Romanisers : is it not a sufficient answer that we are
soldiers of the King of kings, and that these traitorous thieves
not only rob the King's subjects of the gospel, but the King
himself of his glory?   Our churches need just now a strong
detachment of bold and qualified champions to occupy themselves with hunting down the Popish brigands by faithful
preaching, and hanging them up upon the gallows of scorn.
Cursed is he that doeth the work of the Lord deceitfully in
this matter at this momentous hour, when men's souls are
destroyed, and Christ's name is dishonoured.   Carbineers of
the cross, take sure aim, and give good account of the foe.

WARNINGS.

A VERY skilful bowman went to the mountains in search of
game.   All the beasts of the forest fled at his approach.   The
lion alone challenged him to combat.   The bowman immediately let fly an arrow, and said to the lion, " I send thee
my messenger, that from him thou mayst learn what I myself shall be when I assail thee."   The lion thus wounded
rushed away in great fear, and on a fox exhorting him to be
of good courage, and not to run away at the first attack :
" You counsel me in vain, for if he sends so fearful a
messenger, how shall I abide the attack of the man himself ? "

If the warning admonitions of God's ministers fill the
conscience with terror, what must it be to face the Lord
himself?   If one bolt of judgment bring a man into a cold

sweat, what will it be to stand before an angry God in the last great day?

WATCHFULNESS.

WHILE the Austrian general was staying at the Hotel de Ville, upon the Grand Canal, at Venice, we lodged at the same house, and so often as we passed his rooms, whether by day or night, we encountered two sentries on guard at the door. Our heart said to itself, whenever the King of kings deigns to make a chamber of our spirit, let us set holiness and devotion to be sentries at the entrance. When our Beloved visits us he must not be disturbed; ill thoughts must be repulsed, and carnal desires kept at a distance. With drawn swords let watchfulness preserve the sanctity of Immanuel's rest. " I charge you, O ye daughters of Jerusalem, by the roes and by the hinds of the field, that ye stir not up, nor awake my love, till he please."

WATCHFULNESS—when Special Need of.

When cast by providence among sinful persons who respect us, we ought to be peculiarly watchful. The hatred of the ungodly when poured upon Christians in the form of persecution, is seldom harmful to their spiritual nature, but the friendship of the world is always to be suspected. When the servants of the high priest allowed Peter to warm his hands at the fire, had Peter been a wise man, he would have been afraid that evil would come of it. We are disarmed by kindness, but it is never safe to be disarmed in an enemy's country. "Who," says the old proverb, " could live in Rome and yet be at war with the pope?" Who can have much to do with sinners and not have something to do with their sins? The smiling daughters of Moab did more mischief to Israel than all Balak's frowning warriors. All Philistia could not have blinded Samson if Delilah's charms had not deluded

him. Our worst foes will be found among our ungodly
friends. Those who are false to God, are not likely to be
true to us. Walk carefully, believer, if thy way lie by the
sinner's door, and especially if that sinner hath acted a
friendly part to thee.

WEALTH—Involves Danger.

IT was as much as we could do to keep our feet upon the
splendid mosaic floor of the Palace Giovanelli, at Venice: we
found no such difficulty in the cottage of the poor glassblower
in the rear. Is it one of the advantages of wealth to have
one's abode polished till all comfort vanishes, and the very
floor is as smooth and dangerous as a sheet of ice, or is this
merely an accidental circumstance typical of the dangers of
abundance? Observation shows us that there is a fascination
in wealth which renders it extremely difficult for the possessors
of it to maintain their equilibrium; and this is more especially
the case where money is suddenly acquired; then, unless
grace prevent, pride, affectation, and other mean vices stupify
the brain with their sickening fumes, and he who was respectable in poverty, becomes despicable in prosperity. Pride may
lurk under a threadbare cloak, but it prefers the comely
broadcloth of the merchant's coat : moths will eat any of our
garments, but they seem to fly first to the costly furs. It is
so much the easier for men to fall when walking on wealth's
sea of glass, because all men aid them to do so. Flatterers
haunt not cottages: the poor may hear an honest word from
his neighbour, but etiquette forbids that the rich man should
enjoy the like privilege; for is it not a maxim in Babylon,
that rich men have no faults, or only such as their money,
like charity, covereth with a mantle? What man can help
slipping when every body is intent upon greasing his ways, so
that the smallest chance of standing may be denied him?
The world's proverb is, " God help the poor, for the rich can
help themselves;" but to our mind, it is just the rich who

have most need of heaven's help. Dives in scarlet is worse off than Lazarus in rags, unless divine love shall uphold him.

WILL—the Seat of Inability.

NELSON could not see the signal for suspending battle because he placed the glass to his blind eye, and man cannot see the truth as it is in Jesus because he has no mind to do so. Ungodly men are, as the country people say, "like the hogs in a harvest field," who come not out for all your shouting ; they cannot hear because they have no will to hear. Want of will causes paralysis of every faculty. In spiritual things man is utterly unable because resolvedly unwilling.

WILL—Not Violated by Grace.

WHEN we see a casket wrenched open, the hinges torn away, or the clasp destroyed, we mark at once the hand of the *Spoiler;* but when we observe another casket deftly opened with a master-key, and the sparkling contents revealed, we note the hand of the *Owner.* Conversion is not, as some suppose, a violent opening of the heart by grace, in which will, reason, and judgment are all ignored or crushed. This is too barbarous a method for him who comes not as a plunderer to his prey, but as a possessor to his treasure. In conversion, the Lord who made the human heart deals with it according to its nature and constitution. His key insinuates itself into the wards ; the will is not enslaved but enfranchised ; the reason is not blinded but enlightened, and the whole man is made to act with a glorious liberty which it never knew till it fell under the restraints of grace.

WILL OF MAN—Adverse to the Gospel.

WHEN the dove was weary she recollected the ark, and flew into Noah's hand at once: there are weary souls who know the ark, but will not fly to it. When an Israelite had slain, inadvertently, his fellow, he knew the city of refuge, he

17

feared the avenger of blood, and he fled along the road to the place of safety; but multitudes know the refuge, and every Sabbath we set up the sign-posts along the road, but yet they come not to find salvation. The destitute waifs and strays of the streets of London find out the night refuge and ask for shelter; they cluster round our workhouse doors like sparrows under the eaves of a building on a rainy day; they piteously crave for lodging and a crust of bread; yet crowds of poor benighted spirits, when the house of mercy is lighted up, and the invitation is plainly written in bold letters, "Whosoever will, let him turn in hither," will not come, but prove the truth of Watts's verse—

> "Thousands make a wretched choice,
> And rather starve than come."

'Tis strange, 'tis passing strange, 'tis wonderful!

WISDOM—Our, under Differing Circumstances.

IT is a wise thing to exhibit prudence and hopefulness in their proper degrees and seasons. Some are so exultant at success as to become rash, and thereby secure for themselves a disaster, others are so depressed by a defeat as to be incapable of future action. The old Latin distich is worth quoting.

> "Si modo victus eras, ad crastina bella parato;
> Si modo victor eras, ad crastina bella paveto."

> "If conquer'd, for to-morrow's fight prepare;
> If conqueror, of to-morrow's fight beware."

When we are most unsuccessful in our Lord's work we should rally all our forces for new attempts, hoping that the tide will turn, and believing that to perseverance the crown is certain. On the other hand when the Lord favours us with the largest degree of blessing we must watch with holy anxiety lest by any negligence or sin we should grieve the Holy Spirit and so forfeit all hope of future triumph.

WISDOM—To Win Souls.

WE are not wide enough awake in doing good. Pardon the reference, for the sake of the lesson ; it shall be borrowed from Dr. Marigold's cart. When a Cheap-Jack has a little knot of people round his van, he eyes them all, and feels sure that the man who is standing over there is a butcher, and that yonder young lad has more money than brains, and that the girl near him is out with her sweetheart and is soon to be married; now, mark, he will hold up the exact articles which are likely to attract these customers, and in his harangue, he will have jokes and telling sentences which will turn butcher, and lad, and lass into purchasers. He cares not a jot for elegance, but very much for force. He knows that his trade will be better pushed by homely remarks and cutting sentences than by the prosiest prettinesses which were ever delivered ; and he gains his end, which is more than those of you will do who talk to people about their souls with as much richness of diction as—

> " The girl who at each pretty phrase let drop
> A ruby comma, or pearl full-stop,
> Or an emerald semicolon."

Dr. Marigold is sharp and shrewd, because self-interest makes him so, and his extemporary observations are so patly uttered and adroitly arranged, that he wins the attention of all, and the custom of many. Would to God that preachers and other workers for God had a tithe as much common-sense as Cheap-Jack, and were half as earnest to bring men to Jesus Christ as Cheap-Jack is to bring them to buy that tea-tray and set of real china! O that we were as wise to win the ear and heart of the particular case with which we have to deal, as he is in extorting a laugh and compelling the attention of the passer-by !

WOMEN—Preaching.

WHEN Boswell told Johnson one day that he had heard a woman preach that morning at a Quaker's meeting, Johnson replied, " Sir, a woman preaching is like a dog's walking on his hind legs. It is not done well; but you are surprised to find it done at all." We will add that our surprise is all the greater when women of piety mount the pulpit, for they are acting in plain defiance of the command of the Holy Spirit, written by the pen of the apostle Paul.

WORD—Ways of Treating it.

THERE are two ways of treating the seed. The botanist splits it up, and discourses on its curious characteristics; the simple husbandman eats and sows; sows and eats. Similarly there are two ways of treating the gospel. A critic dissects it, raises a mountain of debate about the structure of the whole, and relation of its parts ; and when he is done with his argument, he is done ; to him the letter is dead ; he neither lives on it himself, nor spreads it for the good of his neighbours ; he neither eats nor sows. The disciple of of Jesus, hungering for righteousness, takes the seed whole ; it is bread for to-day's hunger, and seed for to-morrow's supply.—*W. Arnot.*

WORD OF GOD—Everliving.

HOW wonderfully has the Lord provided for the continuance of the vegetable world; he causes the plant to scatter broadcast a multitude of seeds, and bids the winds convey them far and wide. The fowls of the air are commissioned to bear berries and fruits to their proper soils, and even to bury them in the earth ; while scores of four-footed creatures, engaged in storing up food for themselves, become planters of trees, and propagators of plants. Seeds bear a charmed life about them, they will germinate after being buried for centuries ; they have been known to flourish when turned up from the borings of wells from the depth of hundreds of feet, and when ponds and lakes have been dried, the undrowned vegetable life has surprised the beholders by blossoming with unknown flowers. Can we imagine that God has been thus careful of the life of the mere grass of the field, which is the very emblem of decay, and yet is negligent of his Word which liveth and abideth for ever ? It is not to be dreamed of. Truth, the incorruptible seed, is ever scattering itself, every wind is laden with it, every breath spreads it ; it lies dormant in a thousand memories, it preserves its life in the abodes of death. The Lord has but to give the word, and a band of eloquent men shall publish the gospel, apostles and evangelists will rise in abundance, like the warriors who sprang from the fabled dragon's teeth ; converts will spring up like flowerets at the approach of spring, nations shall be born in a day, and truth, and God the Lord of truth, shall reign for ever.

WORKS—and our Salvation.

WILLIAM WICKHAM being appointed by King Edward to build a stately church, wrote in the windows, " *This work made William Wickham.*" When charged by the king for assuming the honour of that work to himself as the author, whereas he was only the overseer, he answered that he meant not that he made the work, but that the work made him, having before been very poor, and then in great credit. Lord, when we read in thy Word that we must work out our own salvation, thy meaning is not that our salvation should be the effect of our work, but our work the evidence of our salvation.

WORLD—Deception of.

ÆSOP'S fable says :—" A pigeon oppressed by excessive thirst, saw a goblet of water painted on a sign-board. Not supposing it to be only a picture, she flew towards it with a loud whirr, and unwittingly dashed against the sign-board, and jarred herself terribly. Having broken her wings by the blow, she fell to the ground, and was killed by one of the by-standers."

The mockeries of the world are many, and those who are deluded by them not only miss the joys they looked for, but in their eager pursuit of vanity bring ruin upon their souls. We call the dove silly to be deceived by a picture, however cleverly painted, but what epithet shall we apply to those who are duped by the transparently false allurements of the world!

WORLD—a Huge Desert.

LIVING in the midst of the church of God is like sailing down the Nile in a boat. One is charmed with the luxuriance of either bank, and with much that is beautiful immediately around; but, alas! at a little distance on either side lies a vast uncultivated, we had almost said hopeless, desert. Some are at rest because they never look beyond the borders of the church, but those whose sympathies reach to all humanity will have to carry a life-long " burden of the Lord."

WORLD—its Instability.

QUEEN ELIZABETH once said to a courtier, " They pass best over the world who trip over it quickly; for it is but a bog : if we stop, we sink."

WORLD—Not to Build too Confidently on it.

IN Chili where the ground is subject to frequent shocks of earthquake, the houses are built of lowly height and of unen- during structure; it is of little use to dig deep foundations, and pile up high walls where the very earth is unstable; it would be foolish to build as for ages when the whole edifice may be in ruins in a week. Herein we read a lesson as to our worldly schemes and possessions : this poor fleeting world deserves not that we should build our hopes and joys upon it as though they could last us long. We must treat it as a treacherous soil, and build but lightly on it, and we shall be wise.

WORLD—Vanity of Pursuit of.

My friends, do you remember that old Scythian custom, when the head of a house died ? How he was dressed in his finest dress, and set in his chariot, and carried about to his friends' houses ; and each of them placed him at his table's head, and all feasted in his presence ! Suppose it were offered to you, in plain words, as it *is* offered to you in dire facts, that you should gain this Scythian honour, gradually, while you yet thought yourself alive. Suppose the offer were this : You shall die slowly ; your blood shall daily grow cold, your flesh petrify, your heart beat at last only as a rusty group of iron valves. Your life shall fade from you, and sink through the earth into the ice of Caina ; but day by day your body shall be dressed more gaily, and set in higher chariots, and have more orders on its breast, crowns on its head, if you will. Men shall bow before it, stare and shout round it, crowd after it up and down the streets ; build palaces for it, feast with it at their tables' heads all the night long ; your soul shall stay enough within it to know what they do, and feel the weight of the golden dress on its shoulders, and the furrow of the crown edge on the skull ; no more. Would you take the offer, verbally made by the death angel ? Would the meanest among us take it, think you ? Yet practically and verily we grasp at it, every one of us, in a measure ; many of us grasp at it in its fulness of horror. Every man accepts it who desires to advance in life without knowing what life is ; who means only that he is to get more horses, and more footmen, and more fortune, and more public honour, and— *not* more personal soul. He only is advancing in life whose

heart is getting softer, whose blood warmer, whose brain
quicker, whose spirit is entering into living peace.—*John
Ruskin.*

WORLDLY MERRIMENT.

I THINK the men of this world like children in a dangerous
storm in the sea, that play and make sport with the white
foam of the waves thereof coming in to sink and drown them;
so are men making fool's sports with the white pleasures of a
stormy world that will sink them.   But, alas! what have we
to do with their sports which they make?   If Solomon said
of laughter that it was madness, what may we say of this
world's laughing and sporting themselves with gold and
silver, and honours, and court, and broad large conquests,*
but that they are poor souls, in the height and rage of a fever
gone mad?   Then a straw, a fig, for all created sports and
rejoicing out of Christ.—*Samuel Rutherford.*

WORLDLINESS.

THERE is a poor creature at Aosta who does not know the
value of money, and only cares for eating, drinking, and
sleeping.   He is undoubtedly an idiot; but what is he who
does not know the value of his soul?

WORLDLINESS—its Blinding Influence.

SUPPOSE I were shut up within a round tower, whose
massive wall had in some time of trouble been pierced here
and there for musketry; suppose, further, that by choice or
necessity, I am whirled rapidly and incessantly round its
inner circumference, will I appreciate the beauties of the
surrounding landscape or recognise the features of the men
who labour in the field below?   I will not!   Why?   Are there

---

* Acquisitions.

not openings in the wall which I pass at every circuit? Yes; but the eye, set for objects near, has not time to adjust itself to objects at a distance until it has passed the openings ; and so the result is the same as if it were a dead wall all round. Behold the circle of human life! of the earth, earthy it is, almost throughout its whole circumference. A dead wall, very near and very thick, obstructs the view. Here and there, on a Sabbath or other season of seriousness, a slit is left open in its side. Heaven might be seen through these ; but, alas! the eye which is habitually set for the earthly cannot, during such momentary glimpses, adjust itself to higher things. Unless you pause and look steadfastly, you will see neither clouds nor sunshine through these openings, or the distant sky. So long has the soul looked upon the world, and so firmly is the world's picture fixed in its eye, that when it is turned for a moment heavenward, it feels only a quiver of inarticulate light, and retains no distinct impression of the things that are unseen and eternal.—*W. Arnot.*

WORLDLINGS—Brutishness of.

LUTHER was told of a nobleman who, above all things, occupied himself with amassing money, and was so buried in darkness that he gave no heed to the word of God, and even said to one who pleaded with him, " Sir, the gospel pays no interest." " Have you no grains?" interposed Luther; and then he told this fable :—"A lion making a great feast, invited all the beasts, and with them some swine. When all manner of dainties were set before the guests, the swine asked, ' Have you no grains?' Even so," continued Luther, "even so it is, in these days, with carnal men ; we preachers set before them the most dainty and costly dishes, such as everlasting salvation, the remission of sins, and God's grace ; but they, like swine, turn up their snouts, and ask for money. Offer a cow a nutmeg, and she will reject it for old hay."

YOUTHFUL PIETY—Advantage of.

IN an election the first votes recorded count all the day
long, and so encourage the party all through the anxious
hours of polling.   When men give in their names for Jesus
and his cause in the morning of their lives, their whole
existence influences their time, and their encouragement to
the good cause is life-long.   Young people, remember this !

ZEAL.

HUMBOLDT, in his travels, observes, " It seems remarkable
that in the hottest as well as the coldest climates, people
display the same predilection for heat.   On the introduction
of Christianity into Iceland, the inhabitants would be bap-
tised only in the hot springs of Hecla ; and in the torrid zone,
in the plains as well as on the Cordilleras, the natives flock
from all parts to the thermal waters."   The fact is not less
noteworthy that men love spiritual warmth.   Cold truth, even
cold gospel truth, is never attractive.   Ministers must be
fervent, their spirit earnest, and their style energetic, or the
many will not resort to them.   Religion is a dish to be served
hot; when it once becomes lukewarm it is sickening.   Our
baptism must be with the Holy Ghost and with fire if we
would win the masses to hear the gospel.

ZEAL.

WHEN the Spartans marched into battle they advanced
with cheerful songs, willing to fight ; but when the Persians entered the conflict, you could hear, as the regiments
came on, the crack of whips by which the officers drove the
cowards to the fray.   You need not wonder that a few Spartans
were more than a match for thousands of Persians, that in fact
they were like lions in the midst of sheep.   So let it be with
the church ; never should she need to be forced to reluctant
action, but full of irrepressible life, she should long for conflict
against everything which is contrary to. God.   Were we

enthusiastic soldiers of the cross we should be like lions in the midst of herds of enemies, and through God's help nothing would be able to stand against us.

ZEAL—Causing Unity.

THERE was a blacksmith once who had two pieces of iron which he wished to weld into one, and he took them just as they were, all cold and hard, and put them on the anvil, and began to hammer with all his might, but they were two pieces still, and would not unite. At last he remembered what he ought never to have forgotten ; he thrust both of them into the fire, took them out red-hot, laid the one upon the other, and by one or two blows of the hammer they very soon became one.

ZEAL FOR SOULS.

A TRAVELLER was journeying in the darkness of night along a road that led to a deep and rapid river, which, swollen by sudden rains, was chafing and roaring within its precipitous banks. The bridge that crossed the stream had been swept away by the torrent, but he knew it not. A man met him, and after enquiring whither he was bound, said to him in an indifferent way—"Are you aware that the bridge is gone ?" "No," was the answer. "Why do you think so ?" "Oh, I heard such a report this afternoon, and though I am not certain about it, you had perhaps better not proceed."

Deceived by the hesitating and undecided manner in which the information was given, the traveller pushed onward in the way of death. Soon another meeting him, cried out in consternation. "Sir, sir, the bridge is gone !" "Oh! yes," replied the wayfarer, "some one told me that story a little distance back ; but from the careless tone with which he told it, I am sure it is an idle tale." "Oh, it is true, it is true !" exclaimed the other. "I know the bridge is gone, for I barely escaped being carried away with it myself. Danger is before you and you must not go on." And in the excitement of his feelings, he grasped him by the hands, by the arms, by the clothes, and besought him not to rush upon manifest destruction. Convinced by the earnest voice, the earnest eyes, the earnest gestures, the traveller turned back, and was saved. The intelligence in both cases was the same ; but the manner of its conveyance in the one gave it an air of a fable, in the other an air of truth.

So it is only through a burning zeal for the salvation of the lost—a zeal glowing in the heart, and flashing out in the look and action and utterance—that the confidence of unbelief can be overcome, and the heedless travellers of the broad way won to the path of life and happiness. Love is the most potent logic : interest and sympathy are the most subduing eloquence.—*Christian Work.*

INDEX OF SUBJECTS.

The reader will please to note that this is NOT A COMPLETE INDEX, but, as the illustrations are already arranged alphabetically under distinct heads, this is a SUPPLEMENTARY index to make the work more useful. Persons seeking any subject should first look to the alphabet of the work, and failing there, the supplement may be helpful.

18

INDEX OF SCRIPTURE TEXTS.

THE END.